THE
THROWAWAY
CHILDREN

There is in every child at every stage a new miracle of vigorous unfolding, which constitutes a new hope and a new responsibility for all.

Erik Erikson
Childhood and Society

THE THROWAWAY CHILDREN

BY LISA AVERSA RICHETTE

J. B. Lippincott Company

Philadelphia and New York

For my son, Lawrence Anthony Richette II,
who proposes that I dedicate this book
to all the throwaway children
I shall never know and thus never have
the opportunity to defend

ACKNOWLEDGMENTS

For much of the case material I have relied on personal notes and files gathered in the course of my work. Although court records are, under Section 245 of the Juvenile Court of Pennsylvania, "open to inspection by . . . persons having a legitimate interest," I have applied the principle of anonymity in all cases where children were actually defendants charged with delinquency. I have altered their backgrounds and used fictitious names for them and other participants—lawyers, probation officers, psychiatrists—in order to spare them further trauma. Only the identity of Judge J. Sydney Hoffman is authentic.

Where the children themselves relinquished their anonymity by becoming plaintiffs (the Rittenhouse Square hippies discussed in Chapter 14) or appealed to higher courts, as in the case of Gerald Gault, I felt justified in using their correct names. I salute these courageous young people and their lawyers who brave the furor of publicity to correct manifest injustices.

Many magnificent professionals in the juvenile field have helped me, and I respect their wish to remain unnamed.

Ephraim R. Gomberg, Executive Director of the Philadelphia Crime Commission, and his Assistant Director, Ian H. Lennox, supplied valuable statistical information. Commissioner Frank Rizzo of the Philadelphia Police Department graciously granted me lengthy interviews with Inspector Charles Dittmer and Lieutenant Joseph Rich, two experienced senior officers in the juvenile field.

For sharing his rich knowledge of classical antiquity I am indebted to Kenneth D. Matthews, Lecturer in Classical Archaelogy at the University of Pennsylvania. For his invaluable encouragement and support I salute Bernard A. Bergman, Book Editor of the Philadelphia *Evening Bulletin*. Bernard Landolfi and Claude Lewis, also of the *Bulletin*, helped in my newspaper research. My colleague, David Pittinsky, Esquire, and Father David Gracie, Urban Missioner of the Episcopal Diocese of Philadelphia, offered many valuable suggestions on the mini-flower children. I am grateful for the candor with which Robert M. Landis, Esquire, Chairman of the Committee on Juvenile Rights of the Philadelphia Bar Association, confronted the complex question of legal counsel for juveniles.

Mrs. Rebecca Segal, whose brilliant contributions are highlighted in Chapter 13, generously gave me time, materials, and her warm understanding. My friend, Robert C. Taber, former Associate Superintendent of the Philadelphia Board of Public Education, guided me through some of the labyrinth. Mrs. Charlotte Kline, Executive Director of Teen-Aid, Inc., answered my every call for assistance.

Eugene V. Armao offered valuable suggestions for several chapters. I am grateful to him and to Jerre Mangione for encouraging me to undertake this book. Spencer Coxe, Executive Director of the Greater Philadelphia Chapter of the American Civil Liberties Union, has given me due process challenges over many years. And my husband, Lawrence J. Richette, Esquire, helped by overlooking some of the disorders of the creative process. Mrs. Blanche McClinton, patient and ever helpful, maintained my household routine throughout the wrting.

Some time ago, Professor Fred Rodell of the Yale Law School challenged me and the other students in his famous writing seminar to communicate lucidly to the citizenry of this land on the murkiest of legal topics. He has been a lively inspiration throughout.

Finally, I wish to acknowledge the greatest debt of all—to Mrs. Betty Jane Corson, my editor and friend. Her devotion, skill, and faith were the rare catalysts that brought forth this book.

L.A.R.

Philadelphia, Pennsylvania
January 1969

CONTENTS

PART ONE———

THE "NOW" CHILDREN CONFRONT THE JUSTICE ESTABLISHMENT

PART ONE ———

PROLOGUE

At nine o'clock on a Monday morning the huge room is as desolate as a wintry beach, yet its human purpose is unmistakable. The high bench, the railing, the rows upon rows of straight-backed wooden chairs indicate clearly that this is a courtroom, the traditional setting for confrontations with justice. Presently a few men and women carrying papers and files begin to drift in. As they take their places to the right and left of the bench, their low-pitched conversations reflect the studied nonchalance of minor players who sense that they are part of an important but unpredictable larger drama.

They adjust their props: a reading lamp over a writing desk to give a clerk enough light to make his handwritten entries, concealed boxes of paper tissues and cough drops to alleviate the coughing and sneezing that may interrupt the proceedings, loose coins for a furtive coffee break later on in the morning if things are going well.

I move past the empty stretches of chairs, glancing down at the duplicates of case summaries marked *Assistant District Attorney* I have just been handed. I sit down at my table just below the bench and read them intently, underlining sentences I will want to refer to later. Before I have completed less than half the sheaf I hear the familiar muezzin cry of the bailiff:

"Oyez, oyez, oyez. The Juvenile Court of Philadelphia is now in session, the Honorable J. Sydney Hoffman presiding!"

We all stand and smile a good morning to the judge. He nods, indicating that he is ready to begin. At the far end of the courtroom a wall clock chimes nine-thirty. The chairs are still empty. Two doors open. The one opposite my desk is the entrance to watch. Out springs a slight black boy somewhere between eight and ten years of age, dressed in the drab denim uniform of the detention center. His eyes glitter—I cannot yet tell whether with ferocity or tears. Shepherded by a court officer, he is led to the railing. He looks back, just in time to see a shabbily dressed man and woman enter. The man makes a half-gesture of greeting to the boy; the woman merely nods grimly as she sits down in the front-row seat to which she has been directed.

"Are you this boy's parents?" I ask.

"I'm his mother. I'm Mrs. Preston." The woman's voice is gruff. "That's his stepfather." Her finger jabs the air in the direction of the man, but she does not move her head.

"'Julius Preston, age nine,'" the judge reads aloud from his portfolio of papers, "'charged with carrying a concealed deadly weapon.' What kind of weapon does a nine-year-old boy usually have? A penknife?"

"No, your Honor," I reply. "Not this boy. He was carrying his own 'atom bomb'"...

1

BEHIND
CLOSED DOORS

Americans vaguely know that "bad" kids end up in a place called Juvenile Court. Most citizens have never been inside one. They are not particularly eager for the experience.

It seems paradoxical that a nation otherwise obsessed with child-rearing techniques should treat so casually the official machinery it set up to deal with children who get into trouble or need protection. General indifference on the part of white, middle-class Americans may have been understandable thirty years ago. In their view, Juvenile Court was a miniature police court into which neighborhood toughs were hauled by the scruff of the neck to give them a good scare. And, if that didn't do the trick, they could always be "sent away." "Nice" children never came near such a place.

Today, Dicks and Janes from all social levels are increasingly part of the juvenile delinquency scene. Obviously, there are individual differences; the life experiences of the middle-class child are unlike those of the more traditional "deprived" youngster. But on the meeting-ground of the Juvenile Court those differences narrow.

Affluent or poor, these children have one thing in common: they are about to be cast off because society has run out of answers.

The fact is that these children have been, in Justice Earl Warren's apt phrase, "swept under the rug" for decades because the American people have been content to regard juvenile courts as sanitation departments whose job is to keep the community clean by picking these kids off the streets. No one pays too close attention to *how* a sanitation department does its job as long as it does it reasonably well. But when the storage bins overflow and the waste-disposal system clogs, people begin to notice. Initially, it occurs to us that maybe we ought to build bigger bins, install up-to-date equipment. But when the jammings and the breakdowns persist, it is time to take a long, hard look at the system itself.

A logical place to start is at the beginning. Established at the turn of the century, the Juvenile Court was designed to reclaim America's lost youth by providing a valid second chance, a moment of hope, which a child and the adults in his world could seize upon to reconstruct his life. For was it not obvious that a troubled, deprived, or needy youngster might otherwise perish or turn to crime as a way to survive in an alien environment?

And so the court extended the sheltering arms of a substitute parent, for it understood the needs of these unfortunates and knew that its resources were adequate to fulfill its purpose. The institutions to which some of the children were dispatched remained at heart nineteenth-century orphanages, slightly updated. The relatively small number of "probationers" who stayed behind in the community under court supervision presented few problems, for until World War II, the court could summon and receive assistance from budding, idealistic social-work agencies.

But during the last quarter-century, changes in the way and meaning of life in the United States have been so rapid that the guidelines for behavior and value judgments have become increasingly unclear and unstable. The individual and his problems are easily lost in this age of big government and big business. It is not surprising, then, that the Juvenile Court has found it harder and harder to mobilize resources needed to redeem young lives in realistic human terms.

Obviously, one reason why the traditional approaches to juvenile problems are no longer effective is that there are more problem juveniles. Though their arrivals and departures are largely hidden from public view, these children move through the nation's courts in increasing numbers. In 1967 over a million American children were arrested on criminal charges. From 1960 to 1967 there was a 59 per cent increase in the volume of juvenile arrests. Other cold-print statistics contained in the 1967 FBI *Uniform Crime Reports* released on August 27, 1968, are equally startling: More than 9 per cent of all persons arrested for murder and voluntary manslaughter were under eighteen years of age, marking a 56 per cent increase of juveniles in this category. Of all persons charged with aggravated assault, 30 per cent were minors; the increase since 1960 in this category is 121 per cent. Juveniles under eighteen charged with forcible rape constituted 21 per cent of all persons arrested for this offense.

Young people are even more deeply involved in crimes against property than in offenses against persons. Although 37 per cent of all robberies were attributable to juveniles, young persons under eighteen comprised 54 per cent of all burglary arrests, 55 per cent of all larceny charges, and 62 per cent of all car thefts. Automobile snatching is the preferred crime of youth; 80 per cent of all persons arrested nationally on this charge are under twenty-one years old! Perhaps the most dramatic peaking of all occurred in the arrests for narcotics possession and use. In just one year, from 1966 to 1967, the number of these arrests spurted 131.4 per cent for urban children, 222 per cent for suburban children, and 132.5 per cent for rural-dwelling young people.

Numbers, however, do not reveal the nature of failure any more than the clichés and dogmas that pass for expertise provide solutions. Apathy, indifference, and deeply-rooted hostility on the part of the public have in large measure caused the juvenile court system to be diverted from its original goal of rehabilitation and perverted into a throwaway process, whereby children receive "the worst of both worlds."

It will not suffice for "thinkers" and "planners" to draw up multi-million-dollar programs outlining administrative reforms and elaborate departmental recommendations as long as middle-class white America views these children as bad seed, incapable of change, and hence justifiably consigned to community storage bins—out of sight and out of mind.

Boys like Julius Preston don't *go* away, even though we *send* them away. In a year or two, or five, they return, taller, stronger, more hell-bent on vengeance, even if it means blowing themselves up with the rest of the world.

The 1967 *Report of the President's Commission on Law Enforcement and the Administration of Justice,* citing FBI statistics, concludes that "enormous numbers of young people appear to be involved in delinquent acts." Confidential studies of youngsters reporting their misdeeds show that 90 per cent of them have committed at least one delinquent act for which they could have been taken into court. Then the *Report* delivers the clincher. According to rough estimates by the Children's Bureau of the Department of Health, Education and Welfare, *one* out of *every six* American boys will go to juvenile court on a delinquency charge before he is eighteen years old.

Like all statistics, these figures wobble a bit under close scrutiny.

Point A: In order to participate in FBI surveys, local police departments must fit youth offenses into the FBI's crime-classification system. Any statistics based upon those police reports give a distorted impression of the situation, because the categories in which arrested children are placed represent adult crimes, and these involve technical definitions of adult "legal intent." A ten-year-old boy who breaks a freight-car seal and gets caught in the act is officially called a burglar. A second-grader who successfully makes off with a few nickels from a broken parking meter has committed larceny. A youthful sexual liaison becomes statutory rape on the part of the boy. I recall my astonishment when I looked up from an arrest report handed to me by a police officer and saw that the alleged rapist was a nine-year-old boy. Even the harsh eighteenth-century English law courts conceded that children under the age of thirteen were incapable of such criminal intent. But the police, within the modern crime-reporting system, can find no other pigeonhole for a boy's aggressive sex play with a seven-year-old neighbor.

Point B: There are more unsolved adult crimes than there are juvenile ones because children get themselves arrested more easily than adults do. For one thing, *savoir-faire* is not the strong point of most delinquent children. For another, many of them unconsciously *want* to be caught and punished. They are like the neurotic criminals described by psychiatrists studying the connection between an individual's sense of guilt and his antisocial behavior. As proof, consider the fact that many teen-agers steal flashy convertibles and one-of-a-kind sports cars on bustling city streets where visibility is at a maximum.

Nevertheless, the trends behind the statistics are true enough. The next question is, Where do all these children come from?

For years juvenile delinquency was equated with big-city problems, especially those facing the offspring of parents aptly termed by Claude Brown in his *Manchild in the Promised Land* the present-day "disillusioned colored pioneers." And it is true that in many cities black children are arrested in greater numbers than any other group. In Philadelphia, for example, out of 12,000 delinquency cases initiated in Juvenile Court in 1967, 71 per cent involved blacks; the remaining 29 per cent included poor as well as middle-class white children and Puerto Ricans, according to the official court records.

But the 1967 national FBI statistics show that juvenile delinquency is no longer the exclusive problem of the big cities. In fact, for that year the urban percentage of juvenile arrests was lower than the rural! With 34 per cent of all offenders children under eighteen, the suburban communities actually led the dismal parade. These facts should shake up suburban and rural legislators who have traditionally ignored the entire juvenile area because it was outside their domain of interest. Ignoring the appeals of city officials for additional juvenile court services, they felt aloof and secure from the pressures of juvenile crime. Now these youthful offenders are solidly at their doorstep, and every indication points to the fact that they will remain there in decades to come.

It is logical to ask, What constitutes "delinquency" in the eyes of the court?

Juvenile misbehavior includes not only most crimes that adults commit but also attitudes and behavior patterns unique to children. Truancy, violating curfews, and running away are examples of child behavior that provide grounds for court intervention. In the case of truancy, although parents can be fined for not making certain their children attend school, the persistently errant child often pays in other currency. He may find himself in a correctional training school where the atmosphere is even more confining than the conventional schoolroom. Edgar Z. Friedenberg, in his classic *Coming of Age in America*, presents a convincing case against the practice of equating truancy with delinquency. A closer examination of the causes of classroom absenteeism in any given case might lead to a more constructive solution to that problem.

Many things a youngster does are construed as defiance of parental authority and lead to his being branded "incorrigible." Some of these acts are the child's response to the complicated process of growing up—a process that involves different behavior and actions from one generation to the next. The courtroom may not necessarily be the most desirable place to deal with problems of this nature; nevertheless, the law allows adults to seek court solutions. It is true that as a child grows up, his multifingered reaching out for identity often looks instead like the shaking of a defiant fist. But, as educators and psychologists keep reminding us, some measure of rebellion against parental and other authority is an essential part of this search for self.

The home, as the place a child spends his earliest formative years, should be both a training and a testing ground. In this basic setting he forms his first image of himself and the world and develops patterns of response to what goes on around him. If that foundation is shaky, the child's chances for getting into trouble increase. Therefore, it is imperative that parents try to demonstrate as much love, understanding, self-control, and consistency of attitude as they are capable of, and to both teach and learn from their children. Those who are too neurotic, indifferent, immature, or faint-hearted to shoulder the responsibilities of parenthood fail to establish guidelines of acceptable behavior for their offspring—and thereby themselves invite whatever trouble the children get into. Juvenile Court affords a convenient "out" for such parents—but not for their children.

There is a catchall category in juvenile law into which are dumped children who are destructive or potentially dangerous to themselves or others. Since they present such a difficult problem at home and in school, they need special handling, which the court should try to provide. The brilliant researches of Dr. Bruno Bettelheim at the Sonia Shankman Orthogenic School, in Chicago, and other scientists prove that these children are emotionally ill, *not* bad. Careful study and patient effort have demonstrated that each child's destructive acts, like obscure palimpsests, can be deciphered. And through understanding comes a treatment program that leads him back into the world. Unfortunately, too few of these treatment centers exist. The large sums of public monies needed to implement such effective therapeutic work are now being budgeted for superhighways, elaborate sports arenas, and salary increases for high-echelon officials.

How heavy a burden society places on the juvenile justice system becomes evident when we consider the children who arrive in court not as a result of delinquent behavior but because they have been badly neglected. Sometimes even the minimal conditions needed for physical survival appear to be absent. Whether or not the parents are legally at fault, and no matter what legal category the children fall into, the court must act immediately to relieve the suffering of these youngsters and find shelters for them.

Many people wonder, By what process do children arrive in juvenile court?

Like all procedures that isolate "undesirables" from the rest of society, the juvenile justice system operates as an anonymous bureaucracy. Once children are caught up in it, they become part of a large invisible population governed by special laws—laws that permit secrecy on the grounds that it ensures family privacy and shields young persons from notoriety that may damage their future. Laudable sentiments, to be sure—but the informal and sublegal modes of operation have had unfortunate consequences. People who function behind those closed doors have absolute dominion over their charges. Since few checks and balances exist, punitive treatment, repression, arbitrary actions, depersonalization of individuals, and institutionalized thinking often replace genuine measures of protection and rehabilitation.

Usually, one of the first adults to spot children in trouble is the policeman. (In 1967, two-thirds of the delinquency cases heard in Philadelphia were the result of police arrests.) To both ghetto and middle-class children, the policeman is known as the "fuzz" or just simply the "Man": the embodiment of white prejudice or despised adult authority. What happens in a police-child encounter may confirm these preconceptions for life.

Despite the 1967 decision in re *Gault*, 387 U.S. 1, which entitles juveniles to the same constitutional guarantees that adults have, *in court*, outside the courtroom, police still frequently treat young persons as subcitizens without rights, still routinely frisk and question them virtually at will. If taken to a police station, children are required to answer questions about their associates, their school attendance, and their sex life; sometimes their honest replies lead them to juvenile court. Guidelines for the police to follow in dealing with juveniles remain regrettably vague, despite the permanent stigma that arrest and referral to court may carry.

Even though many police forces have special juvenile aid divisions to handle young offenders, the officers themselves have no special qualifications for the job. In *Crisis in the Courts*, Howard James, the *Christian Science Monitor* reporter who investigated juvenile and other law enforcement problems, states that juvenile police are selected for their work because they have the right temperament. The practice is to allow them to "adjust" trivial matters when no citizen presses hard for prosecution. James cites an Illinois procedure under a 1965 Juvenile Court Act that allows police to act as judges in certain cases. After reviewing the evidence, they decide whether or not the child is guilty, and they can order him and his parents to report to the police district for counseling sessions. Thus does the *ad hoc* development of our juvenile justice system make it possible for police, who are basically security officers, to lay claim to the judge's bench and the therapist's couch.

There is another group of security personnel—the guards and matrons employed in detention centers, shelters, and juvenile prisons —who are usually chosen because they have a robust physique and a taste for the work. Jobs in these places are often political plums, and the holders enjoy the power they can exercise over their prisoners.

Harold Lasswell, the distinguished Yale social scientist, once suggested to a group of law students embarking on a research project at a state prison that if they really wanted to find out how the jail was run, the guards were the ones to study most carefully, *not* the warden and the professional staff. Most people—including grand juries—who inspect juvenile facilities overlook completely these custodians, unaware of the deep and potentially detrimental effect that their close contact with the children has.

Usually the next person after the policeman to deal with the child is the court's probation officer. Specially designated members of probation departments conduct interviews to determine the vital issue of whether or not to keep the youngster in custody pending his official court hearing. Because overwhelming numbers of cases need "processing," detention can extend into long periods of confinement that are more like punitive sentences, *even though* the evidence has not been sifted or weighed by a judge. To remedy this evil, some courts hold special early hearings to decide the question of custody. But usually a probation officer just telephones the judge to obtain approval.

The probation officer assigned to a child is the court's personal emissary and becomes both confidant and watchdog. Essentially a therapist, he also occasionally plays detective, conducting the interviews and investigations that provide essential background information for the case report that accompanies the child into court.

Ideally, the probation officer should be a skilled social worker with special training in corrections work. For years the National Association of Probation and Parole has been lobbying for this goal. It is far from attained. In large cities, however, most of them are, at the very least, college graduates; some have an M.A. in social work. Since they are generally appointed by judges who are themselves successful products of a political system of election or appointment, extraprofessional factors sometimes creep in. On the whole, written tests are administered, candidates are interviewed, and some semblance of professionalism is maintained.

Unfortunately the wage scale for these court workers is so pitiably low that demand often exceeds supply and standards have to be relaxed in order to fill the job. (In Philadelphia, during most of the period covered in this book, probation officers earned between four and six thousand dollars a year.) Thus, many probation officers are forced to "moonlight."

Probation supervisors receive better salaries, but income exceeding ten thousand dollars a year is reserved only for the cruelly overworked top echelon who are called upon by judges to produce instant cures for troublesome children or to conjure up community resources that just don't exist.

A well-organized juvenile court department often includes other therapists—psychologists, social workers, psychiatrists, and other physicians—who function as a team, studying the children who are placed under observation and making recommendations in their behalf. It is not always easy to maintain a relationship with a child who has learned not to trust adults, and this creates the added problem of having to decide what confidential information should, in the child's best interest, be divulged. Their task is made easier when they are confident that the court has the resources to provide particularized help. The more limited community services are, the harder it is to arrange for treatment suited to the nature and degree of any one child's problems.

The latest—and most controversial—arrivals on the scene are the lawyers. Before the Supreme Court ruled that children must be advised of their right to legal counsel and that a lawyer must be appointed by the court when parents cannot provide their own, youngsters rarely had legal representation at their hearings. (Cases discussed in this book precede that ruling.) Now, trial lawyers are beginning to trickle into the juvenile justice system.

One of the most crippling crises facing juvenile courts all over the country is how to pay fees to the court-appointed lawyers who represent poor children. Poverty-program funds are insufficient to cope with the huge backlog of untried cases. Meanwhile, children languish in detention centers while bar association committees and municipal councils try to find the cheapest way to shoulder this new financial burden.

Fortunately, young lawyers are becoming interested in juvenile court work after field-work experience in the Peace Corps or as VISTA volunteers. I believe that face-to-face contact with disadvantaged children outside the courtroom is the most vital preparation a lawyer can bring to this work—this, and wide reading in the field of child development and growth, including the classic accounts of therapists like August Aichhorn and Erik Erikson, who have worked successfully with problem youth.

The judge is usually the last person to see a child as the system's conveyer-belt carries him to his day in court.

According to Matthew Matlin, editor of *Crime and Delinquency*, only 79 per cent of all the juvenile court judges in the United States are lawyers. Howard James's book *Crisis in the Courts* documents the pitiable level on which many juvenile courts function when ill-prepared and casually chosen judges preside. He reveals that one-fifth of all juvenile court judges have never gone to college, that one-fifth are not lawyers (hopefully the same one-fifth!), and that three-fourths of these judges spend less than one-quarter of their time hearing juvenile cases. These are not very reassuring statistics.

James saw at first hand that many of these judges, having no clear-cut understanding or philosophy of troubled children, operate on whim. The late Judge Jerome Frank of the U.S. Court of Appeals for the Second Circuit, who himself had been psychoanalyzed, maintained that the unconscious hostilities and drives of judges predetermine their rulings. Lawyers and laymen alike characterize a particular judge as "tough" or biased against certain children. But after having worked closely with at least five judges in Philadelphia's Juvenile Court and having observed others in my practice, I believe that any occasionally erratic behavior stems from the unique role they must assume in court. Practically every judge decides fairly early in his assignment what that role will be: sympathetic Big Daddy, stern teacher, guardian of private property, watchdog of community morality, or a mélange of all four.

But playing any one role consistently is difficult because the ever-changing human panorama unfolding in the courtroom each day demands flexibility. Moreover, despite the informality of the court, the aura of law is omnipresent, compelling the judge to add to his self-assigned role some conventional judicial attitudes. The best juvenile court judges have a very hard time of it, for they are acutely conscious of the great power they wield, the absence of clearly defined guidelines for exercising it, and their own uncertainty as to what role will work best with each child. To make matters worse, even if a judge arrives at an ideal solution to a youngster's difficulty, he may have to scrap it or settle for the pathetically inadequate half-measures which are all the community makes available.

Virtually everyone involved in the process—police, guards, matrons, probation officers, social workers, psychiatrists and other therapists, lawyers, and judges—struggles with a sense of frustration. The system calls itself a missionary effort to effect genuine change in the lives of the young. Yet the brutal reality is that all too few individuals and communities support this goal. "You're coddling them!" is the familiar hue and cry.

Control and punishment, not treatment and rehabilitation, are what the public *really* demands. And what it gets is an anonymous army of a million or more throwaways who, with the stealth of a nighttime convoy, are being shipped out—destination unknown.

2

WHERE
THE ACTION IS

When I first walked into Philadelphia's Juvenile Court as an Assistant District Attorney in the mid-1950's, the only judge assigned to that court—an authoritarian who wanted no interference—ordered me to leave. Somewhat dismayed, I obliged. My boss, Richardson Dilworth, then District Attorney and later to become Mayor of Philadelphia, told me to go back into the courtroom and hold my ground, no matter what the judge said. As the highest elected law enforcement officer, Dilworth wanted to know what went on behind those closed doors. For a year and a half I was required to stand leperlike at the far corner of the bar of the court. Furthermore, I could not ask questions or address the judge directly; I had to communicate through an intermediary, an elderly factotum who was the judge's political and court adviser.

Defense lawyers appeared rarely. The most prominent juvenile lawyer at that time was the late William Woolston, an ardent early defender of juvenile rights, who was even more of an anathema to the judge than I. His simplest requests were routinely denied without so much as an upward glance.

When Judge Victor J. Di Nubile was appointed to the bench, a new spirit prevailed in the courtroom. With the barriers removed, I even acquired the ultimate status symbols of a chair and a writing desk. With the appointment in 1956 of J. Sydney Hoffman as presiding judge of the Juvenile Division, the closed doors were literally opened to the press and interested citizens of the community, and the windows of the courtroom figuratively flung open to let in air, light, and hope.

Legally, I had received no special preparation for juvenile court work for a very good reason: none was available. However, while at Yale Law School, I spent three years as a cottage parent in a Connecticut institution for emotionally disturbed children. I lived around the clock with thirteen youngsters between the ages of six and eleven, all of whom had been committed to the Children's Center of Hamden, Connecticut. Because there is a perennial shortage of cottage parents in all children's institutions, positions of this kind are often filled by amateurs—which I certainly was. The other cottage parent in my section was an aristocratic widow in her mid-seventies forced by economic need to seek work. Childless herself, she alternately regarded the children as pets to be spoiled or nuisances to be pushed away. The psychiatrist who consulted with us weekly and the social workers who saw us daily had long ago given up on the widow, but they gladly answered my questions and gave me invaluable help in coping with disruptive behavior: tantrums, fire-setting tendencies, nightly bedwetting, bad dreams, and even the refusal of one boy, aged eight, to wear anything but girl's clothing.

If the Yale Law School provided the intellectual turning point in my life, my parallel experience at the Center represented the emotional equivalent. My interest in throwaway children was born when I became part of a team effort to rescue them—and a successful mission it was in all but a few instances.

I came to love those tortured, difficult, yet beautiful boys and girls, and determined then to direct my energies, talents, and skills as a lawyer toward changing the legal and social status of their counterparts, and above all to fight for humane, intelligent, and compassionate treatment of problem children wherever and however I could.

After graduation, I was made administrator of an interdisciplinary project in psychiatry and law, headed by the late James H. Dession, professor of Criminal Law, and Dr. Lawrence Z. Freedman, then an associate professor of psychiatry at the Yale Medical School. Dr. Fritz Redlich, head of the Yale Psychiatry Department who has since become dean of the Yale Medical School, was interested particularly in finding new ways to treat delinquents, and this aspect of the project appealed to me. As it turned out, the work afforded little opportunity to deal directly with children, and I missed the contact with them that my job as cottage parent had provided. I became restless and left after two years when, by a stroke of extremely good fortune, Mr. Dilworth offered me the chance to serve in the juvenile court in Philadelphia—a setting that reflects the national pattern of justice for children.

I soon learned that the judge is the real powerhouse in a juvenile court; he is where the real action is. Everything that precedes the confrontation between him and the child is in preparation for that moment.

Daily work is conducted by many people in various places. The children themselves are often "warehoused" nearby—after they leave the police station, their first stop.

In most major American cities, these police way-stations look like disaster areas. Paint is chipped and peeling, ceiling plaster sifts down in gentle snowfalls, dim electric bulbs barely illuminate the corners. The furniture is Early Flea Market; not one piece is comfortable, no matter what position the human body assumes. The police working there must surely be as unhappy as anyone with these surroundings. It seems strange that a nation publicly espousing law and order cannot provide decent office space for those who labor to uphold community safety.

Children often spend hours stretched out on long, hard benches, waiting for the Juvenile Aid Division officer to appear. They do not know that the division is understaffed and one man may have three, or perhaps five, calls a night. For the most part the youngsters behave; unruly ones can end up in a cell.

Eventually these children must be fed if they have to wait around long enough. Since there are no cooking facilities—except for the occasional hot plate or electric coffee-maker a policeman brings in— the menu is limited: dry sandwiches and a bottled soft drink from one of the vending machines that line the corridors.

If the police decide to charge a child with delinquency, he is moved to the juvenile detention center. By comparison with other cities, Philadelphia has a fairly new detention home, the Youth Study Center on the Benjamin Franklin Parkway, established in 1952. The Parkway itself is an imposing, tree-lined avenue, copied from the Champs Elysées in Paris. Like its model, it boasts stunning fountains and carefully tended flower-bed ovals; the great Art Museum with its Corinthian columns presides over the avenue at its far end, on the bank of the Schuylkill River. Along its seven traffic lanes stand the city's temples of high culture: the Academy of Natural Sciences, the Free Library, the Rodin Museum. What is a juvenile detention center doing in the midst of all this splendor . . . ?

No signs are visible from the Parkway to identify the building. Strangers have difficulty finding the entrance, which is on a side street that ends in a cul-de-sac. After it opened, the City of Philadelphia ornamented the grounds with statuary costing $100,000 which the children can't see from the Band-Aid-slim windows. The planners forgot to include an outdoor play area in the blueprint: it has never been added. Boys and girls are kept in separate wings that are connected by moatlike ramps and tunnels. Every door is locked —opened as a person goes in or out, bolted after he passes through. The gymnasium has served a dual function almost from the very first day the Center opened: by day, an *indoor* recreation area; emergency sleeping quarters at night. The overflow is such that, at this writing, between fifty and sixty children have to sleep on thin mattresses which have been placed on the floor, only a few feet of space between each.

The Center's well-staffed medical department has physicians and psychiatrists as well as a psychological testing unit acting in tandem with them, a dentist and a technician-aide, and specialized nurses who together with psychiatric social workers step in when needed.

The Youth Study Center is the "jail" where children under sixteen are detained while awaiting court hearings or removal to other institutions. A few teachers conduct classes under the supervision of a "principal" who heads the unit. No special training for this work is required; the teachers are chosen for their endurance, strength, and patience.

Interviews are conducted early each weekday morning by specially designated probation officers known as intake interviewers. In medium-sized conference rooms, several rows of chairs face long tables behind which sit the intake interviewers, the J.A.D. police officers assigned to the Youth Study Center, and stenographers using shorthand or stenotype machines. The children sit several feet away in the first row of chairs, next to their parents or guardians. Outside, down the long hall, is a waiting area. No books or magazines are kept around to help pass the time: this area is a bleak way station and pretends to be nothing more.

The Center has had two able executive directors since it opened: E. Preston Sharp, who became executive secretary of the American Correctional Association in 1965, and Robert F. Perkins, its present chief. Both men have decried the bottlenecking which plagues the Center and similar jails in other states. They concede that the Center is misnamed, since its primary function is not to study children but to keep them locked up. As Mr. Perkins says, it is a "storage bin" for hundreds of children who have no other place to go. In an interview in the Philadelphia *Evening Bulletin* on May 20, 1968, he pointed out that 93 per cent of the counties in the United States provide only jail or jail-like facilities for youth detention; Philadelphia's juvenile jail has a fancier title and better statuary.

Across the Parkway eastward are twin buildings, elegant French-looking gray stone replicas of Gabriel's design for the Plâce de la Concorde in Paris. One, the headquarters for the Free Library of Philadelphia, is a repository for the flowerings of our civilization. The other building is a gathering place for the human weeds of our society: young, middle-aged, and old. Here are the administrative headquarters for the Family Court Division of the Court of Common Pleas, Philadelphia County, which handles such diverse matters as disputed paternity, child custody, support for deserted wives and children, suits by elderly indigent parents to compel their children to support them, and problems caused by alcoholic or mentally ill family members.

As an important component of this court, the Juvenile Division occupies many office cubicles, for juvenile matters form a very big chunk of the workload.

It is a cold, austere place with high vaulted ceilings and *No Smoking* signs everywhere to placate the fire underwriters. In the impressive main entry hall is a statue of the man who forged the present image of the Court: Judge Charles Lincoln Brown, father of one of the two women judges currently on the court, the Honorable Hazel H. Brown. Beneath Judge Brown's statue is an inscription which states the credo of the court:

> The Municipal Court of Philadelphia looks for guidance to a justice that is not blindfolded as is the traditional figure, but to one who removes the bandage from her eyes to see her suppliants; a seeing justice.

Most of the courtrooms are on the ground floor, where hearings in juvenile delinquency cases are regularly held. In 1968, several of the newly appointed County Court judges assigned to the Juvenile Division tried to speed up matters by also hearing cases in conference rooms ordinarily assigned to the medical department, but the experiment has been temporarily abandoned. Security is better in the regular courtrooms, which connect with cells and anterooms on the basement level. The sheriff's vans and cars pull up to convenient ramps and the children enter the basement and go directly to the cells or wait on benches in the anterooms until their cases are about to be called. Then they are led up narrow stairs to small waiting rooms adjoining the courtrooms. It is from here that each child walks into the judge's view.

The basement cells, life-size and real, are also used by adult prisoners. Each has an open toilet in the center of it, and holds as many as eight to ten people at one time. If a child becomes hysterical, difficult to manage, or has a serious arrest charge, the security officers may decide to put him in a cell. (They may also handcuff him, although the judges disapprove of this practice.) I remember seeing one distraught eight-year-old boy huddled on the floor, his face against the toilet. The matron and sheriff in charge explained that it seemed best to put him in a cell because he had threatened to run away!

Boys and girls over sixteen have to ride some distance to the courthouse since there is no room for them at the Youth Study Center. Some girls are spared these rides because their hearings are held in an old building that serves as both a jail and a courthouse.

Until late in 1968 the vans that were used to transport children from one place to another were large, metal-bodied convoy trucks with no connecting partition between the driver's cab and the truck itself. They were airless, locked human-freight cars. Many of my young clients would plead with me to arrange some other means of transportation for them, so great was their terror of the van. I never succeeded in making other arrangements for them. The typical response to such requests was to dismiss them as children's "attention-getting" devices.

In the spring of 1968, a teen-age boy, while traveling to the courthouse in a van from Pennypack House, a detention center at the far northeastern end of Philadelphia, was the victim of a savage homosexual assault by a group of fellow prisoners. The attack lasted the duration of the trip, which was an hour or more. There were the usual outcries from outraged citizens and newspaper editorializing, but the vans still lumbered on for a few more months. Finally, station-wagon-type vehicles, which had been available all along, were authorized for service until better-designed vans were delivered.

As one might expect of a system rooted in law, the juvenile justice process bristles with "papers." A case is born when someone files a *petition*, a request to the court to intervene. Under the law, a petition can be filed by parents, police or court officers, friends, teachers, neighbors—almost anyone who wants the child brought to court. Before lawyers became involved in these proceedings, petitions were loosely worded, often merely repeating legal definitions of a delinquent, neglected, or dependent child and nothing else. Parents served with these papers had little inkling of what would happen to them or their children. Since 1967, these petitions have been revised somewhat and will certainly improve as the due-process requirements set down by the Supreme Court are more fully met.

No petition, however, no matter how specific, contains the full story of the child. That information, together with vital reports by probation officers, doctors, teachers, and others, is kept in a *record* or *file*. Only probation officers and court personnel have access to these documents; lawyers—including the Assistant District Attorney —who deal daily in confidences, are seldom permitted to read an entire case file.

At the time of this writing, a heated battle is being joined between lawyers and social workers over the accessibility—and use—of these secret records. When a child appears in court, his file is placed before the judge, who sometimes has had an opportunity to read it prior to the hearing or who knows the child from past court contact. Lawyers argue that his reading the record *before* the facts in the current case have been presented may prejudice the judge. Or, if he reads it *after* he has heard the case, he may base his decisions on items in the record that the lawyer has no knowledge of and which he can never explain or refute.

Another area of tension between counsel and social workers is the latter's tendency to reduce the hearing to a chatty conference. Whispered exchanges take place out of earshot of lawyers—a practice contrary to the mandates of legal fairness. These secret conversations also have the effect of further weakening the youngster's trust in the adult world.

Long after a child has been discharged, his secret file remains in the courthouse archives. It is a quaint irony that in later years these zealously guarded records are made available to such people as Army recruiting officers, prospective employers, FBI agents, and *adult* court personnel. Most of them are looking for information to disqualify or condemn an individual, whereas the lawyer who had sought to defend him *as a child* had been denied the assistance that such a file could have provided.

In order to discharge a child or amend a court order, a motion must be filed. To obtain a rehearing of a case requires a special petition. Here, too, some lawyers disagree with this practice, arguing that another hearing should automatically be granted. Others believe that newly discovered evidence justifies reconsideration.

After hearing a case, the judge has to consider which of the rehabilitative measures that are available might be most effective. Release is possible, but often some kind of supervision is desirable, and so the child is placed on probation. Unfortunately, court personnel are so overloaded with cases that supervision and help tend to be minimal. Repeated offenses for serious crimes mean prison confinement. In many instances there is a clear-cut need to remove the youngster from the home environment. Sending him to one of a sad little collection of institutions is the most drastic decision the court may take. If the child is lucky, he doesn't have to wait too long to be admitted. These institutions are maintained by the state, the county, or private religious or charitable organizations with their own trustee boards.

The public institutions maintained by the city of Philadelphia are makeshift operations, mainly for boys, grafted onto facilities designed for other uses. One institution, the Youth Development Center, is housed in a former tuberculosis hospital. After the opening of a new ultramodern adult prison, boys and girls over sixteen were committed to the old jail. Recently, a new juvenile facility was opened at Fort Mifflin on empty barrack grounds far from the center of the city. For years, another fortresslike prison—Moyamensing—was talked about as a possible "youth development center." Outlandish as the proposal seems in this day and age, it has a certain inescapable logic: throwaway buildings for throwaway children.

Some critics of the miserable institutional setup in Pennsylvania believe that the state does even less than the city of Philadelphia. For one thing, no one is sure whether juvenile delinquents are criminals or children in need of special services. Since the state has yet to decide whether these young persons should be under the exclusive jurisdiction of the Department of Justice or the Welfare Department, they are at the present time under both.

The State Welfare Department runs institutions for the physically afflicted and handicapped, the mentally ill, and the mentally retarded. It also has responsibility for needy and dependent children; it maintains only a few facilities for young delinquents.

Several years ago, under the vigorous prodding of Dr. John Otto Reinemann, then Director of Probation for the County Court of Philadelphia, the State Welfare Department opened up two forestry camps where older boys can live out-of-doors and work on conservation projects. This small endeavor struggles on, but it has never been properly evaluated or amplified. No other innovations have been tried, despite the fact that, even for the neglected and dependent children, accommodations are not available.

The best that the City Department of Welfare has to offer this same group of juveniles are bargain-rate foster homes and two shelters, one large and one small.

Mentally retarded children who are awaiting transfer to the State Welfare Department school—a shockingly inadequate and neglected facility called Pennhurst—may have to remain at the Youth

Study Center for as long as two to four years before space becomes available.

Mentally ill or disturbed children are really in desperate straits. The state runs a number of large mental hospitals, some far superior to others; but without special dispensation a child can go only to the mental hospital in the county in which he lives. If there are no beds he waits at home, if he can stay there. In Philadelphia the state mental hospital known as Byberry, like many others, has no separately developed program for children and adolescents. It has no teachers, no separate recreational facilities, not even a separate dining or lounging area for these children.

The city's psychiatric facility, which is part of the Philadelphia General Hospital complex, is even less adequate. The children live in a locked, grimy seventh-floor ward, mingling with psychotic adults. On one occasion, when I went to see one of my youthful clients, I found five severely disturbed people in their early and mid-twenties sitting around an old wooden table, playing cards with a half-dozen teen-agers. Only one person was on duty. The doors were locked and no attendants were visible along the long corridors. One adult woman patient I noticed had a particularly menacing expression. Any one of the six children could have been assaulted, molested, even killed, and no one could have come to the rescue quickly.

State officials admit that even for severely schizophrenic children there is absolutely no bed space. A former Secretary of Welfare spent fifteen years of his life getting a separate psychiatric facility for children. When it was finally built, no psychiatrists could be found to run it. In desperation, officials implored the several top-flight medical schools in the Philadelphia area to fill the void by assigning residents and in-training psychiatrists as staff members. The schools agreed, but exacted a crippling condition: *they* would decide which children to admit. The Department of Welfare was forced to agree. Today it finds itself in the position of having no control over a facility it is supposed to run, and still without beds for the many sick children the doctors turn down as uninteresting or unsuitable cases.

The Pennsylvania Department of Justice has only prisons to offer juvenile delinquents. The State Correctional Institution at Camp Hill is a maximum-security prison to which boys over fifteen and young adults up to the age of twenty-five are sent. Until 1968, delinquent boys who scored somewhere between 65 and 85 on outmoded I.Q. tests were shipped off to another prison in the remote mountain village of Dallas, Pennsylvania. The prison was severely run, with solitary confinement and a Kafka-like "badge of honor" system for awarding the inmates pathetic privileges that led to ultimate release perhaps a decade later when the warden saw fit to unlock the door.

While representing an inmate who at the age of fifteen had been confined there for ten years because he had stolen a bicycle, I discovered that the Justice Department required that all boys sent to Dallas be committed not as juvenile delinquents but as "defective delinquents." In effect, this practice "legalized" indefinite confinement beyond the automatic cutoff age of twenty-one.

The practice stopped after we filed hundreds of writs of habeas corpus for the release of these prisoners. The court hearings on these writs resulted in the untombing of some three hundred boys—many of whom had become middle-aged men—who had been thrown away and forgotten behind the locked doors of Dallas.

Early in July, 1968, Governor Raymond P. Schafer signed legislation repealing the whole Defective Delinquent Act. Yet there are several hundred boys and men still at Dallas for whom the officials have no definite plans.

The two state facilities for girls are Laurelton Village for defective girls and women—another abomination—and the State Correctional Institution at Muncy, the women's prison. A few girls are committed to Muncy each year when the various counties cannot find a privately managed institution that will accept them.

In the nonpublic sector, the institutional picture is a bit brighter. The Roman Catholic Church is long experienced in the delinquency field, having opened up the first institution for wayward boys in Rome in the early seventeenth century. In the wake of the French Revolution, the Good Shepherd Order of Sisters arose to shelter the hundreds of homeless and wayward girls who roamed the countryside. Since the nineteenth century, American priests and nuns have built and run institutions for delinquent, dependent, and neglected children of all denominations and races. The Protestants have their homes and shelters too, although these are in the main oriented toward the dependent rather than the delinquent child. The Association for Jewish Children has a highly articulated program with its own residential facility. All of the religiously sponsored efforts in Pennsylvania have accepted children from the Philadelphia area.

A few of the older orphanages have adapted their facilities to handle socially disturbed children. Sleighton Farm School for Girls and Glen Mills School for Boys, both in rolling countryside settings, now accept children who have been in legal trouble. Southern and Northern Homes admit youths with behavior difficulties that have definite psychiatric overtones, and offer therapeutic treatment as part of their service. Not too long ago, the Young Men's Christian Association of Philadelphia established a "halfway house" for boys in one area of its large downtown residence-hotel. Walton Village, as it is called, helps small groups of boys make the transition from institution to home.

Only this one pioneer program exists for boys in Philadelphia, and regrettably no comparable experiment has been tried for girls—even though social planners agree that this halfway-house concept has validity and has worked wherever it has been tried. It is strange that Americans, otherwise so receptive to changes in technology and modern living, are reluctant to see the wisdom of providing an intermediate arrangement whereby problem youth can begin to resume a normal life within the community under trained supervision instead of being thrust out of locked-door institutions at the end of the commitment period.

The Catholic girls' institutions in Pennsylvania managed by the Good Shepherd Sisters have the most attractive and imaginative facilities of all. Apartment-type living units with kitchen, dining, and lounging facilities are attached to each dormitory. Color schemes vary from apartment to apartment, and the atmosphere is markedly less institutional than in other places. Their rehabilitative program is as up-to-date as the decor, since the nuns use the latest methods in educational and group psychology.

All these private institutions have far fewer locked doors than the prisons, but even for them security affects architecture as well as program. The problem of institutional runaways is eternal. Every director must guard against doors left carelessly open as well as against theft, homosexuality, and possible insurrections against the staff.

Inhibited by lack of sufficient funds from the state and county and unable to recruit proper personnel who will initiate bold, new programs, the people running these private facilities struggle to hold their own heads above water while keeping their young charges afloat. Despite their efforts to decentralize, to make the atmosphere as "homey" as possible, institutional patterns crystallize, largely from necessity. It is cheaper to run a well-disciplined army camp than a preparatory school.

This, then, was the world I entered. My official corner of it was a tiny rectangle the size of a makeshift walk-in closet. It had once been a storage room for nursing equipment. The office that I shared with my staff colleagues contained five desks wedged together to form a crazy-quilt pattern irregularly striated by telephone wires. An ancient wheelchair left behind by the nurses waited dolefully against a wall.

Everywhere there were castoffs: typewriters that jammed and desk drawers that stuck. But the sign on the door was fresh, the hand-lettering bold:

DISTRICT ATTORNEY'S OFFICE
FAMILY COURT DIVISION

And taped to the scarred surface of my desk was that real morale-lifter from St. Paul's letter to the Thessalonians:

> You are all children of the light
> and children of the day . . .
> We are not of the night, or of darkness.
> Come then, let us put on the breastplate
> of faith and love,
> And for a helmet the hope of salvation. . . .

So armed, each morning we walked down the hall to meet the children of the night.

3

NEW FACES
IN JUVENILE COURT

Like most of the children brought before the secret tribunal
Julius Preston, the nine-year-old who wanted to blow up the world
with his "bomb," wore a self-imposed mask which few adults would
ever be able to make him remove. Just when he had first put on the
mask one could not be sure, but after observing him at the detention
center for four days, a social worker had noted that it had hardened
into a second skin.

I scanned the rest of his evaluation while waiting for the Juvenile
Aid court representative to locate the arrest report.

At my reference to the A-bomb, the mask began to slip slightly.
For a moment Julius's eyes flashed with pride. Now, as the J.A.D.
officer came forward carrying a strange wooden crate bound together
with a network of wires, the boy's face stiffened and his stubby
fingers clenched the court railing.

Because a J.A.D. officer does not make the actual arrest, but is
called in after the child is taken into custody, correct procedure
requires that the arresting officers themselves appear in court to

testify. In Julius's case, the two men in the squad car who had actually apprehended him had been excused from appearing in court because the boy had readily admitted his purpose and had in no way resisted arrest. Instead, the J.A.D. investigator summarized the long written accounts of the neighborhood police officers, and although his testimony was based wholly on hearsay, he had the court's permission to offer it, since no formal objection had been raised.

The week before, officers patrolling the shadowy ghetto streets where Julius lived had been alerted to reports of a boy carrying a suspicious box. They finally cornered Julius in a schoolyard where he was crouched over a large object. He went quietly enough but insisted on carrying the crate himself. Once inside the police district, the officers pried it out of his grasp and, despite the boy's protests, opened it. Inside they found a maze of wires coiled around a small vial of what smelled like gasoline; next to it was a safety-match box taped to the slats with adhesive. Across this crude inner section the word DEATH had been crudely emblazoned with black crayon.

At first Julius had refused to talk about his box. Reluctantly he told the police his name and the address of the second-floor rear apartment he lived in with his mother and six brothers and sisters. Of his father he knew nothing. There had been a stepfather but he had left some time ago; Julius thought he might be living nearby since he saw him now and then on street corners. A third-grade pupil at the school where the police had picked him up, Julius shook his head No when the officers asked him if he was a good student.

While the Juvenile Aid officer questioned Julius, the men in the patrol car tried vainly to locate his mother. She was nowhere in the general area, and when they knocked on the apartment door a sleepy childish voice said she was still at her job. Finally, at 1:30 A.M. the J.A.D. man decided to take Julius from the district to the Youth Study Center. As he began to fill in the official arrest report, he stopped short when he came to the specific charge against the boy. Was it just a loitering and prowling case? Or was there more? He glanced at Julius. The boy was leaning forward, staring intently at the box. Despite the four hours he had spent on the wooden bench he did not seem tired or even drowsy. What did that crate mean to this kid, the officer wondered.

"Julius, what is this thing, anyway?" he asked.

"None of your fucking business," the boy muttered.

"Well, it looks like good-for-nothing junk to me," the J.A.D. man countered.

"It's the best damned bomb there is," Julius retorted. "It can blow up the whole fucking world."

He had, as children often do, just written his own bill of indictment. The officer quickly wrote in the blank space; "Carrying a Concealed Deadly Weapon."

When the J.A.D. court man finished his testimony, the judge asked to see the bomb. The officer excused himself for a moment, went to his little table at one side of the courtroom, and reached into a stockpile of sawed-off shotguns, rifles, knives, pistols—all the prosecution's exhibits for the day's batch of cases—and gave the box to the judge.

"We had it analyzed, your Honor. It's harmless; you can handle it," he explained, noticing the judge's slight apprehension as he received the "bomb."

Julius lunged forward, screaming, "Don't touch it! Give me back my bomb. You don't know nothing about it!"

"All right, Julius," the judge said quietly. "Enough of that. Settle down and tell me why you want to blow up the world."

The boy was silent. The judge had not really expected any reply. Perhaps only one out of a thousand children ever answers the adult's inevitable query: *Why?* If children like Julius could say why, or verbalize even a small part of their inner turmoil, they would not race relentlessly down the paths that end in this courtroom.

"Will Julius's parents please come forward?" Judge Hoffman asked.

The man fingered a torn cap, giving the woman a moment's head start. Instead of taking his place at her side, he stopped short a few steps behind her. The boy, I noted, sidled away from his mother. As the three of them stood waiting, I glanced down at the hastily written summary the Probation Department's court representative had just handed to me.

It was a familiar recital that fills many of the records of the children we saw every day. Mr. and Mrs. Preston had been separated for three years; he left after the birth of the youngest child. Mrs. Preston was a domestic worker for a suburban family. Mr. Preston, drifting in and out of handyman jobs, was out of work. For months he had not paid a penny toward a support order for Mrs. Preston and four children (excluding Julius).

Mrs. Preston jutted her chin forward expectantly. Despite her energy, her face had the bitter lines one sees in poor people who have struggled long, and lost.

"You don't live together, I see," the judge noted. "Your husband is supposed to send twenty dollars a week for four of your seven children." He paused a moment. "Let Julius wait in the anteroom for a few minutes."

As the boy walked out I observed his gait. A child's mode of locomotion tells, I believe, a great deal about his reaction to things that are happening to him, as well as how he feels about the world around him. At nine, Julius had not yet mastered the teen-age tough's full swagger, with its menacing shadow-bumping against invisible enemies, but he was giving a fair imitation.

The judge looked directly at Mr. Preston. "Is Julius your son?"

"I don't think so, Judge. She had him and the two oldest ones before we got married. I was going with her then off and on, but she says those three ain't mine. They was born in South Carolina. The other four came after we moved North."

"Why don't you help this woman to raise these children?"

"We can't make it, Judge," he replied.

"Judge, your Honor." Julius's mother was determined to have her say. "I go to work every day and I support my children in the best way I can. He does nothing but run out on every job and lay around bars. When he comes back real drunk, he beats me and the kids up. For no reason. I can't have it."

"Did he beat up Julius?" the judge asked.

"No more than the others."

"What about this boy's school report?" the judge wanted to know.

Briskly moving forward, the School Board's representative epitomized neatness and order. She carefully enunciated every vowel and consonant of her dismal report. In spite of normal intelligence test scores, Julius was doing very poorly in school. He probably could read and spell (I glanced down at the boy—he knew how to spell "death"), but he didn't participate in the classroom, and when called upon to recite he just mumbled incoherently. The teacher and the principal thought something was wrong with him and had asked to see his mother, but she had never answered the notes they sent home with Julius.

Mrs. Preston had been glaring fiercely all through this report. Now she interrupted testily. "How can they expect me to be running to that school during the day? I have to work."

She left her apartment every day before her children were awake, and traveled ten miles to and from her job in the suburbs. Her employers, a young couple with two model Dick and Jane children, thought well of her and had sent along a letter of verification which she thrust forward. She worked for the kind of people described in textbooks her children could not read at the school she had no time to visit. On the night of Julius's arrest she had been baby-sitting for her employers and hadn't arrived home until two-thirty in the morning. She was telling the truth and Judge Hoffman knew it, even before he checked the probation report to see if anyone had verified her story.

When Julius was brought back into the room, the judge had another question for him. "Julius, if you blow up the world, don't you realize that you will die, too?"

"That's all right. As long as everybody else dies, I don't mind."

"How long have you worked on your bomb?" I asked.

"Since last year. My big brother, he have a science class—he tell me all about bombs and things like that. But I make it myself."

Judge Hoffman stood up and leaned over the high bench in an effort to get nearer to the boy.

"What would you really like to do now, Julius?"

Quickly, "Make another bomb, if I can't have *that* one back."

The judge had been adding up the possible actions he could take. There were only a few beads on the abacus. He could put the boy on probation and send him back home. But his mother was so busy working and caring for the other six children she would probably not help with any plan the probation officer might make to enroll Julius in a mental health clinic or to get him interested in recreational activities. His stepfather did not count except as a minus: his alcoholism had blunted any chance there had been to establish a relationship with the boy. The judge knew Julius should be removed from that ghetto setting, from that crowded apartment. But where to send him? Was the boy mentally ill? If he were to be examined by the court psychiatrists and they said he was psychotic, what then? He would have to send him to a state mental hospital for ninety days so that their judgment could be confirmed or repudiated. Probably the hospital administrators would agree that Julius was "disturbed," but not severely enough to oblige them to keep him beyond the three-month observation period. They would undoubtedly follow the customary pattern of recommending outpatient therapy for the boy, overlooking two realistic considerations: child-guidance clinics have long waiting lists, and clinic hours are not geared to meet the schedules of mothers who work as domestics. If the boy was "normal" and was accepted by one of the few institutions with openings for children his age, the placement would be a temporary one at best.

Theoretically, a foster home was the answer—one with a sensitive, loving mother and a firm but kindly father who would put his arm around Julius and tell him the world is a good place. But there aren't any homes for this kind of boy. Who wants a nine-year-old black boy whose single goal in life is to blow up the world?

But the judge was obliged to try. He decided to consult the professionals anyway, and go the whole sad, futile route. "Julius, I want you to go back to the Youth Study Center for about a month. I'm going to have the doctors and social workers there talk with you. I want to help you, but I have to find out more about you. Please help *me* by talking to them."

A few weeks later Judge Hoffman got his answer. The court team agreed, after studying the boy, that he was disturbed. They recommended a local private treatment center which occasionally accepted young children referred by the court. But for poor and lower middle-class children the weekly rates were prohibitive. To make it possible for a child to stay there, the court had to obtain the cooperation of the City Department of Welfare. If a child was a ward of that department, the monthly bill was no longer an obstacle.

The Welfare Department agreed to help Julius, but in the end the psychiatric center refused to accept the boy—partly, we suspected, because he was not the kind of child the staff particularly wanted to study, but also because Mrs. Preston found it hard to keep appointments with the case worker. The center based its whole approach on family-oriented therapy, and since it had long waiting lists of middle-class children whose parents seemed willing to cooperate, or at least keep appointments, the interviewers saw no reason to put up with the Mrs. Prestons of this world.

The court psychiatrist felt strongly that confinement in a mental hospital, even for diagnostic purposes, might make Julius even more disturbed than he already was. Better to send him to an ordinary correctional school where he would be with normal kids. In the end, the only institution that said Yes was a substandard agency for Negro boys that soon afterward became the target of Welfare Department investigators and citizen groups chagrined by its lack of standards and unwholesome atmosphere.

On the day of Julius's final court appearance before being sent off to this "school," his bomb was not in the courtroom. It had probably become an interesting addition to the weapon collection that spills out of file drawers and cabinets in the Juvenile Aid Division office headquarters. Julius said nothing about its absence until he was being led out of the courtroom. Then, wheeling around, he shouted to the empty amphitheater, "Don't worry about me. I'll build another one. I'll blow up everything in this fucking world."

More and more, children like Julius began to pop up in juvenile court during the mid-fifties and early sixties. Although few of them exemplify their inner rage and alienation as dramatically as he does, the more inarticulate young ghetto-dwellers sense at an unbelievably early age that society regards them as subhuman—not worth caring about or helping. They look around and see that their chances of making it in this world are slim indeed, and they react with varying degrees of hostility. Many of them build up unbearable loads of frustration and hate, which must inevitably be released on society. There is very little anyone—the courts included—can do for such children as long as the right to a future is denied them.

The social institutions we use to mold our youth have been standing a long time, and the spreading roots of delinquency have at last wrapped themselves around their weakened foundations and exposed their inability to support the burdens we continue to place upon them. Only when we admit that random shoring-up efforts are wasted, and we begin to restructure both our thinking and our institutions, can society guarantee today's throwaways any kind of future.

Several months after Julius went off to the ramshackle school, I suddenly thought of him as I watched a regular "client" of the Philadelphia Juvenile Court walk up to the same bar where the little

boy had stood. Perhaps the sight of the strong brown hands clench-
ing the rail with the same fury I had noted in Julius's puny grasp
made me associate the two. At sixteen, however, Dexter Beardsley,
alias Hambone, had outgrown childish weapons. He was now a skillful warrior who wielded knives, machetes, and other assorted blades.

He was handcuffed, the judge told me, because he had been extremely assaultive on the ride down from the jail, which has a
detention section for boys between sixteen and eighteen years old.
His head was swathed in a blood-soaked turban of surgical bandages;
his clothing was so stained and blood-spattered that he seemed to be
wearing a jungle camouflage outfit. This impression was strikingly
accurate. Sixteen-year-old Hambone was indeed a jungle fighter; the
area of North Philadelphia in which he lived, a seething, poverty-
stricken ghetto where three-day rioting erupted in 1964, is known as
the Jungle. His strong, strapping body bore many mementos of past
knifings and assaults by his peers, but Dexter's latest wounds had been
inflicted by other "enemies": the implacable guardians of society who
wear a police uniform.

Hambone's private war against society had begun at the age of
nine when he first was picked up for stealing dimes from parking
meters. Soon afterward he had stopped shattering metal and begun
to pound away at human flesh and bone. His appalling record of
assaults, which filled two full single-spaced columns, made him a
highly desirable recruit for a neighborhood terrorist gang known as
the Purple Panthers. Although he participated sporadically in their
rumbles, he was really unattached, pursuing a solitary pattern of
violence in the streets of Philadelphia's silk-stocking districts. Under
cover of night he confronted men and women with drawn knife,
demanding their money. At the first sign of resistance, he overwhelmed them with ferocious force. Whenever Hambone was in
police custody he was placed in a line-up before the latest victims of
savage beatings and knifings. Only three persons had ever been willing to identify him and to testify against him in juvenile court. Most
of Hambone's arrests were the result of encounters with police.
Whenever they stopped him, he cursed and pummeled away until he
was subdued enough to be hauled in on charges of disorderly conduct, resisting arrest, and assault and battery on a police officer.

"Back again, Hambone?" asked the judge. "You were released
from Pennypack House less than a week ago. And now here you are

in court on a new charge. What brought you here this time?"

Hambone had an experienced probation officer whose special assignment was to work with older gang members. He came regularly into court whenever one of his young charges had to appear. Standing beside the youth, he shook his head sadly as the judge ticked off the dozen or more times Hambone had been arrested during the past year.

"He's a regular guest at Pennypack House these days. We may even arrange to have his name-plate hung on a cell door," Judge Hoffman remarked wryly. "What is happening to your life, Hambone?"

As the police testimony unfolded, the court heard the familiar tale of assault, flight, and apprehension which was Hambone's pattern.

"Is the victim present in court?" I asked.

"No," the probation officer replied, "but his wife is. She can explain."

A pale, sparrowlike young woman stepped forward. In a frightened whisper she explained that her husband was hospitalized and in serious condition.

"What happened to him?" asked the judge.

"He has over one hundred and eighty stitches in his chest, arms—everywhere. He was just slashed all over—" Her sobs silenced her words. Finally she composed herself enough to demand, in a harsher tone of voice, "Does he have to come here? Hasn't he been through enough?"

"He must identify this boy as his assailant and tell us what happened," the judge explained. Turning to the probation officer, he added, "I'm going to send Hambone back to Pennypack House until such time as the victim is able to appear. He simply must remain in detention. I would jeopardize the safety of who knows how many citizens if I let him return home pending the hearing. I know you have many difficult boys to supervise, but in the interim, please prepare a comprehensive list of recommendations for action the court can take if in fact Hambone is guilty of this assault."

It was almost three months before the victim was able to appear before Judge Hoffman. Again, Hambone stood impassively as the arresting officers told how they had seen him race by the small, brightly illuminated police office they man at a major Philadelphia subway terminal plagued with pickpockets, molesters, and thugs.

From behind the plate-glass window they noticed his blood-stained shirt and the wallet in his hand. Just as he was going through the subway turnstile they caught up with him. Imprisoned by the spokes of the stile, Hambone slugged away at his captors, and it was with difficulty that the police succeeded in pulling him free and, after a fierce struggle, subduing him with repeated blows of their blackjacks.

Hambone had a lawyer this time, a young Negro just making his way into criminal law practice. He questioned the amount of force the officers had used.

The older of the two officers answered. "In all my years on the force I have never seen anyone—boy *or* man—fight back that hard. At one point I actually thought he had us both."

The victim identified himself as a thirty-year-old salesman. His story was briefly told. He had just finished a late business dinner with a prospective client and was on his way to pick up his car at a parking lot when he heard footsteps behind him. Turning, he saw a teen-age boy with a dark handkerchief across the lower part of his face. Through the cloth he heard the muttered words, "I want your money, mister."

Knowing that he had several hundred dollars in his wallet from his day's receipts, the salesman decided to take his chances. He tried to push the boy out of his way, but before he knew what was happening, he was slammed to the ground. He could feel sharp, hacking knife-stabs, the strong fingers tearing at his pockets until they found the billfold. In the struggle the handkerchief slipped and he saw the boy's face clearly.

"Are you certain that this is the person who knocked you down and stabbed you?" I asked.

"Yes," the salesman replied softly, "I'm sure. If it was only the money he wanted, why did he keep stabbing me the way he did?"

Although the man's question was stricken from the official court record when Hambone's lawyer objected, it echoed in my mind as the judge discussed the boy with his parents before making his final decision. Hambone's mother and father—neat, law-abiding, thrifty restaurant workers who one day hoped to own a small take-out restaurant—seemed as baffled as anyone by their son's repeated hold-ups and assaults. His younger brothers and sisters gave little trouble, apart from running around with the neighborhood toughs from whom their parents, like many other trapped ghetto-dwellers, could not shield them. Hambone's father explained that he gave the boy a small allowance and that he had disciplined Hambone when he was younger by whipping him with a belt when he played hookey or came home too late.

At thirteen, Hambone had been so disruptive in his junior high school that he had been transferred to a special disciplinary school. His parents had approved the move, even though attendance there carried a stigma in their neighborhood. They had hoped that the school's rigid code of punishment for even small infractions would keep the boy within manageable limits. But he continued to get into difficulty. The probation officer, impressed by his parents' character traits, had recommended that the boy continue to live at home with them. His mother had usually minimized the reports the probation officer had received from other children that Hambone was menacing them with a knife.

"Mrs. Beardsley," said the judge as he scanned Hambone's dossier, "it's clear to me that you kept seeing improvement in the boy when in fact there was none at all. Didn't you realize that you were just covering up?"

"I know, your Honor." She sighed wearily. "I just kept praying he would change. I don't want him to be a jailbird—his daddy and I have worked too hard, trying to give him everything we could. It seems to me he's gotten worse since he's been at the Youth Study Center and Pennypack House. The last time he was there he came out even more full of hate. I know there's something wrong with him, but what is it?"

"The psychiatrists feel that he needs to be controlled because he can't control himself. They don't think he is crazy or sick. They think Hambone is responsible for the things he does. They suggest that I send him to the State Correctional Institution at Camp Hill."

Mrs. Beardsley broke into loud sobbing. The very mention of this prison terrified her. In Jungle parlance, Camp Hill is the end of the line.

As the lawyer tried to comfort her, she whispered something to him. He shook his head vigorously No. Catching my quizzical glance, he walked over to me and explained in low tones that she wanted the boy to be transferred to an adult court for a jury trial. Such a transfer, known as a certification, is usually requested by the District Attorney's office in cases of the utmost severity short of murder; but a defense lawyer may ask the court to consider such a move if the facts in the case are hotly disputed. Hambone's lawyer refused outright because he was afraid that his client would receive a much longer sentence than the usual eighteen-month stay ordinarily decreed at Camp Hill. I agreed with him.

None of us could have foreseen that in the end Hambone would spend five long years at Camp Hill anyway. But then, since we understood so little about him, how could we possibly have anticipated the explosive impact which commitment to that institution would have on him? On the three-and-a-half-hour ride to Camp Hill, Hambone kicked in an entire side of the sheriff's van in a futile attempt to escape. Once he was inside the institution, defiance became his daily routine. He destroyed everything his hands could reach. The isolation cell became his regular habitat. During the brief intervals that he was allowed to eat with other prisoners he lashed out at everyone, including even his cronies from the Purple Panthers, who kept urging him to play it cool, the way they were doing, so that he would be released quickly. After eight months, Hambone was too much even for Camp Hill; he achieved the unique distinction of being one of the few prisoners the jail failed to control and refused to keep.

When Hambone reappeared before Judge Hoffman I watched him closely. Despite the widespread newspaper publicity attendant upon his return to the court at the request of the Camp Hill superintendent, he was not swaggering. He seemed tough as ever, but also, I thought, older and exhausted in a strange way. When the judge told him that no mental hospital would accept him and that there was no alternative but to send him back to Camp Hill until he reached twenty-one, Hambone received the news with head bowed. I felt an enormous sense of failure as he was led out. Somehow Hambone had stopped communicating with any of us. At that moment, his fury seemed muzzled—but whether temporarily or permanently, who could know? And I asked myself what would happen after his cell door was unlocked and in full manhood he returned to society. But at present, what kind of manhood is possible for the Hambones in this country?

Even for middle-class children, passage from childhood to maturity has become increasingly tortuous. The rebellious behavior of this group of teen-agers has taken on an antisocial cast similar, at least on the surface, to the chaotic behavior of less privileged children. Some of the most striking of these "new faces" in juvenile court are those of boys and girls who "drop out" of their comfortable niches into an indefinable and confused existence that all too often leads to an abyss.

The Juvenile Court, which had originally sought to help lower-class children who lacked parental guidance, has neither the philosophical bent nor the machinery to cope with children who reject the whole concept of parenthood as it is currently interpreted in Western culture. Ever since the Juvenile Court began to serve as a superparent for this "now" generation of the late fifties and early sixties, it has found itself as frustrated and impotent as the well-dressed parents who stand helplessly before it.

The first reaction to the presence of these middle-class children in the courtroom was, "What are *they* doing here? It must be a horrible mistake!" But it wasn't.

In the beginning, officialdom suspected that some deep-seated pathology was causing the vandalism, theft, drug addiction, and sexual license that these teen-agers were being charged with. And it was true that many of them had frequented psychiatrists' offices and clinics off and on for long periods of time. But, as privileged youngsters continued to be hustled into sheriffs' vans along with the children of the poor, it became evident that in both groups the alienation, the rage, the destructiveness are linked to changes in the American way of life—changes that affect every segment of society. It is not surprising that judges, probation officers, therapists, and superintendents of juvenile institutions face their tasks with uncertainty and anxiety.

Take Margo Ellis, for example. She had the kind of small, beautifully featured face that graces advertisements for expensive hair preparations. It was a face one expects to see at coming-out parties, football games, proms—anywhere that nice upper-middle-class children usually congregate; it was not a face I was accustomed to view across my desk in court. How had she got here?

At fourteen she was the elder of two daughters of a well-known physician with an excellent practice in one of Philadelphia's upper-crust Anglo-Saxon enclaves. I quickly scanned the arrest report. At four-thirty in the morning a park guard had flashed his light upon her nude body pinioned to the turf of a remote area of Fairmount Park; she was surrounded by seven boys between the ages of sixteen and eighteen. Before I could read further, the case was called and the park guard made ready to testify.

Margo was standing next to him, near my desk, trembling from head to toe.

"Are you all right?" I whispered to her.

She nodded, covering her mouth with a limp handkerchief.

Through the courtroom door strode a distinguished gray-suited man carrying a briefcase. As he approached the bar of the court and chatted with a few of the seven disheveled boys who were Margo's alleged assailants, I recognized Guy Hotchkiss, a pillar of the Philadelphia Bar Association and an outstanding corporate lawyer. He greeted Judge Hoffman, pulled out a yellow pad, and signaled to me that he was ready. Hotchkiss, I thought, must be in juvenile court for the first time in his life. Obviously, one of the boys' parents, perhaps an old business client, had engaged him to represent all of them. At his appearance, whispers buzzed among the well-dressed couples who sat in the front-row seats reserved for parents of children who have business with the juvenile court.

The park guard's account followed the text of the written report in front of me. He was red-eyed from lack of sleep, having come directly from his all-night tour of duty. His testimony was crucial because he was an eyewitness and could identify the boys who encircled the nude girl. His first question when he came upon the park scene, he reported, was normal enough: "What's going on here?" The boys were silent, but Margo pulled on a coat that was lying crumpled on the grass, stood up, and said calmly, "Nothing is going on, Officer. There's been a slight misunderstanding, that's all."

He took them all to Park Guard headquarters and notified his superior officers, who in turn called the special Juvenile Aid officers who had the authority to interrogate the youths. A policewoman was also dispatched to take charge of Margo. While waiting for their arrival, the boys—all students at an exclusive preparatory school—asked about the automobiles left behind in the park; they were apparently new and fairly expensive sports models. It was the only concern any of them expressed. One boy begged the park guard to drive him back there so that he could remove the keys he had left in the ignition. The guard acceded to this request.

At that point in the story the Juvenile Aid investigator took up the narrative after Hotchkiss indicated that he had no questions for the park guard. The young police officer seemed embarrassed by the testimony he was about to present; he stated at the outset that he would be quoting the kids directly.

At first Margo and the boys had insisted that she had only taken off her clothes and that nothing else had happened. Then one boy had made a snickering reference to Margo's underdeveloped breasts. Outraged by his gibes, Margo had burst forth into a torrent of accusation. "You like me well enough to screw me—each of you! Not once but twice!" she shouted. Then the park guard had appeared. She had repeated her story to the policewoman who took down her statement and typed it out. Margo had signed it with a great flourish. The guard handed me that statement.

A mink-swathed mother jumped up, screaming, "She's a lying little tramp!"

The man next to her tried to restrain her, but she continued to shout, "Tramp! Tramp!"

The judge rapped sharply with his knuckles. "One more outburst, madam, and you will be put out of this courtroom," he told her matter-of-factly. "By the way, are Margo's parents here?"

An attractive couple stood up. He was prematurely gray, goodlooking in well-tailored tweeds. She was smartly turned out and looked somewhat brittle.

"Go to her," the judge instructed them. "She looks fairly shaky." Neither parent moved an inch.

"I don't want them near me." Margo tossed her head. "I'm okay."

Before I began to ask her questions on direct examination, I handed Mr. Hotchkiss a copy of the girl's statement. He read it carefully, looked up, made a *moue* of disbelief, and passed it back to me. He probably hadn't read anything like it since *Fanny Hill*, I thought.

My voice was, I hoped, friendly, even though my queries to Margo were crisp.

How had she met these boys? How long had she known them? Had she ever had relations with any boy before last night? In her own words, would she tell the court what exactly had happened?

Fortunately, the policewoman had already asked Margo these questions, so I was covering familiar ground. In cases involving sexual episodes where the investigation was often less thorough, I had faced the awkward situation of having to put intimate questions to strange children for the first time in the constraining atmosphere of the court-room. Under such circumstances, it was difficult to achieve rapport, or even coherent answers. But Margo was not at all self-conscious. With the flat, slightly petulant voice of a child recounting an unsuccessful shopping expedition, she told her story.

The day before, Bruce Jenkins ("Yeah, the blond crew-cut one over there") called her for a blind date. She vaguely knew who he was. She used to go to a private day school for girls near the prep school Bruce attended, so she knew lots of the guys. She met him that same night at nine-thirty outside a hamburger spot to which her father had given her a lift. She told Dad she was meeting some girl friends. Bruce said they would just ride around for a while. He had a flask of scotch, filched from his parents' supply of liquor, and they shared it. Margo had three or four swigs before Bruce finally stopped the car somewhere in the park. There were several other cars parked nearby; Bruce told her some of his buddies wanted to talk to them. They got out and walked over to the other automobiles.

Six boys poured out—yes, they were all here in court now. She knew most of them by sight. Bruce said they wanted to try something with her because they knew she was so "hot." They wanted to "pull a train" on her. "That means," volunteered Margo, "that all seven of them would screw me, one right after the other."

A loud gasp arose from the parents' section.

I had understood what "pulling a train" meant. Just a few weeks earlier, I had prosecuted twelve teen-age school dropouts who raped an eleven-year-old girl in the fire tower of a large public housing project. The child, a virgin, fainted after the first two boys had raped her, so she couldn't identify the others, who fled long before she was discovered, unconscious and bleeding, by a tenant.

Margo's case was easier to establish. She was a good witness.

She agreed to take the boys on, with one proviso: she would direct the action, telling them when she was ready to start with the next boy. They were all going to have their kicks—but it didn't turn out the way she thought it would. They crowded around and mounted her like beasts, without saying a word to her. After his second turn, Bruce suddenly decided that he wanted her to suck him, but Margo refused. When she began to struggle, saying she had had enough, one boy held her arms, another her legs, while a third boy got ready to take another turn. The nightmare ended with the blaze of the park guard's flashlight.

Anticipating the defense lawyer's line of questioning, I shifted to Margo's sexual past. Better to have her tell it willingly now than reluctantly later under cross-examination. I read the medical report. Early that morning Margo had been given a vaginal examination by the woman physician assigned to the Youth Study Center each day to examine children involved in sexual assaults.

The report read: "Old, healed tear of hymen. Vaginal opening admits four fingers." Margo's sexual past was extensive—of that, there could be no doubt.

Her first sex relations, she stated, occurred with her consent when she was twelve years old. She had been with lots of boys, she guessed.

"How many boys, Margo?"

"I didn't stop to count, your Honor. Eighty, a hundred—I don't know. But nothing like last night ever happened to me!"

Margo's mother moaned, then covered her face. The girl glanced back and then said almost inaudibly, "Oh, Mother, for God's sake." I noted that she was close to tears.

"Cross-examine, Mr. Hotchkiss," Judge Hoffman instructed.

The lawyer looked down at his jottings, lifted his head, took off his glasses, and then addressed the judge. "I really have nothing more to ask this young lady. Mrs. Richette has elicited a full and shocking statement from her. I do not minimize what my young clients have done. It is revolting. Yet I feel that *all* of them—these boys, this young lady—were involved in a joint venture. Frankly, I am as baffled as anyone by this kind of thing, but it does happen. The important thing now, from our viewpoint, is to make sure that these boys are truly repentant for the abuse they inflicted while under the influence of liquor, and that they stop *all* drinking. I cannot really find any element of coercion, your Honor. I would ask that you give these young men a stern warning and leave them to the tender mercies of their parents. I am certain they will not find them very tender."

Judge Hoffman smiled slightly. It was the kind of skillful, persuasive advocacy for which Hotchkiss was famous. But this was not a meeting being held to reach a gentlemanly agreement about stock certificates or minority shareholders' voting rights. It was a court case involving seven boys charged with disorderly conduct, intoxication, assault, and statutory rape of a girl under sixteen years of age.

"Mr. Hotchkiss," the judge began, "I am aware that these boys have never been in juvenile court before this morning. I know they come from fine homes and good schools. This knowledge does not make my task any easier; on the contrary, I find it harder to believe and to accept than if they came from a slum. If their families eked out an existence on welfare funds, I might find that mercy comes more easily, although usually those children, because there is nothing to hold onto in their homes and communities, are dispatched to reformatories. A good whiff of institutional life for a few months might do your clients some good."

Shocked, disbelieving, a few of the boys began to cry. Their parents sat numbly.

"I want full school reports on these boys, and complete psychiatric examinations. It will take the Probation Department at least two weeks to prepare these background studies. Meanwhile, I want them to remain in detention. As you know, Mr. Hotchkiss, the Youth Study Center is so overcrowded that we are using a wing of the House of Correction, Pennypack House, for detainees between sixteen and eighteen years of age. None of these young men is under sixteen, so they will spend two weeks at Pennypack. I will see you and them in a fortnight."

Hotchkiss made one last appeal for the boys' return to their homes while the studies were being made. Judge Hoffman summoned us both to side-bar. He felt certain, he said, that the boys' records would prove excellent, but he wanted to teach them a lasting lesson. Too many middle- and upper-middle-class children think their parents can get them off simply by hiring a top-flight lawyer or writing a check. These boys needed to experience some hardship and suffering in order to understand that they were being held responsible for their actions. He promised that he would list the cases as soon as he received word that the studies were ready. Their next hearing would be held in chambers, he added. Hotchkiss nodded understandingly and expressed hope that the boys' full cooperation would result in their discharge.

Still not believing that they were actually going off to jail, the boys filed out, followed by their parents and their lawyer. Dr. and Mrs. Ellis and Margo remained behind.

The judge addressed the parents. "Let's go into my chambers. Margo, will you please wait here? I want to talk with your mother and father." He beckoned to me. "Come along, too. But no stenographer. This will be off the record."

I joined them in the small office behind the courtroom. Dr. and Mrs. Ellis sat forward apprehensively on the leather couch; Judge Hoffman stood in front of his desk, holding the sheaf of arrest reports, statements, and other papers that formed part of Margo Ellis's permanent court file. I lit a cigarette to ease the tension; Mrs. Ellis also began to smoke after Judge Hoffman nodded affirmatively to her silent question.

"What on earth is happening to this girl of yours?" he asked quietly. "Didn't you realize that something of this sort was going on in her life, Mrs. Ellis?"

A slight forward movement of her carefully coiffured head was her only reply.

"What did you do about it?" he pressed.

"Well . . . for one thing, she's a bright girl with a very definite mind of her own. She has her own ideas, your Honor. She thinks I'm a complete square. I saw nothing wrong with her dating boys, but I warned her to be careful. She made some flip remark like 'The trick is to see that the *boys* are careful!' I guess she has been careful—still, it's a wonder she isn't pregnant. I suspected she was—mmm—having relations, but I couldn't be sure. I didn't want to come right out and confront her—she's just a little girl, really—and she does resent me. And she's terribly jealous of her eight-year-old sister, you know. She feels that the youngster is our favorite and that I have turned her father against her. She absolutely *adores* her father."

"Did you tell your husband what you suspected?"

"Yes," she replied, somewhat reluctantly I thought, "but he said I was being unfair. He thinks I'm too hard on her, that I don't bend enough. At home, she's impossible with me. She explodes constantly and calls me terrible names. I never answer her—I just don't talk to her until she has offered a proper apology. Days, weeks, even a month, can go by without our speaking to each other. When she was expelled from private school last year, she said it was our fault for sending her there in the first place."

"What did happen at that school?" I asked.

"Well . . ." She hesitated a moment. "I want to be fair. Her grades *were* terrible, especially toward the end. She used to be a good student and a great reader when she was younger. But as soon as she hit her teens, she changed. She never did homework, and she took tests without even reviewing subjects. I think what really happened was that the headmistress found out about Margo's activities with the boys. At our final conference, she would not come right out with it, but hinted that Margo was not quite normal, that she might be upset emotionally. In fact, she advised us to take her to a psychiatrist."

Judge Hoffman looked up. "Did you?"

"Yes," came the reply. "She went five times. I'm sure the doctor will give you a report, if you want one. He's a very good man, but Margo said he 'turned her off.' She refused to go back after the fifth visit, saying it was a complete waste of her time and our money. At twenty-five dollars an hour, I think she had a point."

"Psychiatry is not my specialty," Dr. Ellis interjected, "but I don't think it's the answer in this case. Not as long as she is at home and can push her weight around. We've all been too easy with Margo. She needs to be punished. That's what we both want, Judge Hoffman. Put her in a school or an institution for as long as is necessary to make her snap out of this thing. The past two years my wife has been sick over this girl. When Margo was asked to leave school, we were so embarrassed we couldn't tell our friends. They found out on their own, anyway, that Margo was in public school. But this situation is different—those boys and their families live right in our neighborhood. How do we go on living there after all this? If I could, I'd move my practice to another—" He broke off suddenly. "Excuse me," he mumbled, turning his face aside.

Judge Hoffman broke the painful silence. "Margo will be studied, of course; but regardless of the outcome, I was hoping you would take the major responsibility for her. After all, you are her parents; you are people of means; you are intelligent; and it is her *first* brush with the law. Furthermore, she needs you both desperately, even if she can't admit it."

"No!" her mother cried out bitterly. "I have to think of my

other child and my husband's position, not to mention my own health. She has to go away. She can't come home."

"What about one of these schools for disturbed children?" I suggested, mentioning two highly rated private facilities on Philadelphia's Main Line.

Apparently, Dr. Ellis had already looked into both schools. The financial strain would be too great, he claimed, especially when it was likely that Margo would have to stay there for the entire high-school period.

"We just can't afford eight thousand dollars a year, your Honor. It's not fair to the rest of us, especially to our other child. We don't expect to get off scot-free. We'll be glad to pay any fee or costs the court orders, wherever you send her."

They remained adamant in their determination that the girl be sent away. As they left, the judge asked them to visit Margo at the Youth Study Center. Mrs. Ellis shook her head.

"I can't, Judge Hoffman. I've taken too much. Her father can visit her if he wants to." We knew it was pointless to try to change her mind.

The probation department studies of the boys showed nothing grossly abnormal in their backgrounds. At the boys' hearing two weeks later, Judge Hoffman adjudged them delinquent, placed them on short-term probation, and sent them home in the custody of their parents.

The next time Mrs. Ellis saw her daughter was two months later in Judge Hoffman's chambers. The studies had been delayed because, apart from Catholic-run schools which Margo absolutely refused to consider, the only available place to send her was a training school and farm that took in less intelligent, less sophisticated girls from a different social stratum. Reluctantly, the probation officer finally recommended that Margo be sent there. The court workers had tried to find a foster home, but they had been turned down by both agencies and private citizens who feared that the girl's sexuality was so dominant that it would disrupt any household.

Margo did not blanch when Judge Hoffman told her she was committed to the farm school. She walked out, flanked by a matron and a sheriff's guard, without a backward glance. Sitting next to Mrs. Ellis, I heard her whisper as the door closed behind Margo, "Good riddance to bad rubbish!" I stared at her in disbelief. She was dry-eyed, composed. Her manicured hands, folded quietly in her lap, looked incapable of violence, just as her face appeared to reflect all the decent middle-class virtues. Yet she had just thrown away her daughter.

Margo lasted six months at the farm school; then she ran off, to be picked up weeks later by the Morals Squad in a flophouse hotel where she was sharing men with an older streetwalker. Her steady boyfriend was a young black sailor who had been an early customer.

This time her father came to court alone. He turned away from the sailor and barely looked at Margo. He was there because in his world people obey court subpoenas; beyond that, he would not become involved.

The school refused to take her back. After another long stint at the Youth Study Center while the authorities cast about futilely for an institution closer to the city, she was finally sent off to a state training school for girls almost four hundred miles away from Philadelphia. Since her parents never visited her, the distance was actually of no consequence. But this institution (since closed down by the Pennsylvania Department of Welfare) was not well run; schooling was minimal and lesbianism was rampant. For a girl like Margo, such a place must have been hell.

When she turned eighteen she was finally released. Her record was poor. She told Judge Hoffman she wanted to take a business course, and Dr. Ellis agreed to pay. She told me that she had arranged to live with a friend who had been a fellow inmate at the training school. The address was not a good one, but she had no place else to go. She was able to stay out of trouble so she was discharged from probation a few months later.

Not long afterward I caught a glimpse of her as I walked through the theater district late one evening with friends. They noticed her first and called my attention to "the girl with the garish make-up, hanging on the arm of that paunchy sailor." Margo's hair was a frizzled henna aureole that seemed to accentuate her elaborately outlined eyes. If she recognized me, she masked her reaction well. She turned down a narrow alley with her companion and that was the last I have seen of her.

Julius, Hambone, Margo, and the thousands of new, troubled—and troubling—clients of America's juvenile courts are part of a frightening reality that has superimposed itself on the hopes and visions of the past. The new faces crowding out the old ones have created a tumult in the children's tribunals. A crisis of unparalleled dimensions threatens to undermine the juvenile court system, and the pessimism, sense of futility, and especially indifference of citizens everywhere in the land make prospects for immediate change unlikely unless everyone takes a new look at those new faces. Meanwhile, many of these youngsters are trapped in a downward spiral of delinquency that leads to further branding by society and its courts. Their young lives spin in the vortex of a self-fulfilling prophecy:

We are what you say we are—the throwaway children.

PART
TWO⸺

BORN
TO BE
THROWAWAYS

PART TWO ═══

PROLOGUE

In classical antiquity, with its extensive system of private property —which included the holding of human beings as personal possessions—children were regarded as the chattel of their parents. Courts did not intervene to change parent-child relationships, no matter how devastating the effects upon young people were. The children of slaves, lacking even vestigial legal rights, differed from free children only in that most of them received no special nurturing and, as soon as they passed through early childhood, became work-units subject to the will and discipline of their owners.

Orphans, however, came under the scrutiny of special tribunals. Interestingly, from the ancient cultures of Mesopotamia down to the present, society has expressed concern for homeless, neglected children. As early as the third century A.D., the Roman emperor Antoninus Pius, in memory of his adored wife Faustina, established a series of institutions for children who, lacking adult protectors, were victimized by unscrupulous exploiters.

The idea that *all* children are the special concern of a state which protects their right to childhood is a relatively new one. Indeed, the whole concept of childhood as a special, unique phase of human development is a twentieth-century idea, as Philip Aries, a French cultural historian, has brilliantly shown in *Centuries of Childhood*. Child labor has been outlawed for less than a hundred years. For the past century the children of American slaves have been engaged in a continuing struggle for equal education, housing, recreation, and the undisputed right to select freely a life style that will carry them into meaningful adulthood.

This change in attitude made possible a change in their legal status. Juvenile Court Acts established special tribunals for children and stated the conditions or circumstances under which these courts could intervene to change a child's environment. These new laws set up an arbitrary division between dependent and neglected children, with individual parental fault as the legal dividing line. If a child's home conditions are bad as a result of a parent's mental or physical infirmities, the child is considered *dependent*. If, on the other hand, a child has been "willfully" neglected or brutalized by a parent who is capable of providing a better home environment, he is labeled *neglected*.

That legal distinction serves no useful purpose today, for a juvenile court judge can do little more than administer a tongue-lashing to a parent, who generally needs much more than that. If there is an available therapy program, the court can only suggest firmly to the individual that he or she seek help. A parent who has contributed to a child's delinquency or undermined his morals can be so charged and the case sent to an adult trial court. The real muscle of the Juvenile Court is reserved for children.

The mechanism that brings these children to official attention is the petition. Often a parent will file this formal request for legal assistance, but he or she frequently hides parental failure under harsh words denouncing the child's seemingly intolerable behavior. In cases of gross abuse or neglect, a relative or a neighbor sometimes musters sufficient courage to appear in court as the parental adversary. More frequently, however, interested parties make anonymous reports to one or another public or private agency, which then investigates, and if the circumstances are compelling enough, presents its own petition to the court.

There has been a dramatic decline in the number of dependency and neglect cases presented to the nation's juvenile courts. In Philadelphia, the number has dwindled from 2,828 cases in 1931 to 1,206 in 1967. This decrease, however, is not the result of overwhelming success in the prevention of these problems. Rather, it reflects in part a growing tendency on the part of social welfare workers to bypass certain legal steps in helping these children. For example, the Philadelphia Department of Welfare, once entrusted with the actual custody of these dependent children, makes its own internal processes flexible enough so that these children can be helped without going into court again. Furthermore, aid-to-dependent-children programs, Title IV of the Social Security Act, and other new measures give administrators rather than courts the power to dispense the largesse that enables children to remain in homes that are deemed adequate. In 1931, 71 per cent of all the dependent and neglected children appearing in juvenile court were removed from their homes and placed elsewhere. In 1967, only 48 per cent of the children were actually shifted.

The attention officialdom gives these children is often of the fly-swatting variety. For the handful of children discussed in this section, and for the thousands who remain faceless, society does not, as Erik Erikson observes in *Childhood and Society*, "lighten the inescapable conflicts of childhood with a promise of some security, identity, and integrity. . . . [or] create the only condition under which human growth is possible."

4

DEATH-DEALING
HOMES

Clipped to a pile of messages and interoffice memos on my desk
when I returned from a morning assignment in juvenile court was a
note my secretary had marked "Urgent," asking me to call Lieutenant Andrews of the Homicide Division, the section of Philadelphia's
police department which investigates all suspicious deaths.

The number I dialed did not have the usual "Municipal" prefix
assigned to police headquarters and I realized that George Andrews
was calling me from the street. Considering his work-style, this was
not extraordinary. An intelligent, resourceful Negro—himself a graduate of ghetto streets—he was a thorough, even dogged, investigator
who patiently pieced together the jagged, raw chunks of background
to murder. Whether he was studying the bloodlettings of the poor—
shootings, knifings, lye-throwings—or investigating violence in a
more elegant setting, Andrews had a relentless drive to nail down
every last detail before he had marked his investigation "Completed."
When he testified in the courtroom, his ability to marshal facts and

relate them authoritatively had a stunning impact. He was one of the most respected men in the police hierarchy; the common belief in the District Attorney's office was that with Lieutenant Andrews as a chief police witness, an otherwise difficult murder case would be won hands down. The last time I had seen him, a few months earlier, he had casually told me that he was attending graduate seminars in sociology at a university that offered evening programs.

"It helps you to understand people better," he had said in reply to my unspoken query. "Also gives you an idea about how to change a lot of things that go on."

The phone at the other end rang once. "Lieutenant Andrews speaking." He had been standing by for the call.

He spoke more rapidly than usual, almost excitedly, I thought. "Thanks very much for calling me back, Lisa. Can you get away from your desk for about an hour? We're investigating something you ought to see. It's ——" His voice broke off, then resumed curtly. "This is something we need you on."

In a few minutes I was heading my car toward the teeming, cluttered slums that lie a few blocks to the north of the courthouse. The address Andrews had given me was not in the Jungle but on its perimeter—a thin line along which hundreds of Puerto Rican families had settled in the last two decades, pushing the original Negro inhabitants farther away from the center of the city.

The house I sought was unnumbered and—except for the first-floor luncheonette with a sign offering Spanish food at cheap prices—indistinguishable from the other dingy four-story brownstones on the block. Working my way around the barricade of a mammoth juke-box in the front of the shop, I found Andrews, two uniformed officers, and a police photographer, all waiting by a wall telephone. The phone rang, and the photographer answered it.

"The Assistant D.A. just walked in," he said. "I have a few more shots to take. Give me another half-hour. This case is pure murder," he added. "Excuse the lousy pun."

Lieutenant Andrews came up to me. "Glad you got here so quickly. We want you to see this just as we found it. The call came a few hours ago from the mother—a Mrs. Margaret Blake. To make the call she had to run to a house down the street where a friend lives. She was completely out of her head with alcohol and shock, so a policewoman took her to the hospital. We haven't touched anything in the apartment. It's on the third floor," he explained, indicating the dilapidated stairway in the hall.

"What have you got there?" I asked Andrews, for his character-istic pipe-and-trenchcoat neatness was marred by the ludicrous addi-tion of a battered saucepan he held in his hand. Peering into its un-scoured depths, I saw a congealed gray lump stuck on the bottom.

"Tell you about that later," Andrews replied. "Easy on the steps. They're very loose."

I needed no warning about those corroded corridors. The rotting woodwork, the gaping banisters, the peeling paint of this house, were part of the general squalor I had come to associate with the lives of many throwaway children. Both official assignments and my own incurable curiosity about how these families lived had propelled me up and down many such rickety flights of steps.

The mingled stench of urine and garbage triggered a faint nausea that I was fortunately able to control. On the third landing, Lieuten-ant Andrews stopped short and, without looking back, knocked on the door. It flew open forcefully and the doorknob clattered to the rough wooden floor. From inside the apartment came a whimpering cry, "Mommy, Mommy!"

In the harsh sunlight streaming through the grimy, unshaded windows I recognized the young woman holding a naked, tousled child of about two. She was Policewoman Bea Straight, an exception-ally sensitive and competent member of the corps of women police officers assigned to work with the juvenile police division.

"We're sorry you have to see this," she explained. "The am-bulance hasn't come for the body yet, and the kids are stuck here because the Department of Public Walfare says it has to clear special space at the shelter for them. They are overcrowded, as usual."

Feeling a tingling, whirring sensation, I brushed my hand against my face and hair and glanced down at my clothes. In those few seconds I had been in the room, dozens of huge, winged insects had landed on me.

"They're jumpers—flying roaches," said Lieutenant Andrews. "Better stand in the middle of the room. They usually stay near the walls."

The roaches terrified me more than the large sewer rat that scurried into a dim corner as I stepped forward.

We were standing in a makeshift bedroom. Three foul-smelling, unmade beds, pressed against the unpainted walls, jutted out into the room. The light from an exposed overhead bulb spotlighted three thin brown forms on one of the beds. I stared down at the sleeping children lying huddled against each other. A filthy sheet had torn on one of the exposed coil-springs of the mattress; large dried urine puddles had created a counterpoint design to the faded floral print of the mattress cover. Oozing from the smallest of the children was a pile of feces.

The rest of the furnishings were so miserable that they were worthless even as firewood. A gaping dresser-frame boasted only one drawer into which odds and ends—tattered clothing and scuffed shoes—had been thrown helter-skelter. A battered end table leaned crazily against a broken plush armchair that was alive with vermin.

Through the doorless opening into the room beyond, a boy and girl were visible, seated quietly on the rough planked floor.

"Woodrow! Ruth!" called Lieutenant Andrews and hurried into the kitchen, waving me to follow.

There, on the floor between the two children, was a contorted pink-and-violet-striped object resting on a pile of newspapers. I stared at it in disbelief. It had feet, hands, a human head; a few patches of curly black hair clung to the skull. It was the corpse of a baby less than a year old. But what had happened to the outer skin?

The staccato sounds of water dripping from a nearby faucet finally penetrated the shock that had immobilized me. I walked over to the sink, and my nausea returned. The grime-encrusted bowl was blood-stained, and from one side of the sink hung a pale-brown oblong membrane. I knew instantly I had found the answer to my question.

Next to the sink was a refrigerator; its broken door hung open, revealing utterly bare shelves. A terrible stench emanated from it as well as from the wooden ledge that had served as a kitchen table. A sliver of meat lay moldering on a tin pie-plate. As I turned away, my foot brushed against two empty soda bottles; the rattle of the glass broke the ghastly silence. The walls of the kitchen, I saw, like those of the entire apartment, were thin partitions pock-marked with literally hundreds of tiny holes. I remember wondering absently what could have caused them. Here and there were larger holes, like the gaping wounds left by a severe bombardment. Pieces of plaster had fallen, leaving a film of fine gray dust everywhere.

"Don't miss the bathroom." Policewoman Straight pointed to a tiny, windowless area to the right of the kitchen. A half-hinged wooden door sagged against a grime-ringed tub; the toilet bowl had no seat or flush handle. Peering into the uncovered tank, I saw that the inner tubing was old and worn out. I realized that the apartment's foul stench was compounded by the lack of workable plumbing.

When we returned to the bedroom, the children were still sleeping. I looked at the other beds more closely now and saw that the mattress of the smallest one had been almost entirely eaten away. The stiff coils had survived, and clinging to several of them were bits of the same substance I had seen on the sink.

Lieutenant Andrews motioned to the photographer. "Get it all. Everything. You can do the body later."

The photographer went to work immediately, recording each horrifying detail.

Lieutenant Andrews maneuvered around the farthest bed and pointed. There, almost hidden from sight, stood a magnificent color television set. "It's new," he noted unnecessarily. "The price tag is still on it." He read aloud the name of a large merchandising outlet store specializing in installment sales to poor people. Once the buyers —many of whom were on relief—signed the payment contract, the store through its own finance company sold the contract to a prominent bank, which then assumed the task of extracting payments from persons it never would have accepted as credit risks on its own. Complaints about this practice flooded the Business Frauds Division of the District Attorney's office every day.

"The set isn't even connected," Andrews observed. "Mrs. Blake must have purchased it before her last binge."

"How does she support herself?" I asked. "How could she possibly afford that TV?"

"She receives a welfare check—one of her children told me," the policewoman answered. "We don't know the amount, of course, but with six children, it must have been nearly two hundred dollars a month."

I did some quick mental arithmetic. At the standard monthly rate of twenty-nine dollars per child—the bare subsistence rate allowed under government regulations—Mrs. Blake had been receiving one hundred and seventy-four dollars a month.

Just a few minutes later in walked a young man who identified himself as a social worker from the Philadelphia Department of Welfare. After a brief discussion, we agreed that he should take the three younger children to the Department's shelter for homeless children. Ruth and Woodrow, because of their direct involvement with the circumstances of baby Rita's death, would go instead to the Youth Study Center on charges of delinquency.

The sleeping children were roused, wrapped in blankets, and carried off; they were so numb with fatigue, hunger, and fear that they barely uttered a protest. Ruth and Woodrow sat motionless when I explained to them why their younger brothers and sisters would be in one place and they in another. Despite the apartment's near-freezing chill, which penetrated the heavy coats we wore, the handsome boy, who was nine, was bare-chested, wearing only a torn pair of jeans. His bare feet, like his sister's, were heavily coated with dirt. Younger by a year than her brother, Ruth, too, wore a single layer of clothing: a tattered print summer dress.

A careful search of the single dresser drawer yielded neither shoes nor garments that fit the two youngsters. Fortunately, the detention center to which they were to be taken by police squad car was a little more than a mile away; the emergency blankets that Andrews had ordered would keep them warm on the way. At the Youth Study Center they would be given clothes immediately.

Shortly after Woodrow and Ruth left, two men from the Medical Examiner's office arrived to remove the last member of the Blake family—the infant, Rita. Despite his deft movements, the man whose task it was to collect the body trembled as he knelt on the floor to slip the tiny form into the pillowcase in which it would be taken to the city morgue. When I saw the photographs several days later I knew why he had flinched. In contrast to the devastation of the body, the features of the little face were beautifully distinct, and the innocent eyes, glazed with pain, were intact.

Across this filthy death chamber, Andrews, Policewoman Straight, and I faced each other, still speechless with horror. Now that the official details had been attended to, my strongest impulse was to run down the steps in a quick escape. But Andrews seemed rooted to the floor. I waited. The roaches continued to buzz; the rat rustled in its corner.

"We'd better take a last look around," Andrews murmured at last. "This is probably as bad as it can get."

We walked through the apartment once more, poking around, inspecting, trying to memorize the sickening details that are not included in official reports, to which only the camera would bear silent witness.

As we finally closed the lockless door behind us, Andrews reminded himself to place a call to the furniture store to remove the television set before it was stolen or damaged by vandals.

"Are you also going to call the Department of Public Health?" I asked. "If ever there was a place truly unfit for human habitation, that is it. And imagine—they sell *food* on the first floor!'"

After Andrews finished his calls, we stood in the deepening twilight and made an appointment to meet the next day in my office to work up the case for presentation to the juvenile court. The whole family would come under the legal scrutiny of this court; the three children at the welfare shelter because they were dependent; Woodrow and Ruth as possible culprits in the baby's death; the mother to review her credentials as a fit custodian for the children. For her, it would also be a preliminary hearing to assess whether or not the charge of homicide should be filed against her for trial by jury in an adult court. As usually happens with adults charged with criminal neglect of children or corrupting them morally or otherwise, evidence and background information would be gathered and presented by the Juvenile Court's own investigative staff first.

That evening I sat at my desk at home writing out the facts that Andrews had presented to me. Mrs. Blake had received her last welfare check four days earlier, and according to Mr. Diaz, the luncheonette owner who had cashed it for her, she had immediately gone out, not to reappear until a few hours before the police arrived. While she was away—not very far apparently, since she was seen in neighborhood bars and coming in and out of various houses throughout the four-day period—Ruth and Woodrow took charge of the household. There was nothing at all to eat in the apartment, and after his mother had been gone a full day, Woodrow went down to the luncheonette and asked Mr. Diaz for some food. He came away with a few stale rolls.

Two, possibly three, days passed and the laments of the hungry children became louder. Baby Rita wailed incessantly and would not sleep. Woodrow and Ruth decided that a bath might calm her a bit and give them some peace. She might even go to sleep. The kitchen sink was the only place to bathe her, so Ruth held the baby under the faucet while Woodrow turned on the water. It was sizzling hot and Rita screamed in pain as the water beat down on her tiny body. Panic-stricken, the children ran to the bedroom, flinging the baby onto the nearest empty bed. But the burned skin stuck to some exposed mattress coils as Rita moved, causing her to shriek louder. Woodrow, pushing aside the hysterical Ruth, ran back to the kitchen with his bleeding baby sister and placed her in the sink. Soon the tiny body stopped quivering and was still. Both Ruth and Woodrow sensed that Rita was dying—perhaps even dead—so they hid her on the floor where the other children could not see her.

They waited and their hunger pangs became unbearable. Finally Woodrow found some old flour, added hot water from the sink, stirred up the sticky mess with an old spoon, and told his brothers and sisters that it was fresh bread. Each of them ate a little. The pot in which he had "cooked" it had caught Andrews' eye; it was this object that he had been holding when I arrived at the luncheonette.

On that fourth morning, at eleven o'clock, Mrs. Blake finally came back to her children. Even though she was heavily intoxicated, she realized that Rita was missing. Woodrow and Ruth, at first evasive, soon collapsed under her heavy blows and took the baby's body out of its hiding place. Mrs. Blake ran screaming out of the house to tell a neighbor what had happened, and her friend called the police. When Andrews saw her, he decided she needed to be hospitalized.

As I came to the end of the account, I could feel again the chill, the poverty, the degradation of the Blake apartment—a strange contrast to the warm, comfortably furnished study in which I was sitting. John Donne's words, "No man is an island, we are all part of a vast continent, a dominion," kept echoing in my mind as I considered how to end my report. Finally, I wrote:

So, when the child Rita Blake died in her naked filth, her undernourished flesh impaled on the rusty springs of an infested mattress, there in that unheated, unlit twentieth-century dungeon, all of us were involved in her death. If a bell tolls for that seedling life, it tolls for all those who turn away their unseeing eyes from these death-dealing homes.

The next morning, before going to my office, I went back to the brownstone. Mr. Diaz followed me up the stairs, all the while explaining that there was a new door and Lieutenant Andrews had asked him to escort me when I returned. I couldn't help smiling. Andrews, whose obsession with the case I had detected the day before, had been perceptive enough to sense that I, too, would be haunted by the hideous reality of the Blake household and would return to it.

When I arrived at the third floor I gasped in surprise. If I had not known better, I could easily have assumed I was in the wrong building.

A new, unpainted wooden door with a shiny brass knob opened into a freshly plastered and painted apartment. Even the windows had been scrubbed down. Every room was bone-bare but clean. The firewood furniture, the maggot-ridden beds, had vanished. The color television set had already been picked up, at Andrews' request, by the credit store. How many hands had wrought this miracle, I wondered. Set away from the still-moist walls in the kitchen were a gleaming refrigerator, a gas range, and even an attractive dinette set. Those former implements of death, the sink and the unspeakable faucet, were both gone. In their stead was new equipment still bearing the manufacturers' labels. Even before I opened the new bathroom door I knew what I would see. The only reminder that less than twenty-four hours ago this room had been a garbage heap came from a faint stench that mingled with the strong odor of disinfectant.

With many gestures I scarcely heeded, Diaz explained how crews engaged by the landlord had worked through the night in a fever to complete everything before the Public Health inspectors arrived to investigate Andrews' complaint. The Herculean effort, I thought to myself, had paid off: the Augean stable was indeed cleaned out. And the higher rent the slumlord could now charge would bring in far more money than he had had to spend to obtain that nighttime labor. Only the police photographs and our testimony could attest to the brutal squalor he had imposed upon people who could afford nothing better.

Mercenary motives in part accounted for his lack of concern for his tenants—after all, he was a property owner, not an overseer of the poor. But what about the Department of Public Assistance, out of whose monthly checks Mrs. Blake had paid her rent? How could even the most case-calloused and overburdened social worker have approved of such living quarters? And what about the other links between this family and the community—the Board of Education truant officer, for example, or the visiting nurses?

Returning to juvenile court, I found Andrews waiting in my office with a packet containing the photographs, and together we went down to the courtroom to confer with Judge Hoffman. Before uttering a single word, we showed him the pictures. Halfway through them he stopped, livid with anger.

"I want a *full* investigation of this tragedy," he exclaimed. "Why was Mrs. Blake allowed to keep those children? I'll call the Welfare Commissioner to be sure that he finds foster homes for all five of them—yes, even Woodrow and Ruth. I realize that you had to file delinquency petitions, Lieutenant, since they accidentally scalded the baby and then hid the body for several days. But unless you and Mrs. Richette can come up with additional evidence of actual criminal behavior on the part of these poor children, I will discharge them of any delinquency and hold them instead as dependent or neglected children—depending on what we find out about Mamma Blake. Is she still in the hospital?"

Andrews nodded. "I spoke with the doctor earlier this morning and he tells me she is an advanced alcoholic with some brain deterioration."

"Astonishing for a twenty-six-year-old woman," Judge Hoffman observed.

Andrews agreed. "She also has another interesting condition," he added. "She is in her fourth month of pregnancy, and she is not sure who the father is."

Mrs. Blake's preliminary hearing before Judge Hoffman on charges of homicide and criminal neglect was scheduled for the following week. During the interval, I spent most of my out-of-court hours working on the case. I had lengthy telephone conversations and face-to-face interviews with all the officials who should have known about the Blake children—but did not. The truth was almost inconceivable.

For example, the Board of Education did not know that these children even existed. Neither Woodrow nor Ruth had ever been enrolled in school. I learned that Mrs. Blake had moved around so frequently that even if a complaint had been filed, a school representative would have been hard pressed to find them.

"But there must be hundreds of lost children like them," I exclaimed.

"Yes," came the brisk reply. "We just expect a small percentage of such kids to escape us. Children of migratory workers are a good example."

I was rocked. Even with my court experience, I still assumed that every six-year-old child automatically fell into one of those neatly lined-up rows of students waiting for the school bell to ring.

Since the State Department of Public Assistance case records were regarded as confidential communications between a social service agency and a client, I was not permitted to read the entries made by the Blake family's case worker and her supervisor. But the chief administrative officer who met with me said he could find no notation or complaint about Mrs. Blake's drinking bouts or her appalling neglect of home and children, despite the fact that during the nine years that she had been on Public Assistance rolls, she had been "seen" by almost twice as many case workers as was customary. Why so many? At that time, the turnover in social service personnel was about 50 per cent a month. The case loads, in some instances as high as two hundred families per social worker, were so staggering, and the kind of help that could be offered was so minimal—in many cases even nonexistent—that sensitive college graduates and in-training social-work students found the experience too shattering and quit. Mrs. Blake's present case worker, for example, had been assigned to the family about two weeks earlier, but had not been able to make a home visit. New applications for public assistance had required her services as an investigator.

"We're running an espionage system," the administrator said bitterly. "We're more concerned with whether or not adults lie than with whether or not children eat. It's perfectly understandable to me why, given the present system, once Mrs. Blake was found eligible for a grant, she just slid by month after month."

He pulled a folder out of his briefcase. It was bulging with type-written and mimeographed sheets.

"These are the proposals and recommendations that I and other directors throughout the state have made for additional family counseling services for our clients. Every year we send them to the top brass at Harrisburg; they send us back their grateful endorsement. And every year the Appropriations Committee of the legislature flatly turns down our requests for additional funds. The name of the game is 'Saving the Taxpayers' Money.' Just once, I wish we would try playing the game called 'Saving the Children's Lives!'"

At the Center, Woodrow and Ruth were at first so shy and withdrawn that the group supervisors feared that they might be incipient schizophrenics. But, at Judge Hoffman's request, two social workers saw them daily and reported that the children's problem was that they were totally confused by the new world they found themselves in. Even though many of the daily activities of the Center were commonplace routine, any organized pattern was foreign to Ruth and her brother. They had to learn, in a few days' time, the socialization patterns that most children absorb in the first six years of life.

For example, they had never tasted the simple ordinary foods of American culture. Neither Woodrow nor Ruth knew what hamburger was. When asked what they ate, they shrugged their shoulders. Since they were both illiterate, they could not identify the numbers and letters that marked their rooms at the Center; they remained in them, afraid that if they left they would never be able to find their way back. Even the very act of communication between adults and children was a new experience. Because Mrs. Blake usually screamed obscenities at them, both children peppered their conversation with four-letter words.

"It's fantastic," one of the group of workers said to me. "These children are so far out of it that sometimes I almost find myself viewing them as visitors from another planet!" I agreed. The distance that separated them from society could have been measured in terms of light-years.

The Blake children made good newspaper copy. Reporters referred to the case as the "boiled baby story." Letters began to come into the District Attorney's office. Some of the letter-writers viewed the grim story as proof that public welfare programs were worthless. Others were viciously racist, citing the Blake home conditions as evidence that "these people" were nothing more than "animals." I decided to save all this mail and set up two files—one labeled *Community Response*, the other *Crackpottery*. The second file was far more voluminous than the first.

Among the letters was a postcard with these pencil-scrawled words:

> Miz Blake got another baby. She safe at
> Fernwood Schol. Find out. You see I right.

The card bore no signature. Anonymous messages are common working materials in police departments and prosecutors' offices.

I took it with me when I went to the Fernwood School to check out this tip. Outside, the building had the moldering Victorian stone façade that marked it as a ghetto elementary school, but as I stepped inside I could feel a happy vitality in the air. John Sloan, the school's principal, was a middle-aged Negro whose dynamism and dedication were well known. Several years ago, two of the children who attended his school had been burned to death in one of those devastating fires that sweep through the papier-mâché firetraps in which many poor families live.

Sloan, it had been reported to me, wept at their funeral, but he dried his tears quickly and did two things. First, he called together the most responsible mothers he knew and spurred them into forming a Mothers' Committee. The women serving on it were to act as neighborhood social workers, each one checking on the dozen families of school children assigned to her and reporting home conditions to him. Second, he established a special fund to buy an organ for the school in memory of the dead children, both of whom had been musically gifted.

Sitting down in his office, I asked him about both projects. He smiled in a pleased way.

"Sure," he said. "We're moving along. The Mothers' Committee has uncovered some bad situations which we are trying to get real help on. The biggest problem we discovered is that these kids come to school without breakfast. We already have a hot-lunch program, you know—thanks to a special private grant we received a few years ago. So I went back to the foundation and got some extra money for cereal, milk, and eggs. A group of mothers volunteered to come in to prepare the food, so I didn't have to ask the Board of Education for a penny, thank heaven. As for the organ, we raised enough money to buy it. I hope you will come to the official installation ceremonies next month." (I did attend. It was a beautiful lesson to me of what people can do for themselves even under tragic circumstances.)

I showed Sloan the postcard and told him the purpose of my visit. Apart from that card, I had no other clue about the missing Blake youngster. Suddenly I had a hunch. "Do you have very many severely burned children in this school?"

"About four really bad ones, I think. Do you suppose . . . .?" His voice trailed off as he turned to his files to find their names and addresses.

Armed with the list that John Sloan gave me, I began my quest after I finished in court that afternoon. The first house I called at was clearly not harboring any of Mrs. Blake's children. For one thing, the little girl whose name Sloan had given me was too old; she had just turned eight. The child I was looking for had to be either under eight years old—Ruth's age—or older than nine-year-old Woodrow. Furthermore, I did not think it likely that this woman, who seemed so overwhelmed by her own four children, would accept someone else's child.

The next address was hard to find. The tiny, littered street began and ended abruptly and was really nothing more than an extended alleyway. A polite, exhausted woman in her early sixties came to the door.

"Yeah," she said, "I'm Miz Everett. You say you want to see my baby Joan? What for? She went to the store."

I explained that I was trying to find out what her relationship was to the little girl. Was Joan a foster child?

She answered readily. "I'm Joan's foster mother. And I take good care of her. Who's complaining?"

After I reassured her that nothing was amiss, she invited me into a small but tidy sitting room. A few minutes later, a healthy little girl who bore a marked resemblance to the other Blake children bounded into the room. She was wearing a colorful head scarf, which she kept on even after she removed her coat and sat down to chat with us. As I studied her more closely I saw that one side of her face, which she carefully tried to keep turned away from me, had a network of scars running from temple to chin.

Finally Mrs. Everett sent her to visit a little friend who lived nearby. When we were alone, she leaned toward me and said quietly, "I'm going to tell you the truth."

Six years earlier, Mrs. Everett, a childless widow, had been visiting a friend at a city hospital and on her way out of the building had met a thin young woman carrying a baby whose head and face were bandaged. Two other small youngsters trailed behind her. She was crying as she tottered under her burden, and Mrs. Everett sympathetically asked if she could be of any help. The girl explained that there had been a fire in the apartment she had been living in, and now she had no place to stay. She could manage the other two children, but she just couldn't take care of her badly burned baby girl.

" 'Tell you what—I'll take your baby home with me,' I said to the poor girl, and she handed her over right on the spot. She just said, 'Her name is Joan,' and that was that. The good Lord never gave me any children." Mrs. Everett looked genuinely unhappy about this fact. "But I took care of lots of them on my job—I did domestic work then, and I still do day work to make ends meet. I never asked for relief money for that baby," she added firmly, still unsure of my reason for being there. "Anyway, that girl never came around to see her child, so I became Joan's mamma. You won't tell her, will you?"

"It's not up to me," I had to answer honestly. "The court will have to decide. But tell me, how did you enroll her in school without a birth certificate? The mother obviously didn't give you one—or did she?"

She shook her head. "I told the school she was my niece from down South, and that I was trying to get her birth certificate. I begged them very hard to take her in, and they did."

She assured me that she would bring Joan to court for any tests or studies the judge might order. As I walked down the street with its dwarfed houses, I wondered how many wonderful Mrs. Everetts there were in the city—indeed, the world—who become self-appointed, unpaid foster parents for throwaway children. I wished that for every Mrs. Blake there was a loving, maternal replacement. We needed legions of such women and John Sloan, for one, had realized how helpful they were in the child welfare area.

Judge Hoffman had ordered that the Blake children's case be listed separately from Mrs. Blake's. Since she had been transferred from the hospital to the detention center for women on criminal charges, she was entitled to a speedy preliminary hearing. With her in court was a lawyer from the Voluntary Defender Association, a privately funded agency that provides lawyers for indigent criminal defendants.

Lieutenant Andrews, always a thorough and eloquent witness, at one point stopped, leaned down, and picked up an object which he offered into evidence as a Commonwealth exhibit: the battered saucepan containing the moldy remains of Woodrow's bread. Police-woman Straight was an equally competent witness.

Despite the lawyer's plea that Mrs. Blake was not guilty of the kind of criminal neglect on which a charge of involuntary man-slaughter could properly be based, Judge Hoffman ordered her to stand trial in adult court on that charge. He set bail at a customary low figure, which he knew that Mrs. Blake with outside help might be able to meet. If she had to stay in jail, he added, he hoped that some representative of Alcoholics Anonymous would talk to her. She would soon be a mother again, and unless she was cured of her drinking habit, she might injure another child, possibly several. After all, he said in conclusion, she could not be incarcerated forever.

When she asked permission to say something to Judge Hoffman off the record, I felt that beneath her listless manner there was genuine anxiety about her children. Whenever their names had been mentioned during the hour-long proceedings, she had pressed her lips together as though to control an outcry. Therefore, I was not surprised when she asked the judge for permission to see them. She hoped that Woodrow and Ruth, at least, could live with her when the case was over. It was clear to me that her interest in them was more than financial: although she counted on receiving a public assistance check for them, she was also emotionally dependent upon them. In a twisted way that is common in such situations, her young-sters had become almost parent figures to her. She had taken away their childhood so that she might continue her own.

Ultimately, Mrs. Blake was acquitted of the involuntary man-slaughter charge. Despite the convincing case the prosecuting attorney presented, the visiting judge from an outlying county assigned to criminal court that month was so shaken by the civic apathy that had permitted such home conditions to exist that he excoriated Philadelphia welfare authorities and the community as a whole. Since Mrs. Blake's lawyer had wisely waived a jury, the decision was solely the judge's. Coming from a prosperous farm area, he could not understand how such human misery could be tolerated in the very shadow of the great new plazas and buildings that characterize the "redevelopment" of the city.

Long before Mrs. Blake left the courthouse, a free woman about to give birth to a new life, Judge Hoffman had permanently removed her children from her custody.

The City Department of Welfare found a good foster home in which Woodrow and Ruth could grow up together. The three younger Blakes went as a group to another of the Department's homes. Joan, the child I had found living with Mrs. Everett, presented a more difficult problem.

When the little girl had been examined by a doctor in the court's medical department, she had not wanted to take off her head scarf, and he had to coax her to let him remove it. In spite of himself he stared in horror at the cheap doll's wig that had been crudely stitched to the child's head. The surrounding skin was scarred and somewhat inflamed; Joan told him her head itched constantly. She did not remember when the wig had first been sewn on, but it was a long time ago, she thought. (Mrs. Everett finally confessed that a friend had done it—a "beautician" who assured Mrs. Everett that everything would be all right.) Joan was quickly dispatched to a children's hospital to have the wig surgically removed. An interested dermatologist volunteered to give her special treatments to induce hair growth. A businessman's wife who was an aide at the hospital persuaded her husband to buy Joan a real wig, which she and the little girl selected.

Even disregarding the questionable judgment Mrs. Everett had shown in the matter of the wig, the Department of Welfare would not approve her as a suitable foster mother. She was too old, for one thing. For another, she left the child unsupervised when she went off to do her day work. In her favor, however, was the deep bond between the woman and the child which should not be severed abruptly, if at all. They loved one another, and Mrs. Everett, whatever her limitations, had been a devoted and loyal custodian. She was "Momma" to the little girl.

It was John Sloan who came up with the solution. One of the mothers on his committee was already an approved foster parent for the Department of Welfare; if Joan went to live with her, she could remain at the school with her friends and classmates and visit Mrs. Everett as often as she wished. Mrs. Everett would then be like a grandmother, affectionate and protective, rather than continue as Joan's principal caretaker.

After Rita Blake's body was laid to rest in a tiny pauper's grave, her mother moved to a city in another state. Several years later I received a letter from the Welfare Department of that community asking the whereabouts of the Blake children; their mother, it seemed, was eager to regain their custody. I referred the letter to Judge Hoffman. His reply was so strongly worded that the social worker called him to apologize for making the request; she simply had not been aware of what had happened in Philadelphia.

It was not surprising that Mrs. Blake had been able to move away and start a new family elsewhere; there is no effective system to deal with interstate referral and supervision of irresponsible parents. Although they do serious, and often irreparable, human damage, no federal agency has assumed a watchdog role. The Children's Bureau of the Health, Education and Welfare Department is traditionally concerned mainly with policies, standards, and practices of state and local child welfare agencies, in addition to juvenile court procedures as they affect victimized children.

Apart from the problem of keeping track of the movements of these families, there is the more complex question of how the community can effectively end the unbelievable social isolation that characterized the Blake household, and that Harriett Wilson, an English investigator, finds as the core problem for these children. Her recent book, *Delinquency and Child Neglect*, stresses how damaging antisocial behavior is frequently induced by the family's lack of connection to the broader community. Long years spent under horrifying home conditions almost inevitably make children especially susceptible to mental and physical disorders that cripple them for the future. By chance, Woodrow and Ruth had enough resilience to survive even the trauma of Rita's death. Other children fall apart under much milder stress. Lindy Burton's recent study, *Vulnerable Children*, effectively documents these observations.

How can these children be rescued from death-dealing homes? Certainly the traditional institutions that dispense children's services —the Department of Public Assistance, the Board of Education, Children's Aid societies—should have enough qualified, stable employees to carry out more effective monitoring and supervisory programs. It is shocking to realize that in the nation's fourth largest city no social agency knew or cared that the six Blake children were living in such devastating squalor. Only when one of them died did anyone at all notice them.

To really work, monitoring systems must be set up right in poor communities and the residents themselves called upon to participate. Using the approach that John Sloan found so successful at Fernwood School, grass-roots groups of knowledgeable, concerned men and women can be organized to perform valuable services, and they should receive reasonable compensation for their efforts. They can spot difficult home conditions and act as intermediaries between the family and the social services establishment. They can provide the day-to-day supervision that is so vital to the success of any remedial program. For example, they can make sure that children receive needed medical treatment, that they are attending school every day. These neighborhood monitors can give overburdened case workers more than just a helping hand; by reflecting ghetto thinking and attitudes, they can provide insights and suggestions for new ways to rescue society's throwaways—children and adults alike. Their effective participation in solving thorny community problems will give demoralized middle-class bureaucrats a psychological lift and help draw them out of *their* isolation.

Monitors can also help in the search for sorely needed foster homes by promoting interest in available programs and by actively recruiting parents for this important job. Small storefront quarters opened at key points can become neighborhood centers that provide activities for everyone. For example, troubled and inadequate parents can attend group-therapy sessions; children can participate in recreational, educational, and training programs run by adult neighbors, who also can plan activities of general interest. Any modest monetary earnings they can realize from their projects will further build their sense of accomplishment and self-worth.

In addition to the monitoring system, much more care needs to be given to the child wardship system, which at present places homeless, dependent, and neglected children under the exclusive care of departmental social workers attached to various public welfare agencies. Apart from the inevitable fact that personnel work patterns cause a certain amount of discontinuity, there is also a more frequently controllable—but more serious—problem: the lack of personal accountability for what happens to a child. It is too easy for a child's "case" to get shuffled around in the bureaucratic maze. *All* children are precious. If they lack parents, their lives should be shared and guided by adults who will be vigilant in protecting their best interests and in giving them the devoted attention that every child needs.

The system as a whole has a clinical coldness about it. Agency decisions to turn children back to juvenile court are often made to placate case workers or supervisors who are unwilling to work with the youngsters. I saw hundreds of adolescents literally dumped back into court during the period of inevitable identity crisis—which is, for children who have been institutionalized for years and have never known their parents, generally much more severe than the average teen-ager experiences. When these young people misbehaved, or ran away in search of their parents, the Welfare Department often filed delinquency petitions against them. Although the worker who testified against such a child would often express regret that such a step had become necessary, I rarely detected the signs of emotion that usually accompany a similar statement uttered by a person closely involved—albeit, part of their professional training is designed to help them maintain a certain emotional distance from their clients.

In my view the system needs two things: a broad new humanizing element that will counteract the feelings of alienation and rejection these children experience, and a set of legal controls.

Young persons who are heirs to money receive the services of a well-paid guardian ad litem who supervises the disposition of those funds until they attain majority. Is the gift of life less important? Do property rights prevail over the human rights to growth, development, and the fulfillment of the child's potential?

Under the recent New York Family Court Act, "law guardians" are appointed to defend children accused of delinquent acts. But vulnerable, parentless children also need *full-time* guardians appointed by the juvenile court to look after all aspects of their development but not have actual physical custody. These guardians—private citizens with good credentials—would receive a flat annual sum for their services, in addition to reimbursement for special items approved by the court. The child's legal status would not change. The guardian's responsibility could be terminated by the court at any time. The closest analogy to this arrangement is the European system of "affiliation," a procedure which is halfway between outright adoption and the loose court-wardship concept that is widely used in the United States.

As matters stand now, it is far too easy for parents, and society, to shed their obligations to children, whether by callous neglect or through the juvenile court. Monitors and court-appointed guardians could shore up the sagging system now used to deal with vulnerable children.

5

CHEATED
OUT OF CHILDHOOD

As the community's official superparent, the juvenile court acts to help brutally victimized children when the police department requests intervention as the result of a formal complaint lodged against one or both parents.

Some ghastly cases leap to mind. One day, about five years ago, two little boys whose mother had deserted them stood at the bar of the juvenile court; a few feet away stood their father, who was accused of cruelty to them. Under Pennsylvania law, cruelty to minors is a summary offense and can be tried by a magistrate, in this case the juvenile court judge. The ludicrous penalty is a fine of two hundred dollars or ninety days in jail if payment is not made.

The plucky neighbor who had summoned the police was also in court to testify that for the past month the father had tied the two youngsters to a tree in the back yard adjoining hers before going off. Despite his threat to kill her if she made trouble for him, she could not endure that heartbreaking sight. The police had come, immediately cut them loose, and then sought out the father in a neighborhood taproom. When Judge Hoffman asked the tots about the marks covering their arms and legs, they said that their father held lighted cigarettes against them "because they were bad."

I also recall a tearful, trembling teen-age girl who whispered hoarsely to Judge Hoffman that her father "punished" her for keeping late hours by forcing her to eat food after he had urinated on it. At the end of the meal she had to repeat after him, "Good to the last drop." The elderly grandmother with whom they lived sat placidly by. When the girl and her sister were very young, the mother had divorced the father and not kept up any contact with her children. Only when a school nurse, her suspicions aroused by the girl's daily bouts of nausea, repeatedly questioned her, did the youngster confide in anyone. Summoned by the school principal to investigate, a policewoman interviewed the older sister and learned that she, too, had received this punishment. She had escaped by eloping.

One of the very few sets of twins ever to appear in our court had confided to a sympathetic aunt that for the past two years their father had "kept them in line" by forcing them to be sexually intimate with him. Several nights a week he slept in their bed, a daughter on either side. After holding him in bail for trial on charges of rape and assault with intent to ravish, Judge Hoffman asked their mother how she could have permitted this situation. She replied that he had been a gentleman about it and had promised her that he would not make complete penetration. The medical reports, however, showed that he had not kept his word.

An unforgettably distraught mother in another case said that she had hailed a passing police car after she had been locked out of her house for days by a pathologically jealous husband. Gaining admittance by breaking down the front door, the officers found her five children, whose ages ranged from two to eight years, chained to bedposts in a rear second-story room. On the bed were doggy bowls filled with a meatlike substance, which their father later conceded was canned dog food. If the children became hungry they had to bend down to eat it, as though bobbing for apples. Since he would not release them even to go to the bathroom, they had to perform their natural functions on the floor. He readily admitted his acts to Judge Hoffman: since their mother was a bitch, he said, her children were no better than animals and deserved to be treated as dogs.

Not too long ago, the nation was shocked to read that an Arizona couple, outraged by their daughter's confession that she had engaged in a love affair with a soldier, retaliated by handing her a loaded gun and ordering her to shoot her beloved pet dog. The girl took the gun and shot herself to death instead.

Although police do uncover a surprising number of such home-based horrors, a private social agency, formerly known in Philadelphia as the Society for the Prevention of Cruelty to Children and now more simply called the Society to Protect Children, has tried for years to perform a watchman service in the community.

The "Cruelty," as it is pithily termed by many poverty-stricken citizens, has its counterparts in almost every American major city. After receiving—often anonymously—a complaint of child abuse, the Society sends trained social workers out to investigate. More interested in rescuing children than in pressing charges against the adults responsible for the child's plight, the agency employs a non-punitive approach. Interviews and continuous contact with the parents often result in their agreement to relinquish the child to the Society, which then proceeds to file a dependency or neglect petition at the Intake Department of the Youth Study Center. Victims too young to be housed there remain at the agency's shelter, which is in the same building as its administrative offices. Even a brief tour of this shelter, with its scarred, bruised, and occasionally even crippled children cowering in cribs, is a searing experience that destroys forever any sentimental preconception the visitor has ever entertained about the so-called parental instinct. After such a tour, the medical term "battered-child syndrome" ceases to be a clinical abstraction.

Once the Society's petition is granted by the judge, the child is placed in the custody of either a private child-care agency or the City Department of Welfare, to remain with them until he reaches eighteen or some custodian comes forward to reclaim him.

Although many of the external scars these children suffer in early life eventually become imperceptible, their inner wounds do not heal so readily. Often they carry into adulthood the emotional stigmata of their brutal treatment during infancy. One of their most poignant characteristics is their longing for the parent who has failed them so monstrously but whom they idealize in memory as they become older.

Wiry, tense, thrusting constantly into his mouth grimy finger-nails that had been bitten down to the quick, nine-year-old Timothy Shivers had been a battered baby. When he was two, his mother had voluntarily surrendered him to the Society's social worker and he had been assigned to the Department of Welfare as a ward of the juvenile court. It had been easy to find a foster home for such a likable boy, whose blue eyes flashed merrily but whose face and body were covered with bruises from painful beatings with an electric light cord. These ugly welts and marks had been inflicted by his mother and her boyfriend.

All had gone well in the new surroundings until Timmy at age six entered first grade. Taunted by his schoolmates about his social worker and realizing that they lived with their real mothers, fathers, brothers, and sisters, Timmy became aware that he was "different." His foster mother became annoyed with his constant questions about *his* real mother and the social worker gave him evasive answers, so he decided to find out for himself.

He ran away from home to find his mother and, incredible as it may seem, he succeeded on his first try. Displaying the mysterious instinct of a lost fledgling, he singled out her home from the hundreds of similar row houses in the Kensington section of Philadelphia. Even though Mrs. Shivers called the Society the moment he identified him-self, Timmy was sure she was happy to see him. The Society, of course, called the social worker, and back he went to his foster home. He ran away to her house again—then a third and a fourth time. It became a pattern: a brief reunion with her, followed by a tearful return to the foster home he came to despise. When the social worker suggested to his mother that he might not run away if she visited him regularly, Mrs. Shivers reminded the worker that he was no longer her responsibility.

Even though Timmy had developed an all-too-familiar pattern of symptoms that connote a child's uncontrollable anxiety—tantrums, nightly bed-wetting, and stubborn resistance when anyone tried to reprimand him about running away—he "passed" a battery of psy-chological tests. In three years the boy was placed in *nine* foster homes; in each case the foster parents, finding his frequent runaways intolerable, asked that he be removed.

Now, at nine, Timmy was back in court, no longer as a de-pendent child but as an alleged "incorrigible." The Welfare Department charged that the boy needed a "correctional setting with strong controls." When the social worker told Timmy what was likely to happen, he asked only that his mother come to court with him before he was sent off to a juvenile institution. In an effort to calm the boy, the social worker notified Mrs. Shivers to appear in court. As Judge Hoffman listened to the Welfare Department report, Timmy huddled against his mother. Her presence did not have the desired effect on the boy. Although he scarcely moved a muscle, it was painfully clear that he was overwrought.

When his mother told Judge Hoffman that she could do nothing for Timmy because her boyfriend would have no part of him, the boy cried out, "No, No!" Suddenly he seemed to realize how alone he really was. As he was pulled away from her and taken back to the cell room behind the hearing chamber he screamed repeatedly, "Mommy, Mommy! Don't leave me! Take me with you!"

Even though the judge had been optimistic that with a bit of luck he could get the boy into a wonderful boys' ranch for homeless youngsters set up by a retired FBI agent, the Department of Welfare was reluctant to send him there. The very qualities that made this small ranch so attractive—its open pastures, its horses, its lack of wire-fencing—would also make it easy for Timothy to escape. After months of marking time at the Youth Study Center, waiting vainly each visiting day for his mother to appear, the boy was reluctantly committed by the judge to a Roman Catholic "protectory" for delinquent boys, there to remain until he completed high school. By my calculations, he is now probably a junior of about sixteen years of age. Even if he graduates at eighteen, I ask myself, "Where will he go to live? Will his mother relent enough to let him stay with her even overnight?" Perhaps he may decide, as a few other boys in the Catholic training school have, to enter the priesthood. Or he may spend the rest of his life searching for other refuge.

Instances of gross physical abuse, neglect, and rejection are more easily detected than situations in which a parent is psychologically undermining the normal childhood process. That parents can spiritually cripple a child, regardless of how invulnerable he may appear, is a proposition which psychiatrists, educators, and child care workers can readily prove by citing their many professional experiences. How to cope with and, more importantly, prevent this subtle psychological destruction of young people is a perplexing issue for both lawyers and social workers. Since our legal system reflects society's premise that parents have paramount rights over their offspring, court processes to terminate the parent-child relationship are always troublesome confrontations between private rights and the state's concern for the best interests of the child.

When a parent has openly made his child an accomplice in criminal activity, the juvenile court's right to intervene is clear. The court acts promptly and firmly. Take, for example, a child like Louise Evans who, at eight, had become a seasoned shoplifter under her mother's careful tutelage. Clearly, she had to be taken out of her home and placed elsewhere.

Ingratiating and amazingly fleet-footed, Louise had managed to evade store detectives and guards for a long time. She was literally the bane of center-city Philadelphia department stores. When she was finally caught by a hefty woman who had been employed by one store to catch shoplifters, the little girl was wearing, in place of underwear, an expensive jeweled sweater which she had somehow managed to steal. She told the interviewer at the Youth Study Center that she had gone to a rest room to put it on; her mother had always told her to put on as many of the stolen things as she possibly could. In this way she would not arouse suspicion. A paper bag Louise was carrying when she was caught contained only a few five-and-ten-cent-store items she had purchased before getting down to serious business.

In court, the girl stood next to her mother, giggling as the store detective recited the details of arrest. Louise had put up a terrific fight, biting and kicking, even managing to get away momentarily. Her contempt for her captor was evident. When Judge Hoffman told her at the end of the hearing that he was committing her to the Department of Welfare so that she would live in another home, she said defiantly, "I already have a home. I want to stay with my mother."

Louise refused to budge. Finally, two strong sheriffs had to be summoned to carry her, screaming and protesting all the way, out of the courtroom. In the split second before they took her away, she turned in a blaze of hatred toward the store detective and, taking careful aim, spat neatly and accurately on the woman's neck.

It seemed clear that no matter how many foster homes the girl was sent to, her deepest bond would be with her mother, herself a graduate of the state prison for women. No court order can sever or loosen such a tie, and the services available to families like Louise's are so ineffectual that nothing short of a miracle can rescue children growing up in them.

Louise has many doubles, not only in the United States, but throughout the world. I saw one of them while on an extended holiday in Barbados, B.W.I., in 1968. Interested to see what kind of juvenile problems existed on that sparkling island in the sun, I obtained permission to attend several juvenile court sessions. First on the list that bright morning was the case of an appealing nine-year-old girl who arrived with an older woman. The chief social worker whispered to me that the woman, the child's mother, was one of her probationers, having been recently convicted on several counts of larceny. She said the child, who had been taught to steal from small shops in the poor district in which they lived, had been caught rifling a cash box. After several hearings the magistrate (empowered under law to sit as a juvenile court judge) placed the little girl on probation, together with her mother. His decision was strictly of the *faute de mieux* variety that juvenile judges are so often compelled to make. No foster home could be found for the child, and he refused to send her to a maximum-security "training school," which would keep her locked up for many years. The parallelism between Louise and this little girl went beyond their physical resemblance and their home conditions. Even their personalities were similar; the Barbadian child was as high-spirited and volatile as the Philadelphia girl. The island shopkeeper testified that she had great difficulty holding the child down until the constable arrived. In the poetic idiom that the islanders often use, the woman described her as a "prancing mare."

In addition to these children who are the offspring of criminally oriented, immature persons lacking any credentials for parenthood, there is yet another category of throwaways by birth who frequently escape the notice of any community agency and rarely find their way into a juvenile court. These children are immured in households where the atmosphere is nothing short of psychotic, but whose façades feign orderliness and normalcy; only an out-and-out catastrophe or a quirk of fate causes this sham exterior to collapse. The malignancy that is laid bare surpasses the morbid atmosphere that envelops the innocents in a tale by the Brothers Grimm.

Perhaps it was her own sense of *thanatos*, her death-wish, that impelled Mrs. Elvira Diamond, but whatever dark force thrust her into the Youth Study Center one morning, it set into motion a series of inexorable events that would change the whole direction of several lives.

Her mission was to file strongly worded charges of incorrigibility against her two sons: fifteen-year-old Danny and his thirteen-year-old brother Carl. At the Center she contemptuously dismissed all efforts on the interviewer's part to settle the problem there; she demanded an immediate audience with the judge.

It was so arranged, and as I read the terse summary, less informative than usual because of Mrs. Diamond's noncommunicative attitude, I glanced up at her and wondered if someone had not made a gross error. Tastefully dressed and soignée, she seemed the antithesis of a virago. She stood at the bar of the court, each arm encircling a handsome boy, her classic profile and Junoesque stature suggesting a modern-day Cornelia displaying the paired jewels that were her ultimate adornment. I asked the court clerk for the petition Mrs. Diamond had filed against her sons. Her signature was indeed affixed to the affidavit charging Daniel and Carl as "incorrigibles." I looked back at the case résumé: she was divorced from their father; there was another son, nineteen years of age, but he was attending a Midwestern college.

Part of my task as an Assistant District Attorney was to elicit from witnesses coherent, reasonable statements on which the judge could base his decisions. I began with the usual preliminary questions, but Mrs. Diamond cut me off imperiously. Refusing to answer another of my questions, she addressed Judge Hoffman instead. Her hostility was chilling, but it lessened as she began to speak in a more modulated voice to him.

"I prefer to tell the story in my own way, your Honor. My sons have been torturing me since they were little boys. Danny started it, and Carl learned it from him. Their father was actually the ringleader, but he left home some time ago."

The summary indicated that Mr. Diamond, who was not in court, had been absent from the household for about six years. I realized that the boys could have been only around nine and seven years old during the period that Mrs. Diamond was describing.

"I took care of them and their big brother. He was already in high school at that point. But these two were terrible." Her voice became strident and her face was contorted with anger.

"I washed their clothes, fed them, got them to school, but they were impossible. They made every kind of trouble for me. I fought with my neighbors; *they*, too, were against me. I was completely alone, and these two young devils laughed at me and tormented me from morning to night."

Incongruously enough, she was delivering her jeremiad against the boys without loosening her dual embrace of them! Even more amazingly, they were motionless, heads downcast as though in obedience to a conjurer's command.

In my experience, children do not usually stand by mutely when an adult damns them vehemently. Either by vocal outcry or by physical defiance they react quickly to unrelenting censure. Yet these two boys seemed almost abject as they listened to their mother inveigh against them.

"What is their behavior toward you now?" asked Judge Hoffman, whose puzzled look mirrored my own bewilderment.

"Oh, they are so evil, Judge. They hit me all the time. They plot against me. They do terrible things at night," she hissed.

Danny moved slightly away from her embrace. Looking up, he blinked. He had a finely chiseled face and the same classic head as his mother, but his thin shoulders were beginning to stoop under some invisible burden. He was weeping.

Alert to his movement, Mrs. Diamond paused in her narrative. She turned to him and said with sudden tenderness, "Don't cry, son. We'll be out of here very soon."

Judge Hoffman, I saw, was increasingly disquieted by this scene. He reread the summary and looked sharply at the boys.

"I suppose you have something to tell me about all this. Let's start with Dan. Is what your mother says true? Are you mistreating her?"

"Only in part, Judge," the boy replied quietly.

"Which part?"

"I don't know," Danny muttered.

Judge Hoffman thrust on. "Carl, what have you to say? Are your mother's complaints true?"

The smaller boy, pudgier and more effusive than Danny, seemed eager to answer. Turning to Danny, he caught an admonitory glance and froze.

When Danny finally said, looking at the judge almost beseechingly, "She's right," I heard Carl utter an almost inaudible "No!"

I asked Judge Hoffman if he and I could confer at side-bar.

"This is a puzzling situation," I said. "Mrs. Diamond's attitude is quite strange."

The judge agreed. "What is her real reason for pressing these charges? Even while she's claiming her two boys beat her, she keeps her arms around them. That little one wants to say something, but Danny won't let him. Obviously, we won't get anywhere in an open court hearing. I'm going to send them all up to see a psychiatrist right away—I want to get to the bottom of this. The case would have been thoroughly investigated by a probation officer if Mrs. Diamond had not insisted that it be sent into court as soon as possible.

"She filed the complaint about two weeks ago and she certainly hasn't changed her mind in this interval. I'm going to continue the case for two weeks, and then we'll list it again. She may become troublesome about seeing a psychiatrist, but I am going to insist. If she withdraws the charge, I shall order a dependency petition to be filed so that we may retain control over the situation. There is something about Danny's manner that I neither understand nor like. Do you feel the same way?"

"Absolutely," I said. "But Mamma gives me an even spookier feeling."

Judge Hoffman began speaking to Mrs. Diamond in the patient, sincere manner he always used to explain court procedures to the distraught and the defiant, the young and the old, who came before him by the dozens each day. "I think it will be best if you and your sons are interviewed by our Medical Department. The court nurse will take you upstairs now to make an appointment."

"I don't want any medical advice," the woman interrupted shrilly. "I'm not going to talk to any doctors. If it's Danny's fits you are concerned about, don't bother. He's much better. No doctor or nurse, please. I came here for justice," she concluded.

From the rear of the courtroom where she had been sitting unobtrusively, anonymous in her trim street clothes, the court nurse walked forward until she stood directly behind Mrs. Diamond. She readied an aromatic preparation which she concealed in a tissue, apparently expecting Mrs. Diamond to collapse at the end of her outburst. The ever-present tension of the juvenile courtroom did occasionally culminate in the complete prostration of an overwrought parent; but watching Mrs. Diamond's dramatic performance, I was fairly certain that *she* was not likely to swoon. If she ever had to be carried out of a courtroom, it would be over her loud and unceasing protest. Yet who can be sure of anything? I asked myself.

"This is the first I've heard about any fits," said the judge, somewhat taken aback at this bit of news. Mrs. Diamond glared at him, obviously annoyed at her slip. "That is exactly the reason I want you to see our doctor. My request has nothing to do with your charges. I'm interested in the well-being of all three of you. I want you to go," he said firmly. "It's an order."

Danny whispered quickly to his mother, and she nodded, then turned to face the bench. "All right. We'll go."

They left the courtroom. The nurse, whom Mrs. Diamond had peremptorily waved aside, strode rapidly to keep pace with the trio.

Several hours later, as the court was considering the fortieth—or was it the fiftieth?—case on the day's list, the chief psychiatrist came up to the bar of the court and asked if he could interrupt proceedings for a moment. It was urgent, he added. Knowing well the doctor must have good cause to make the request, the judge acceded and beckoned me to join them in his chambers.

Always direct and nontechnical in his speech, the psychiatrist explained the situation quickly. The Diamonds had come into the department to arrange an appointment, but the boys' mother had been verbally abusive to the secretary and had demanded to be seen immediately. So adamant was she about not returning unless this condition was met that the doctor had been obliged to grant them a short interview despite his jammed schedule. Even that brief meeting had been enough to put him on guard. He was sure that Mrs. Diamond had a psychiatric history and he suspected that her complaints against her sons masked deeper ills. Judge Hoffman agreed to a three-week period of further studies and case-work investigation.

A few days later I met one of the Juvenile Division supervisors in the courthouse corridor and learned that Nick D'Amico, an engaging and dedicated probation officer, was working on the Diamond case. Thirty-six years old and idealistic about his work, Nick had fortuitously been assigned for some time to the geographical district in which Mrs. Diamond lived. I also learned that Nick had already turned in a startling report on the family which Judge Hoffman and I should read before the Diamonds returned to court. With his usual thoroughness, D'Amico had tracked down the boys' school records; he had studied the Social Service Exchange—a central index that listed all the agencies to which a family was known as a result of professional contacts—and he had even conferred with the psychiatric department of Philadelphia's General Hospital, the city-run facility which housed men, women, and children needing emergency help.

"It would take too long to summarize his report," said the supervisor. "I might omit some important detail. Better talk to D'Amico directly."

I wasted no time in passing on to Judge Hoffman what I had just learned, and he arranged a conference with D'Amico, the supervisor, and me in his City Hall offices that same day.

The judge's desk was covered with building-block stacks of records, files, and reports. He picked up a mass of penciled and typed notes clipped to the familiar pink sheets used by the court's medical division and leafed through the pages, visibly affected by what he read. Putting them down, he said to D'Amico, "You have done an excellent piece of work. Perhaps you should tell us the whole thing in your own words now so that we all have the situation clearly before us."

"I'll be glad to, Judge. I think I remember the facts pretty well." D'Amico recounted a family history that transfused our interest and concern with disbelief, revulsion, and, finally, deep compassion. But none of us could fully express our complex reactions—we merely uttered an expletive or a disjointed phrase from time to time as he spun out his narrative.

Married twenty years earlier in a prominent Philadelphia synagogue, the Diamonds had set up housekeeping with substantial help from her father. He had given the young couple a modest two-story house as a wedding present. Until recently he had owned a jewelry business, but it had been sold by Mrs. Diamond's brother because the old man's health was failing.

Mr. Diamond had had a good position as an insurance salesman for a large life insurance company whose home office was in New York. With the birth of Lewis, their first son, a year later, their happiness had seemed complete. Mrs. Diamond's brother, who supplied much of the information on which D'Amico based his report, characterized them as an "ideal family." It was not until almost four years later, while Elvira was pregnant with Danny, that the family's troubles began. Mrs. Diamond took to weeping for hours on end, terrified that she was carrying a deformed child. When the baby was born, he was healthy and normal; yet Mrs. Diamond refused to hold him. She declared that this was not her baby, that the nurses were hiding out of sight the monster she had birthed.

The doctor told Mr. Diamond and her brother that she was in the full throes of a post-partum psychosis and might not recover for many months. A few days later she was wheeled from the maternity ward of that private hospital to a waiting ambulance which sped her to the psychiatric ward of a city hospital. Mr. Diamond was obliged to hire a full-time housekeeper to take care of the infant and five-year-old Lewis. With his commissions already severely reduced because he had stayed home many times to try to calm his pregnant wife, he could not afford even short-term private care for her.

She remained in the psychiatric ward for two months. On his frequent visits to her she begged her husband to take her home, promising that she would "behave"; she was eager to return to Lewis. But whenever Mr. Diamond mentioned Danny, her father's namesake, she fell silent. One day the housekeeper abruptly quit, and faced with this new crisis, Mr. Diamond persuaded the hospital staff chief to allow his wife to return home.

Seemingly able to perform her many chores—both her brother and her husband praised her housekeeping—she nevertheless became distant with both children. She began to complain about the neighbors and to question her husband closely about the frequent late hours and overnight trips that she knew to be a routine part of his job. The accusations increased steadily. Next-door neighbors were conspiring against her, she claimed, telling evil stories about her in the shops and streets. When Lewis started school, she became convinced that these malicious rumors had already reached his teachers. Mr. Diamond stayed as close to home as his work permitted, spending long hours with his wife. In an interview with D'Amico in his small apartment, he confessed that during that period he had virtually ignored both his sons.

When Mrs. Diamond became pregnant with Carl, her family dreaded the possibility of a new breakdown. But she went through a different cycle this time. No longer were her fears directed against the coming baby; now she became convinced that her husband despised both her and the children and was seeking to destroy his family. She screamed and clawed at him; she barricaded herself and the boys in her bedroom at night, shoving a heavy dresser against the door lest he gain entry and kill them while they slept. When she realized that the police, frequently summoned by her harried telephone calls, would not force her husband to leave, she embarked upon a campaign to drive him out of the house. At her brother's mild suggestion that she consult a physician, she denounced him as a traitor. She knew he always hated her, she screamed, so it was no surprise to her that he had joined the destruction team.

After Carl's birth, there were a number of peaceful interludes: a summer at the seashore when Mr. Diamond obediently stayed away, automobile outings when she seemed almost happy. As the boys grew older, they took over the pacification effort that Mr. Diamond had shouldered alone for many years. Then one day, just after Lewis entered high school, she quietly announced to her husband that she was going to seek a divorce. He quickly agreed to pay the legal costs. He placed the title to the house in her name and offered to send weekly cash payments for the support of the children in amounts sufficient to also maintain her, since Pennsylvania law forbade alimony payments to a divorced wife.

Neither husband nor wife ever told the lawyer Mrs. Diamond retained for the divorce proceedings any of the underlying reasons for the separation. Mrs. Diamond charged him with "indignities to the person" (Pennsylvania's version of mental cruelty); what she actually related during the hearing held by the special master (an attorney appointed by the civil court to take testimony and file recommendations in divorce cases) remains locked forever in divorce records that are automatically impounded under Pennsylvania law.

D'Amico then told us that from the first year of his life on, Danny had been subject to severe epileptic seizures—perhaps partly caused by his mother's harsh treatment, he speculated. A family doctor prescribed daily medication for the boy, which Mrs. Diamond frequently "forgot" to administer. After he entered school, the seizures tapered off; now he had them only occasionally and always at night, when the boy was at home.

The day after his father left for good, Danny had a terrible seizure in the classroom. Checking with the family physician, the school nurse learned that Danny was in fact under his care, even though he had not been examined for some time. Since the boy had no more seizures at school, she dismissed the matter, though she did inform the principal that Dan was afflicted with epilepsy. Many chronically ill children, victims of diabetes, heart murmurs, asthma, and the like, often blend into the over-all school population, especially if they do not suffer any symptoms during school hours and thus do not disrupt the routine. With the small medical and nursing staff assigned to each Philadelphia school district (frequently one doctor and one nurse for thousands of children), these children rarely receive sustained surveillance.

Danny himself told D'Amico that he continued to have attacks at home. Lewis had always taken care of him during his seizures; he had been the one to give him his daily dosage of Dilantin, the anti-convulsant drug that had been prescribed for him. But after the older brother left home two years earlier to attend college on a scholarship, Danny's world began to collapse. Once again he experienced the agony he had suffered after his father's departure. His epileptic attacks, he told the probation officer, were very frequent now—sometimes as many as eight or ten in a twenty-four-hour period. He admitted that, without Lewis to prod him, he rarely took his medication.

His school records showed that he was repeating his sophomore year of high school. Absent almost three-quarters of the time the year before, he had failed every one of his academic subjects. His younger brother, whose absences were less numerous, had been promoted, but with barely passing grades. The intelligence examination scores for both boys fell in the 120–130 range, placing them well above average intelligence and marking them definitely as candidates for college and possibly for professional careers.

Thus far, D'Amico's account had catalogued the many disturbances that children manifest when a parent seemingly deserts them during those vulnerable years. Danny's epileptic attacks were the major clue that he had been more profoundly affected than many of the children who came before the court.

"That certainly gives us a clear picture of the home background, D'Amico," said Judge Hoffman as the probation officer fell silent. "But how did you uncover the truth about Mrs. Diamond's relationship with Danny? That developed after Lewis left home, didn't it?"

D'Amico picked up the narrative. He had encountered total resistance when he had tried to interview Mrs. Diamond. She had also refused to let him in the house to talk to her sons, but he had succeeded in engaging both Danny and Carl in friendly chats on the sidewalk directly outside their home. Through the half-open front door D'Amico had been able to see that the living-room area was neat and comfortable. Only after he complimented Mrs. Diamond on her sons' good manners did she deign to discuss the boys. It was in the midst of her complaints about their abusiveness to her that she had suddenly let slip her concern about Danny's sexual experiences. When D'Amico tried to pursue this topic, she had balked and finally denied that there was any such problem.

The alert D'Amico had called the court psychiatrist to report this item, so that when Danny and Carl arrived for their interviews the doctor carefully questioned each boy separately. Danny blushed violently and said his mother was wrong about his sex life. He became extremely uncomfortable and asked permission to walk around the office. The doctor watched him carefully, prepared for a possible seizure. He was relieved when the interview ended without incident.

Carl was more candid than his brother. He said that his mother and Danny slept in the same bed; he heard noises from their room at night. Sometimes when he came home from school his mother would still be in bed and Danny would be with her. When asked by the doctor if he knew what was going on, the boy replied simply that they were like "married people." He remembered that shortly before Mrs. Diamond brought them to court he had overheard Danny screaming to her that she was never to take turns with Carl. Hearing a scuffle, Carl had run into the bedroom. His mother was about to hit Danny with a lamp, so Carl knocked it out of her hand, slapping her hard. It was the only time he ever struck her and, as far as he knew, it was also the first time Danny had quarreled with her. Usually, he added, his brother was the only one who could keep their mother quietly in line.

Armed with this information, the psychiatrist had called Danny back into the room for another interview. After failing to persuade the doctor that he slept in his mother's bed only to help her through her nightly bouts of insomnia, the boy finally admitted that he had engaged in love play with her. Yes, he had fondled her breasts and "down there," pointing to the genital area, but nothing else. He clung to this story, even when the doctor bluntly said he did not believe that Danny was telling him the full truth. The boy became so enraged that he swore he would deny ever having admitted the loveplay. The psychiatrist believed that the boy would go to any lengths to protect his mother from outside intervention.

"I wonder if Mr. Diamond would take his sons for a while?" asked the judge. "At the moment, that appears to be the only choice we have. I see that we have tried various placement agencies and have been turned down because of Danny's medical problem. Well, I'll try to get one of them to reconsider. But meanwhile I want those boys out of that house—and I want it done immediately. It would be best if we could arrange it voluntarily. D'Amico, you seem to have a good relationship with Danny and Carl, and Mrs. Diamond is at least talking to you. Do you think you can work it out amicably, with everyone's consent, until the case is relisted in court?"

D'Amico agreed to try. First he would talk to the boys immediately about living with their father. Then he would ask Mr. Diamond to take them in, explaining that the mother was making sexual advances to Danny and warning him that the boy must never know that his father was aware of the situation. As we got up to leave, we all wished D'Amico luck with his unenviable assignment.

The next day the supervisor told me that the situation had been resolved with unbelievable smoothness. Amazingly, Mrs. Diamond had passively stood by as the boys packed their suitcases and left with D'Amico.

Less than twenty-four hours later, however, we learned that the little scene had been part of a charade in which all the Diamonds—father, mother, and sons—had participated. Determined for their own individual reasons to maintain the status quo, they had deceived D'Amico by acquiescing to the new arrangements Judge Hoffman proposed. That he had been conned was made clear to the probation officer when he stopped at the father's apartment the next evening around dinnertime to see how things were going. The boys were nowhere in sight; Mr. Diamond and a woman friend were having pre-dinner cocktails. The father explained flatly to the astounded

D'Amico that the boys had not wanted to stay with him and had returned home that same night.

As soon as Judge Hoffman heard this news, he ordered the case listed for an immediate hearing, and asked that Mr. Diamond be subpoenaed to appear with Danny, Carl, and their mother.

Trailing behind Mrs. Diamond and boys as they entered the courtroom was a balding, smallish man. He thrust forward his subpoena but when none of the court officers took it and he was instead directed to sit down in the front row, he looked about him in puzzlement and annoyance. I saw Danny nod at him and Mrs. Diamond scowl at this sign of recognition. It was obvious not only that Mr. Diamond was here under duress but that his former wife was displeased that he had been summoned.

"Please step forward, Mr. Diamond," ordered Judge Hoffman. "I am very unhappy with the lack of cooperation all of you have shown. This is a very difficult situation. I have gone over it with the probation officer and the psychiatrist, and everyone agrees that these boys cannot stay with their mother. Mrs. Diamond, through no fault of her own, is not able to exercise the duties of a mother. I believe she is sick and should be in a hospital. Mr. Diamond, you know what is going on in that house, because I asked Mr. D'Amico to explain things to you. We felt that you should take these boys, at least until the court could find either a good boarding school or a foster home for them.

"I had hoped to resolve this in a friendly way, without hurting any of you, but you—all of you—have refused to cooperate. The sad thing is that these two boys will be the ones to bear the brunt of this situation, because I have made up my mind to commit them both as dependents to the Youth Study Center until we can come up with a long-range plan. I'm sorry. I tried to spare them, but you didn't help, any of you."

Mr. Diamond spoke up softly. "There's nothing I can do, Judge. It's true I'm their father, but they won't stay with me. Carl perhaps would have come around, but Danny, never. And what Danny says, Carl does. They want to stay with their mother. They say she needs them."

"They are mine!" Mrs. Diamond spat out the words. "My sons! Why shouldn't they live with me?"

"I have full reports on your home, Mrs. Diamond," Judge Hoffman said firmly. "They cannot stay with you. I think you know why. I am going to sign the court order right now."

As the court clerk handed him the forms authorizing the confinement of the children at the detention center, Mrs. Diamond startled us all by flinging her handbag to the floor and shaking her arms wildly in the air.

"Goddamned papers! Papers, papers!" she shrieked in ear-splitting tones. "They are all poisoned, those goddamned papers! Murderer!" she screamed, pointing a finger first at the judge, then wheeling around to include us all in her accusation. "You are all murderers!"

Two court officers moved quickly to her side, prepared to restrain her. In anguish, Danny covered his face with trembling hands. Carl's face froze in a half-smile.

"Take the boys out of the courtroom," Judge Hoffman ordered the deputies. "Don't touch Mrs. Diamond. Your mother will be all right, boys," he added, looking down at Danny's sorrowful form. "No one is going to hurt her. She is safe with us."

Mrs. Diamond did not even notice that her sons were no longer in the room, so intent was she on delivering her diatribe. Her occasional flashes of lucidity, in which she expressed total exasperation with the ponderous workings of bureaucracy, coupled with her powerful delivery, suddenly reminded me of a hysterical paraphrasing of Magda Sorel's compelling aria in Menotti's *The Consul*.

Then, without warning, all rationality disappeared. Eyes flashing, head thrown back, her body rigid with unbelievable tension, Mrs. Diamond launched upon a forty-five-minute monologue devoid of sense, punctuation, or pattern. The court stenographer, at a signal from the judge, frantically tried to record most of it on his stenotype machine, stopping only to insert more paper. On the basis of that written record, a formal petition for Mrs. Diamond's commitment could be filed immediately, a step which D'Amico had said earlier her immediate relatives would not take, partly because they feared her, but also because they did not want to be saddled with the responsibility of helping to care for Danny and Carl.

Her rage spent at last, she uttered a final obscenity and sat down in her place. Only then did she ask where her sons were. When the nurse whispered that they had been sent out of the courtroom she nodded apathetically. She has already begun to withdraw behind the barricade of illness, I thought.

Visibly shaken, Mr. Diamond accompanied her to the medical department where she was given sedation. An ambulance was ordered, the emergency commitment forms were completed, and in less than an hour she was on her way to a psychiatric hospital. Within a week, the hospital reported that her condition had worsened; it seemed likely that the emergency commitment would be changed to a long-term one.

From the Youth Study Center came equally depressing reports about Danny. More shaken than Carl by his mother's appalling breakdown in court, the boy was overwhelmed with feelings of failure, betrayal, and guilt. All the years spent devotedly shielding her—even to the extent of giving her his body—now seemed to him an utter waste. His epileptic seizures became more frequent. Standing silent on the fringe of all group activities, remaining mute during his counseling sessions, weeping quietly when he thought no one was watching him, he endured the long days of waiting at the Center. D'Amico visited him and Carl frequently but could report no progress in finding a place for the boys to live. Judge Hoffman's entreaties to agency directors to take both boys were defeated by Danny's history of epilepsy. Just when a sympathetic social worker seemed about to say "Yes" to the judge's plea, Danny's electroencephalogram, with its highly abnormal pattern of brain functioning, rose up like Banquo's ghost.

D'Amico even wrote to Lewis, asking for suggestions. In a polite letter of reply, the brother explained that he himself would be working at school that summer and would therefore not be returning to the Philadelphia area, but his suggestion that D'Amico call Mr. Diamond's widowed sister proved invaluable. When the probation officer asked her to take the boys, she was hesitant at first—but only until she learned that her sister-in-law would probably be hospitalized for a long time. Then she agreed to have Carl come live with her. Of Danny she was somewhat fearful: she thought he was "strange—like his mother." After visiting both boys at the Center, she was more determined than ever to take only Carl.

Concerned about Danny's reaction to another separation, Judge Hoffman hesitated a few days before authorizing the arrangement. But when the psychiatrist reported that the boy's depression had become so acute that it bordered on the suicidal, the judge agreed to let Carl live with his aunt since separation was inevitable anyway:

Danny was being sent immediately to the adolescent ward of a nearby state hospital for treatment.

Carl plunged happily into the routine of his new home. Through the efforts of the state hospital's psychiatric social worker, the elderly aunt became less afraid of Danny and she finally agreed to take him when his three-month period of treatment ended. Carl, who had counted every day until his brother's discharge, received this news with whoops of joy.

Danny went back to school and passed his courses, but just barely. He was polite and respectful toward his aunt, pleasant with his cousins and their children. When his father came to the house to give his sister weekly funds in compensation for her care of the boys, Danny spoke to him in monosyllables.

A year later D'Amico filed a motion requesting the discharge of both boys from probation. He alone appeared at the final listing of the Diamond case. He told Judge Hoffman that Carl had become an outgoing, energetic youngster who seemed very happy, but that Danny was still depressed and withdrawn.

"He's like someone who is mourning constantly while making an effort to go on living. But he is trying." D'Amico paused, then added touchingly, "I hope he makes it . . . I will continue to see him from time to time."

Judge Hoffman marked both boys officially discharged from court supervision. The Diamond case was soon buried under the avalanche of work that continued to snow down on the court, but the whole tragic story came back to me months later when D'Amico told me that Danny had turned seventeen and had left school to take a job.

"What kind of work?" I asked, remembering his intellectual potential.

"He's a salesman," D'Amico told me, and mentioned the name of a large chain store.

It was more than idle curiosity that made me go into the shop shortly afterward. Danny walked past briskly, not recognizing me at all. In the crush of women shoppers, busy salesmen, and watchful assistant managers, he moved quietly and aloofly. He was, on the surface, pleasant and smiling, but studying him more closely, I sensed an ineffable sadness about him.

As I turned for a last glance at him, I too was filled with sadness

—for him and all the other throwaways who are cheated out of child-hood. For them, the future is summed up so tragically well in one ominous word, which had been the hospital's prognosis for Danny: *Guarded.*

6

THE
YOUTHFUL ART OF
SELF-RESCUE

Reflecting on the dreary background summaries of the runaway children who were brought before the court each year, I was often struck by the fact that for many of them the act of flight was a desperate dash for life.

Before community attitudes hardened against these fleeing children and their acts became categorized as a juvenile offense, a nineteenth-century writer like Mark Twain could persuade readers to accept his youthful runaway heroes, Tom Sawyer and Huck Finn—juvenile delinquents by present-day standards—as symbols of free young spirits whose motivation was more admirable than that of the adults from whose control they fled. Today, such romanticism is in disfavor with all save the young, who find great appeal in the adventures of Holden Caulfield, J. D. Salinger's version of a twentieth-century free young spirit. *Catcher in the Rye* is a widely read contemporary classic, recounting in first-person form the wanderings of an upper-class adolescent in search of his soul.

Unfortunately, many of the experts who "studied" our less

glamorous young clients were too concept-bound or cynical to view them as picaresque heroes and heroines. And the youngsters themselves were too inarticulate or scared to correct any misjudgments. Only rarely did we encounter a handful who could utter a manifesto of self-emancipation.

Admittedly, we had few imaginative alternatives to offer them, but they could not be permitted to run their own lives; they were too immature, we told them. So, after all was said and done, they, too, were sent off to the usual training schools and institutions.

A better long-run technique of self-rescue for these children involves an almost limitless act of faith in the adult world. It is difficult for them to solicit help from individuals within the power structure. Yet a surprising number of desperate children do exactly this.

Looking up from my desk one day, I saw, through the open doorway between my office and the outer reception area, a teen-age girl wearing the navy-blue jumper and white blouse that was standard garb for parochial school students. She walked up to the secretary and asked wearily if she could talk to a detective, resting her books on the desk as she made her request.

"What is your name?" I heard the secretary ask, pencil poised above the pad. She knew what to do: any information she obtained went straight to Lieutenant Hanes, a specially assigned county detective who conducted investigations for the Family Court Division of the District Attorney's Office. When he was not off on an assignment—bringing back a husband who had defaulted on support payments or a parent who had abducted a child in defiance of a court custody order—Hanes usually worked in a rear cubicle.

"Beatrice Rossi, R-o-s-s-i," the girl replied, carefully spelling out her name. "I don't have an appointment," she added, "but it's very important."

After checking with Hanes, the secretary escorted the girl back to his office. About ten minutes later, the tall, gaunt detective appeared at my desk. He seemed even more preoccupied than usual, his glasses pushed up on his curly gray hair.

"Sorry to intrude," he began, "but there's a young girl in my office, a Miss Rossi."

"I know; I saw her come in. Why is she here?"

"To ask us to arrest her!"

"What has she done?" I asked.

"Nothing yet," he replied, "but she's afraid she will commit a violent act. Up to now, she and her mother and the other kids have been on the receiving end of things. I certainly would like to throw the book at her father, even if only half of what Beatrice tells me is true."

"What did she tell you?" I asked, my interest aroused by Hanes' obvious agitation—a departure from his usual imperturbable professional manner.

"She says he broke up every bit of furniture in the house and now forces her mother, her younger brother and sister, and herself to eat, sleep, and spend all their time in the cellar. He beats them savagely. She showed me some welts he raised on her arms and legs last night."

"Does he drink?" I queried. "Is that his problem? Or is there something more?"

"It's all very jumbled—she said something about a cousin of his who used to live with them. It seems there's hanky-panky between Pop and her. I wish you'd talk to the girl. By the way, she's only been in the United States for a few years, but her English is very good. You speak Italian, don't you? Perhaps it would help if she could talk in her own language. Anyway, I'd like to bring her in to talk to you. Maybe you can get the straight facts so that we can decide what to do."

A few moments later the girl was sitting across from me, flanked by Hanes. Her command of English was excellent, as Hanes had said, but at times she became so overwrought that her narrative faltered.

"*Con calma, signorina,*" I reminded her as her words started to get jumbled.

"*O, che buona fortuna!*" she exclaimed. "*Lei parla italiano! Bravo!*"

Hanes nodded in satisfaction; even though he did not understand a word we were saying, he was sure that now we would find out something significant.

Her story was amazing, and one that had to be either the truth or the outpouring of a sick mind. As though she read my thoughts, she paused from time to time in her recital to say reassuringly, "*Non sono pazza.*" ("I am not insane.")

She had grown up in a small village south of Naples in the lovely countryside of Campania. About ten years earlier, shortly after the birth of the third child (her young sister), her father had decided to immigrate to America. Like thousands of other poor Europeans, he hoped, by hard work, to save enough money to send for his family. A skilled mason, he was able to accomplish his goal in two years.

In his letters he said he had put a down payment on a house, and referred often to a distant cousin, now living near him in the Italian quarter of the city. She had befriended him, he said. When Mrs. Rossi innocently inquired how the cousin was related to him, he answered that she was a newly discovered relative from the maternal branch of his family. Like most Italians, Mrs. Rossi was an avid student of genealogy. Yet, hard as she tried, she could not locate this cousin on Mr. Rossi's family tree; even the oldest and most knowledgeable elders of the village had never heard of her. Her neighbors and friends discussed the matter in letters to *their* American relatives. One day Mrs. Rossi's sister confirmed what everyone else had already suspected: the "cousin" was in reality her husband's mistress.

Impassioned family councils were held to settle the issue of whether or not Mrs. Rossi and her children should go to America. Beatrice, who had long been dreaming of the move, spoke up in favor of the trip; she reasoned that the best maneuver would be to face the cousin and outnumber her. Mrs. Rossi, timid and fearful by nature, agreed one moment, had her doubts the next. In the end, however, amid tearful farewells, the Rossi family flew off to New York by jet. Mr. Rossi met them at the airport, but their happy reunion ended abruptly when he pulled up his car in front of a neat row-house in Philadelphia, and there, standing on the steps to welcome them, was a plump, overdressed woman with a smiling doll-like face.

Mr. Rossi explained that Signorina Di Carlo, his relative, was a wonderful businesswoman who was going to help him set up his own masonry firm. Already she had assisted him enormously by finding this beautiful house and furnishing it for them. For Mrs. Rossi she had found good employment in a tailoring factory; there was no end to the good services she performed. It had been only fair for Mr. Rossi to express his gratitude by inviting her to live with them, since she was alone in the city, without a single relative to fall back on.

Beatrice could barely restrain herself at this news, but she said nothing. Within a few minutes, the girl recognized in the signorina a shrewd, implacable enemy.

Of indeterminate age—somewhere, said Beatrice, between thirty-five and forty-five—the cousin quickly established herself at the head of the household. From selecting daily menus to purchasing even the most trivial home furnishings, she dominated the family's affairs. At first, her fluency in English gave her an overwhelming advantage, but Beatrice enrolled in a nearby school and learned the language quickly. She then perceived that the cousin was really an uneducated woman who spoke ungrammatically and lacked both finesse and competence.

Beatrice shared a bedroom with her younger sister; both her brother and the cousin had their own rooms; and her parents ostensibly shared the large front room. Shortly after they arrived, Beatrice heard her parents quarreling, and later she questioned her mother about it. Her father, it seemed, was paying long nightly visits to the cousin when he thought his wife was asleep. When her father and the cousin went out nightly, her mother would sob that no woman should endure the shame of having her husband put horns on her under her very roof. Finally, Beatrice told her mother that before another day passed she would ask the cousin to leave.

A terrible scene ensued. The cousin protested her innocence, while Mr. Rossi slapped his daughter over and over again for her impudence. Finally the cousin announced with hypocritical meekness that if the girl and her mother objected to her sleeping arrangement, she would find a room near by, but continue to take her meals with them and "help" them.

"Miserable wretches!" screamed Mr. Rossi when it was all over. "You'll pay for this!"

He became a raging tyrant. He ordered his family to take their meals separately from him and the cousin. He moved his clothing to the cousin's former bedroom and slept there, the door firmly closed.

Arriving home from school one day, Beatrice found a truck parked outside the house. As she walked in, she saw that, having already stripped the living room bare, her father and the cousin were now beginning to remove the dining room chairs. When she asked why they were taking them, her father punched her hard in the mouth and went on removing furniture. Later, when Mrs. Rossi returned from work, she joined in Beatrice's protest. This time Mr. Rossi's answer was to take the remaining kitchen chairs and hurl them against the wall.

"We have only our beds and the kitchen table in the cellar,"

Beatrice told me. "We eat standing up. I have to do my homework on my bed, and I can barely see to do it because the light is so bad down there."

"What about the neighbors?" I asked. "Have they tried to help you?"

"They are frightened to death of my father; he's such a wild man. Anyway, what's the use? He and that witch are determined to punish us. You know, she now has a house of her own not far away. I followed her one night and found out exactly where it is. I didn't get a chance to look in—she keeps the venetian blinds drawn—but I'll bet all our things are in there."

She calmly continued her story. After wrecking other parts of the house, Mr. Rossi told his wife that she would be put out on the street because he was not going to make the mortgage payments. Remembering the name of the bank, Beatrice called up to verify his threat. She found out that he was one month in arrears. From her mother's pay checks, Beatrice put aside enough money so that in two weeks she was able to go to the bank and make the payment.

She was fearful, however, that her mother would collapse from worry and grief. Her father, whose rages had become both more intense and frequent, might kill them all. Their situation was unbearable. Could the "law" not help them?

I asked how she had come to find her way to the District Attorney's office. She explained that she had gone first to the neighborhood "politician," a committeeman of many years' standing who performed, like many other ward workers, an informal social worker's role as part of his electioneering activities. She told him her story, disguising it as the plight of a schoolmate whom she was eager to help. At fourteen she manifested, along with maturity and responsibility, a deep shame for her father's conduct toward his family.

I told her that I would send Lieutenant Hanes home with her to investigate first hand; his testimony would be necessary in case her father and the cousin tried to conceal what they had done. If the situation was as she described, her mother would have to sign a formal complaint before Mr. Rossi could be brought into juvenile court to answer charges of assault and battery and cruelty to his children.

For the first time Beatrice became apprehensive.

"When he finds out what we have done, we won't be safe. Is

there some way that he can be brought to court before he has a chance to get at us?"

I assured her that once the warrant was issued, our efficient county detective staff would work out a plan to protect them. As she left with Lieutenant Hanes, she was still nervous, but she turned around and said with a smile, "That's life, I guess. We always have to take chances."

The next day Hanes reported that the home was exactly as the girl said it was. He was on his way now to have Mrs. Rossi sign the complaint. Would I take it to Judge Hoffman and have a warrant issued so that he could arrange to pick up Mr. Rossi at a prearranged place and time?

When I described the situation to the judge, he said that Mr. Rossi should be studied for possible mental illness.

"And the cousin?" I asked.

"Let's issue a subpoena for her. I'm eager to make her acquaintance. She sounds like a real beauty!"

In less than forty-eight hours the Rossi case was called in juvenile court, at the end of the already-assembled day's list. Judge Hoffman's eyes sparkled when he saw the agitated, dowdy woman insisting to the court officer that she be allowed to stand next to the defendant.

"Who are *you*, madam?" he asked pointedly.

"The cousin, your Honor, I help this family," she replied brazenly with a smile.

"Please sit down over there," the judge directed. "I think your helping days are over now."

After Lieutenant Hanes testified, I called Mrs. Rossi as the next witness. Aware of her language difficulty, I tried to ask her questions simple enough to elicit Yes or No replies, which she could answer without great effort. I was counting on Beatrice to flesh out the story.

The girl proved to be a superb witness; she spoke clearly, slowly; her recall was almost total. Throughout her testimony, the cousin squirmed in her seat, shaking her head, even holding up her hand as though she were in a classroom.

"You seem eager to speak to me, Miss Di Carlo," observed Judge Hoffman. "What do you want to say?"

She bustled forward. Mr. Rossi, a handsome, prematurely gray man of brawny build, stepped back deferentially as she came up to the bar of the court.

With the narrative prowess of a Scheherazade, the woman told her version of life in the Rossi household. Those "bad" children were disrespectful to their father; Mrs. Rossi, a woman possessed of the evil eye, was despised by everyone—including her family—in Italy. They had been delighted to be rid of her, she added. In answer to the judge's query about the wreckage in the house, she suggested strongly that much of the damage had been done by Mrs. Rossi and the children as part of their effort to frame that wonderful man who had become their victim. Shaken by Judge Hoffman's skeptical queries, she finally admitted that she had helped remove the furniture, but added that she and Mr. Rossi were "merely fixing up the place" to make it more comfortable.

"You are a very lucky woman," Judge Hoffman told her, "because I am not going to do anything more to you today than warn you to stay away from Mrs. Rossi and her children. But if I hear that you are molesting them, I'm going to put you in jail so fast that your head will swim! You are an outrageous woman and you don't fool me. Keep away from all of them and don't entertain any idea about getting even with this girl," he said, pointing to Beatrice. "You have done enough harm already!"

"As for you, Mr. Rossi," he went on, "I think there must be something deeply wrong with you for you to hurt your family this way. I intend to find out what it is. I'm committing you to the Philadelphia State Hospital for ninety days. When I get the doctors' reports I will decide what has to be done next."

As her husband was led off by the sheriffs, Mrs. Rossi broke down. Taking advantage of this moment, the cousin whispered viciously to Beatrice, "See what you've done, you little bitch!"

Judge Hoffman rapped sharply for order with his knuckles.

"Keep Miss Di Carlo here for a few minutes until the girl and her mother have had a chance to get out of the building," he ordered. "Mrs. Richette, please call the police district and ask the captain to assign a patrol car to the house to make sure that these people are not disturbed. That's all." The judge rose and left the bench.

After I discussed the Rossi situation with the director of Catholic Social Services for the Philadelphia area, he agreed to talk with Beatrice himself before assigning one of the agency's case workers to the family.

Encouraged by the counseling they received, Mrs. Rossi and her children moved out of the ravaged house and into a comfortable small apartment in another area. When her fear of her husband and his mistress became so acute that she could no longer go to work at the factory, Beatrice arranged for her to do piecework at home. She herself got an after-school job in a nearby notions store. From her small earnings, supplemented by full-time work in the shop during summers, she bought her own clothing and school supplies.

Near the end of the ninety-day period Judge Hoffman received the hospital report on Mr. Rossi. The staff had diagnosed him as a severely paranoid man who harbored deep resentments against his wife and children. After his relationship with Miss Di Carlo had supplanted his original loyalty to them, there built up in him a guilt which he could express only in physical violence and brutality. The report recommended that he receive continued treatment, even though he was not strictly psychotic in the accepted sense.

Miss De Carlo hired a lawyer to file a petition seeking his release from the hospital. At the hearing, I opposed this request, pointing out that until Mr. Rossi came to terms with himself, he was liable to do grave harm to his wife and children. But I knew that my argument was futile; on the basis of the psychiatric report, his continued confinement was highly unlikely.

As the lawyer was leaving the courtroom after his successful argument, he stopped to chat. He told me that Miss Di Carlo had loaned the Rossis a large sum of money, for which she had proof in the form of a judgment note signed by the husband and wife. She was demanding payment of this sum, and had instructed him to file suit. Concerned at this development, I wrote a note asking Beatrice to call me. When I told her what Miss Di Carlo's lawyer had said, she replied firmly that her mother had never signed any such paper and that the cousin had never advanced them money.

"It's a trick," she said quietly. "They must want to get the house away from us. My mother's name is still on the title. Can you send me to a lawyer?"

As I gave her the number to call for a lawyer's referral service maintained by the Philadelphia Bar Association, I marveled at the girl's self-possession and resourcefulness. She had taken charge of her own life and her family's destiny, and she did not mean to fail, no matter what adversity she faced.

In the end, the attorney who represented her mother proved that the judgment note was a forgery. The cousin's last maneuver had failed. By the time the matter reached the litigation stage Beatrice, now seventeen, had graduated from high school and had secured an excellent secretarial position in a law office. When she called to tell me the outcome of the lawsuit, I congratulated her. Over the years I had told her I admired her strength of character; she had seemed so embarrassed by my praise that I hesitated to say anything now. Finally I told her that she was one of the most remarkable young people I had ever met. There was a brief pause, and then she replied, "Thank you, Mrs. Richette. But so many people helped me: you, Judge Hoffman, the Catholic Social Service, my teachers, my boss. I guess I was just a lucky girl!"

In a sense, Beatrice was right. Courage and determination are all-important qualities for any young person engaging in a self-rescue mission, but the unpredictable play of circumstances can undermine even the most valiant effort to remake one's life.

Ramon Perez, a shy, serious fifteen-year-old, was, like Beatrice, a newcomer to the United States; he had grown up in a small Puerto Rican coastal town. A few months after his father died, his mother made up her mind to transport her large family to Philadelphia to rejoin a girlhood friend.

At first Ramon was thrilled by the many rooms of their new apartment, located one floor above the one that Carmen, his mother's friend, lived in. There was plenty to eat, good clothes for him and his five little brothers and sisters, even money for a trip now and then to his beloved seaside. Whenever he asked about the source of their bounty, his mother assured him that Carmen had much money and was a wonderful help. At night, Mrs. Perez would leave him in charge of the family while she went down to the apartment below.

One day at school he overheard a boy referring to his mother as a whore. Outraged, he struck the boy to the ground and savagely kicked him. But the boy stood up and said, "No matter how hard you hit me, Ramon, you won't change the truth. She and Carmen have a big business. I even know the names of their customers—my uncle is one of them."

Ramon ran home and confronted his mother. He said he would work and give her his money, if only she would not do bad things. She laughed at him, saying that there was no harm in what she was doing. The children were happy, weren't they? They had a good apartment, didn't they? Ramon should not worry about the silly things his classmates said; he should study and pay no attention to things that were not his concern.

The boy was not reassured by his mother's words. He began to brood for long periods of time and barely passed his last year of junior high. Lying in his bed at night, he would strain to decipher the sounds of laughter and music that filtered up from Carmen's apartment. One night when the noise was particularly loud he went downstairs and sat on the front steps, watching a procession of inebriated, laughing men come and ring her bell.

Too troubled to go to bed, he began to walk through the streets. Perhaps a police officer would arrest him for being out alone after curfew. Then he could just say what was going on in that house, and the police would put a stop to it. But children wandering the streets very late at night are an accepted part of *barrio* life, and attract little attention. After walking for many blocks without spotting a police car, Ramon came to a decision. There was a station house he passed on his way to school; he would go there and ask to be locked up. A cell would be better than his room in the house where his mother carried on her dirty business.

He walked into the brick building and said to the officer on duty at the desk, "Please arrest me . . ."

Now Ramon stood in juvenile court, holding the standard brown paper bag dispensed by the Youth Study Center so that court-bound children can take along their few possessions: an arts-and-crafts project, a comic book, occasionally a book of Psalms. From his shirt protruded a comb and a toothbrush.

I looked down at the summary and saw that Ramon had been charged as a runaway. On the line that usually contained the names of the arresting officers the word SELF had been typed in capital letters.

The Juvenile Aid Division court representative who was presenting the cases that day had a baffled look as he began to testify. He explained that the boy had entered the police district and begged to be sent to jail. When asked why he had run away from home, he told the officers that his mother was a prostitute and that he was afraid he would kill her and Carmen if he stayed there.

Ramon then waited calmly for a Juvenile Aid man to arrive. On

his way to the Youth Study Center several hours later, he asked the
J.A.D. officer if he would have a chance to appear before the judge
before he was sent away.

While the officer was talking, I watched two small women attired
in brilliantly hued satins who had perched themselves on the front-
row chairs. Which one was the boy's mother, I wondered.

At the end of the police report, I asked Ramon if what the
Juvenile Aid man had said was correct.

The boy glanced at me, then turned to Judge Hoffman.

"May I speak to you, Judge? You are a man, and I think you
understand me."

Judge Hoffman nodded encouragingly. "Do you want to speak
to me alone, Ramon?"

"No, sir," he replied. "I can speak here, before everyone. I cannot
live at home. My mother is leading a terrible life. In the house where
we live, she sells herself to men. The other children are too young
to understand, but I know what she does. I am sick. I cannot sleep.
I ask her not to do these things—I tell her I will get a job and get
money for us all. But she only laughs at me. Please send me to prison.
I do not care what happens to me, but please help my brothers and
sisters before they find out."

At the end of this touching plea Judge Hoffman asked the boy's
mother to step forward. The younger of the gaudily plumaged
women came mincingly up to the bar of the court. Carmen followed,
announcing that she was there to interpret because her friend didn't
understand English "too good."

She was told curtly that Mrs. Perez would understand well
enough. Waving the probation officer's investigation reports in his
hand, the judge told both women that they should not even bother
to deny anything to him; he already had the full truth. He announced
that he was ordering the younger children to be taken immediately
to the Welfare Shelter. At his request, the Catholic Social Services
representative, a gentle Trinitarian nun sitting at the rear of the
courtroom, came up to the bar and listened attentively while the
judge explained what he wanted her to do. She was to report to her
supervisor that the Perez children were all to be placed in the best
foster homes that could be found. Mrs. Perez nodded a greeting to
the sister, her long gold earrings bobbing madly up and down. After
Carmen rushed her friend out of the courtroom, Judge Hoffman

explained to the kindly nun that since Ramon's evidence was circumstantial in nature, and not based on his actual observation of any of her transactions, the police department would maintain a surveillance of Carmen's apartment so that some effective prosecution could be initiated against both women.

The younger children were quickly settled into a good foster home run by a Puerto Rican couple. But Ramon's future was more difficult to chart. The few training schools to which he could be sent had no openings. With nowhere else to go, he stayed at the Youth Study Center for months. After celebrating his sixteenth birthday in these unfestive surroundings, he was sent to Pennypack House.

When Judge Hoffman learned that Ramon was still in jail, he became annoyed and personally intervened with the priest who ran a training school to which he had referred Ramon. Finally, after a four-month stay at Pennypack, Ramon was transferred to the Catholic school where he remained for two years. At eighteen he was discharged and went to live at the Young Men's Christian Association residence in mid-town. Through an interested school staff member, he found employment as a busboy in the restaurant of a nearby hotel.

I remember thinking to myself as I looked at him on the day of his discharge that he had changed, and not for the better. He still possessed unusual dignity, but it was blunted now by a streak of coarse sensuality that was troubling. As he walked out of the courtroom I found his strut unpleasant to watch.

Not long afterward, I again came face to face with Ramon in another court. During a Saturday tour of duty in a divisional police court, I had nearly come to the end of the morning's preliminary hearings for adults arrested on various criminal charges when I heard his name called. Even before looking at the charge on the arrest sheet, I knew why he was there.

A morals squad plainclothes officer testified that Ramon had solicited him to commit an immoral act in the washroom of an all-night theater, a notorious center for homosexual activity. Ramon listened impassively.

"I have no lawyer," he said quietly to the magistrate. "Do I have the opportunity to get one?"

Bail was set at five hundred dollars, and the case was continued for a few days so that the young man could engage an attorney to represent him. Since my duty at the police court was only for one week end a month, I was not present at Ramon's hearing, but I learned that he had been bound over for indictment and trial. I found out the name of the attorney who had appeared in his behalf and called him to talk about Ramon. I told him to investigate his juvenile court record and to present it in mitigation. The lawyer thanked me for the advice and said that he already knew about the commitment to the training school.

"He's a real faggot, I'm afraid," he continued. "Interestingly enough, where do you think he had his first sex experience with men? At Pennypack House.* He was seduced by an older prisoner. Of course with a mother like that, he probably hated women long before that episode. But who knows? Had he escaped that experience, he might have been rescued. As it is, he's had it."

I agreed. A jail is not a likely place to practice the youthful art of self-rescue.

---

* A footnote is in order here to explain that months after this section was written, and years after the *Perez* case, a dedicated Philadelphia judge, the Honorable Alexander Barbieri, horrified by homosexual assaults occurring in sheriffs' vans transporting boys and men from the detention center and Pennypack House, appointed an Assistant District Attorney, Alan Davis, as a Special Master to conduct an investigation of sexual assaults in these jail facilities. Davis's report, which indicated widespread involvement of guards, prisoners, and young boys, created such a public furor that reforms were instituted in the adult facility. Despite the demands of citizens' groups that juveniles be removed from the unsavory atmosphere, months later not a single step had been taken by officialdom to move those two hundred adolescents elsewhere.

7

"A" IS FOR ANGUISH

Better leave the handcuffs on him. He's hell-bent on suicide," whispered the detective.

"What do you think, Father Brown?" I asked the priest standing beside the slender, distraught youth. "I hate to see children manacled. He's such a slight boy, and only thirteen years old. I think I'll check with the judge. He's probably still at home. It's not yet nine o'clock."

The priest nodded. His sensitive, thin face, which at first glance appeared ascetic, conveyed briefly a sickening anguish. But when he turned to the boy, his look was fatherly and gentle. A human shepherd is Father Brown, I thought. He follows the strays to the very edge of the precipice.

I had just arrived in my new office on the top floor of the courthouse building when the two homicide detectives arrived with the boy and the priest. Files which needed my attention were piled on the desk, but I pushed them to one side as the priest began to speak.

"I've known Vincent as a parishioner for five years. I trained him to be an altar boy. He wants to talk to you. I think he may be all right now, but perhaps you should talk to the judge about the handcuffs."

I put the call through. "Good morning!" The judge was brisk and cheerful. "I hope we have our usual uneventful day in juvenile court," he said.

"Turn on your radio," I told him. "An hour and a half ago a thirteen-year-old boy named Vincent Danzey emptied a thirty-two-caliber revolver into his mother and father. Homicide brought him right in. He's sitting in my outer office with a parish priest. He's a quiet, clean-looking boy: button-down paisley shirt, pressed chino pants—and handcuffs. I don't want to talk to him while he's in chains. Is it all right with you if we remove them?"

"Use your own judgment, Lisa." He paused a moment. "Great gods! Both parents? How horrible." Another short silence. "Find out as much as you can before they bring him into court. I guess he doesn't have a lawyer at this point. Well, warn him, of course, and ask him about engaging counsel. Whoever he retains will not, I hope, plead for mercy on the grounds that his client is an orphan. Or hadn't you heard that particular definition of *chutzpah?*" he added sardonically.

Gallows-humor had a way of blunting the grimness of tasks like the one that awaited me now. I smiled wryly on my way to the outer office where I motioned to the sheriff's deputies to unlock the handcuffs. After the boy's wrists were freed, he slowly pulled himself to his feet. His brow, which had been contorted and tense, relaxed for a second. I noted the pale skin, the flecked hazel eyes, the golden brown hair that spilled down over his forehead; he could have stepped out of a Renaissance canvas, I thought; he had the look of an agonized angel. Before he could take a single step, two hefty bailiffs flanked him and held him firmly by the arms as they led him into my office.

"Sit down, Vincent," I said quietly. "You can let him go, Sheriff. Father Brown and I want to talk to him. Please wait outside."

The boy sat listlessly, head downcast. As soon as the door closed with a loud click, he shot up out of the chair.

"Are you a Catholic?" He was breathing heavily in agitation.

"Yes, I am. Why do you——?"

The end of the question floated unspoken in the room, cut off by the boy's loud wail. In one lunge he threw himself on the floor, his arms clutched around the priest's legs.

"Please, please!" he screamed. "Kneel down and pray with me. Help me to recite an Act of Contrition! God! O my God! Please forgive me!"

"Get up, Vincent," Father Brown urged softly. "You can make your own perfect Act of Contrition a little later. Now we want to talk to you."

"May I sit in your lap?" he asked the priest in the inconsolable voice of a lost child. "I can talk better that way."

But, as Father Brown drew him close and moved his hand upward to brush the boy's hair back, Vincent pulled away with the same terrifying, ferocious energy and hurled himself against the wall, striking it head first. Almost as if rebounding, he shot across the room and smashed into the opposite wall. His movements were punctuated by a series of pitiful outcries; wordless, shrill, they seemed to well up from the depth of his frail body, which was racked with an anguish too heavy for a young boy to endure.

We had both jumped to our feet to keep him from hurting himself, but before we could reach him his agitation subsided as suddenly as it had begun, and he quietly took Father Brown's hand and sat down beside him. He made no move to return to his lap.

"God!" he wept. "I want to stop my brain. I want to stop thinking and feeling! I want to die, too! Oh, God, please stop her from twitching; make her be still!"

He started to jump to his feet again, but this time Father Brown held his shoulder firmly. They both got up and walked slowly to the long glass window that overlooked the tree-lined Parkway. I hoped that Father Brown, who seemed so responsive to the boy's tension, would not relax his vigil; there was a sheer drop of four stories between the window and the street.

The boy began to speak firmly. In astonishment I realized he was quoting Shakespeare. "'Why is the sun shining so brightly? It is a bright day that brings forth the adder.' Cassius said that," he said, turning to me. "It's *Julius Caesar*."

Before I could answer, he shrieked, "Cassius was an assassin. Like me!"

"Calm down, Vincent." Father Brown led him back to the chair. "Come, try to pray quietly with me."

The priest's soothing voice, his repeated stroking of the boy's forehead soon quieted him, but we both knew that this comfort would only be momentary.

"I don't want to ask Vincent any questions now," I murmured to the patient cleric. "Is there a lawyer—perhaps a family lawyer—who can be called in to represent him? Are there any relatives we could ask?"

"There is an older brother who is in the Army, but he's stationed in Germany. I don't know of any other relatives. Can't the court appoint a lawyer for him? That would be best."

At those words Vincent quickly looked up, fixing his remarkable hazel eyes upon my face.

"I don't need a lawyer, or want one! We have the electric chair for people like me, don't we? I'm guilty—I deserve to die. I don't want to answer any questions, and I don't want anyone to explain what I did. It's done, and that's the end of it." Hunching his shoulders, he began to weep soundlessly.

"Even though you want to die, Vincent, it's not up to you," the priest reminded him, with an undertone of sternness in his voice which was meant to stir the boy out of his despair. "Let God's will be done. It is not for you to decide. God is with you, Vincent. He is merciful. Let the court appoint a lawyer to help you."

It was time for Vincent to return to the basement cell-block where children charged with serious offenses or who are in a severely agitated state are locked up while waiting for their cases to be called. After he left with the sheriffs, nodding in response to Father Brown's promise to rejoin him in a few minutes, I explained to the priest that for the moment Vincent was officially booked on a general charge of homicide, without any specification of whether or not his action was murder, either first or second degree, or manslaughter, voluntary or involuntary.

"The juvenile court judge will, after a full hearing and investigation, determine whether or not Vincent will be certified to adult court on a charge of murder. If he thinks the crime lacks the necessary elements of premeditation and malice that make it murder but decides that it is manslaughter, then under our law the case can stay right here in the juvenile court.

"You see, to a large extent the judge relies on the recommendations of the District Attorney's office, but he isn't necessarily bound by what we say. If the judge finds, say, that Vincent's mental condition was so disturbed that he could not form the intent to commit murder, then he can treat him as a seriously sick boy and see that he gets the proper help. Vincent is a fascinating youngster. How odd that he should quote Shakespeare! He seems terribly bright and sensitive. There must be a dark, terrible story behind this ghastly thing he did. Do you have any inkling?"

"Not a one. I was having breakfast in the rectory this morning when he burst into the dining room. You saw how he hurled himself around like a desperate, trapped wild animal. He almost knocked me off the chair, screaming that he had just killed his mother and father, demanding that I hear his confession. I was stunned, speechless. But I listened to his words. Then I asked another priest to stay with him while I called the police. They brought him here right away." Father Brown obviously felt deeply concerned for the boy, but he had himself in good control as he tried to fill me in on the facts as he knew them.

"Vincent has always been a very good boy, Mrs. Richette. He graduated from our elementary parochial school with a straight A average. He began high school just a few months ago. I noticed that for about a month he was coming to Communion daily; then, suddenly, he stopped. I would see him occasionally, hurrying by on errands for his mother, but I didn't have much of a chance to talk with him. Mr. Danzey was a printer, very well respected by everyone; I seem to recall he was in politics, too—a committeeman, I believe. The mother was an ordinary, matronly-looking housewife perhaps in her early fifties. There's an eleven-year gap between Vincent and his brother. She had her second baby when she was close to forty, I think. Absolutely respectable, decent people, as far as I could see. I'm sure Vincent never had even one conduct infraction on his entire school record. This thing he's done is beyond belief."

Several hours later, Vincent and Father Brown stood before Judge Hoffman. I summarized my earlier meeting with the boy, and requested a month's continuance so that the police and the county detectives could make a complete investigation and the boy could be studied by juvenile court personnel.

Vincent, who had so bravely held in check his terror and guilt until then, burst into tears. "Don't drag it out, Judge, please. Get it over with fast! I don't want to live. O God! Why did I do it?"

The judge could barely find voice to answer. "That's what we want to find out," was his reply before looking down for a moment to regain his composure. Rarely had he seen such naked grief, such relentless, stark remorse. The boy's fair skin was now mottled and bruised; a cut on his cheek, sustained probably when he had slammed against the wall in my office, had reopened, and the tears that coursed down that side of his face were blood-tinged.

"I want a psychiatrist to see him immediately; he should be under some sedation," Judge Hoffman continued. "He should not be left alone. Father Brown, can you arrange to stay with him at the Youth Study Center tonight? He may try to harm himself, and I think he needs your comfort and support."

The priest nodded and placed his arm around Vincent's shoulders in a protective gesture.

"I want this case worked up completely. Please discuss it with your superiors," the judge instructed me, "and advise me of their recommendation. Keep in touch with the psychiatrist assigned to the boy. I want to know what I am dealing with here, and whether or not this boy is dangerous to himself as well as to the community. Where did he get the gun, by the way?" he asked the homicide detective.

"It was his father's gun, Judge. The boy said that his father always kept it fully loaded, usually in a dresser drawer. About a week ago Vincent took the gun from its usual place and hid it in his room. He had been planning this for about two months."

"Strike that whole statement from the record," ordered the judge. "Vincent has no lawyer, and I don't want to hear any admissions he has made. I'll go over my list of lawyers and appoint someone to represent him right away.

"It's very upsetting to know that his father kept that lethal weapon lying around. It's unbelievable how irresponsible some parents are about guns. About ninety per cent of all guns involved in killings by children are, in effect, put in the kids' hands by their own parents," he said, almost musingly. "Maybe this tragedy could have been averted if the gun had not been so accessible."

Later that day, before going off to a briefing session with several division chiefs in the District Attorney's office, I received a call from Senator Sam Shoreham, a distinguished Philadelphia lawyer in his mid-seventies, who had served many terms in the Pennsylvania legislature. Returning to private practice a few years ago, he had become interested in child-welfare problems, and he frequently volunteered his services on behalf of needy children in the juvenile court.

"The Danzey boy," he said gruffly. "Just saw it in the early papers. Does he need a lawyer? Tell Sydney Hoffman he's got one. Me."

"That's wonderful!" I exclaimed. "Why don't you call the judge yourself and tell him? He'll be as glad as I am that you want to represent Vincent. The boy needs you badly. I hope you will be able to get over to the Youth Study Center to see him soon, Senator. Don't be too dismayed when you see him. Father Brown is with him, but the officials report that the boy is very agitated; they say that he refuses to eat or drink, and is on the verge of collapsing. Good luck, Senator. Please keep in touch."

Ostensibly, the briefing had been called to discuss the beginning phase of the Danzey investigation; but before long the talk turned to a legal issue. Should the boy be tried for murder as an adult or be allowed to receive treatment as a juvenile delinquent? Under the first alternative, he might be sentenced to life imprisonment, whereas in a juvenile proceeding, his confinement would end when he reached twenty-one and was no longer under the jurisdiction of the youth court.

I kept remembering the early-morning scene in my office; I was sure the boy had some deep emotional problem. I took a quick head count: those pressing for a murder indictment outnumbered me 4 to 1. The Assistant District Attorney in charge of the Indictment Division summed up the majority view: "The kid had the gun. He planned it for months. He hated one parent—or both. Sure, he has problems. What kid doesn't? But he murdered two fine people, good parents. The community demands a public trial and real punishment. That's our job, gentlemen—and lady. Direct the investigation toward building up a good, tight case. Let's not go off half-assed into the broader manure pile of psychiatry. We'll have trouble enough proving our case: need I remind you that Senator Shoreham is very good at cute defenses?"

His was a widely held, simplistic conception of the job of an assistant district attorney. He was right in saying that the public demanded direct, punitive action against a boy who had perpetrated two seemingly senseless murders. But didn't our commitment to individual justice require us to go beyond public expectation? Were we not obliged also to make clear our duties as lawyers and representatives of the Commonwealth? Should not an Assistant District Attorney strive to be, like the Roman tribunes of old, the conscience of the community rather than its megaphone?

Lieutenant Lindsey, the ranking county detective who would be in charge of the Danzey investigation for our office, came up to me as the meeting ended.

"I don't agree with the others." He lit a cigarette. "I don't think we'll find out a blasted thing if we do just an ordinary run-of-the-mill investigation here. Furthermore, I doubt that we can come up with too many helpful witnesses. The two people who could tell us most are dead. That leaves us the four walls of that house and whatever we can find inside. I intend to comb that place from top to bottom."

My depression, an accumulation of the day's turbulent events culminating in the meeting, suddenly lifted. There was still hope if Lindsey carried out his mission to find at least a partial answer to the haunting *Why?* that Vincent's act had evoked in us.

"Bring in everything you find that seems the least bit unusual," I urged him. "Make an inventory of everything in Vincent's room too: his books, records, and wall pictures. Who were his heroes? Who were his villains? Above all, go through the mother's things. Was she really just a placid, simple housewife? Meanwhile, Dr. Tom Davis, one of the best psychiatrists at juvenile court, will be seeing Vincent daily. In fairly short order, we should be onto something."

In the next two days Lindsey's men accumulated enough cartons marked *Danzey Investigation* to fill a small unused cubicle. The other detectives referred to them jokingly as "Lindsey's Loot," but the visible items were so ordinary and drab that the boxes evoked little curiosity among the office staff. The immediate reaction was: just a pile of junk thrown into grocery cartons. And why not? Who noticed that set aside in a dim corner were two large sealed boxes? I shall never forget the afternoon that, as Dr. Davis and I stood by watching, Lindsey neatly slit open the taped corners of those boxes. How could we have anticipated what we would see?

"The knife I'm using is apparently Mr. Danzey's—he had quite a collection," the detective remarked. "I'll have to ask Vincent about them when I talk to him tomorrow. Senator Shoreham has given me permission to see the boy . . . Okay now, take a deep breath before we plunge in," warned Lindsey as he unsheathed the first thick bundle. "Maybe the shrinkers are right after all," he said, glancing at Dr. Davis. "Who else can explain what the hell this stuff was doing in a 'nice, respectable' house?"

A stunning collection of erotica, of a breadth and scope to quicken the pulse of even a jaded collector, mushroomed before our eyes as Lindsey pulled out layer after layer of photographs, magazines, books, pamphlets, posters, tear-sheets, playing cards—even match covers. It was hard-core pornography by any standard, and its very crudity intensified its impact.

Lieutenant Lindsey stood back, surveying the display.

"This had to take years to accumulate. I've seen a lot of it around, but some of this stuff is pretty wild!"

"Fantastic!" murmured Dr. Davis. "This was a total obsession—but was it one parent or both? Some of it looks like a comic-book version of the Marquis de Sade. Where did you find it all?"

"Oh, almost all over the house. Most of the books were in Mrs. Danzey's cedar chest and in her sewing bench; a lot of the other stuff was shoved into drawers and closets all over the house."

"I'm very glad I came over today and saw this," Dr. Davis said finally. "Now I am beginning to understand some of Vincent's reactions. Yesterday, when he came in for his interview, he seemed calmer than usual. You know, he says that during his second night at the Center he had a purifying experience—that's his term—when he saw and spoke with his parents. His father came and sat on the bed, and forgave him and comforted him. Vincent insists that it was no dream or hallucination.

"Since he was more composed and able to pray quietly with Father Brown, I thought it would be a good time to ask him about his sexual development in a general way. I brought up the subject cautiously, but he immediately turned red, jumped out of his chair, and ran out of the room yelling that he would not listen to any dirty talk. He resumed the interview only when I promised him that we would consider the subject closed for the time being. I have rarely seen such outrage and disgust in a boy his age. This"—waving his hand at the table—"must be part of the answer. By the way, were any of these pictures in Vincent's room?"

"No—but that reminds me: there's another weird thing you should know," said Lieutenant Lindsey. "There isn't a single door on any of the rooms upstairs—not even the bathroom. It seems that privacy was not one of the Danzeys' 'hang-ups.' The only picture we found in Vincent's room is very different from these. Here it is. I almost forgot I had put it in my pocket."

The three of us looked down at a small, yellowed magazine illustration. Someone had framed its edges with a funereal border of black masking tape, transforming a commonplace item into a pictorial epitaph. The photograph, however, far from being poignant, was chilling and sinister. In the foreground, back to the camera, loomed a huge male figure brandishing a belt strap. Beyond him, in a surrealistic perspective reminiscent of a Dali painting, stood a dwarf— no, a cowering little boy, his trousers falling about his ankles, his hands covering his face as if to ward off the impending blows. Mesmerized with horror, I stared at it, and as I did so, the man seemed to close in upon the child. It was unforgettable in its pathos, frightening in what it seemed to imply about Vincent.

"Did he actually have this on his wall?" I asked incredulously.

"Yes. It was directly across from his bed, at just about eye level."

"I would like to take the picture with me, if I may. We're having a staff conference on Vincent tomorrow," the psychiatrist said. "I want the rest of the team to see it."

"A 'model' boy, intelligent, alert, sensitive." I felt sick at heart. "Why did he choose this picture for his room?"

"He must think of himself in those terms. Vincent is the little boy about to be brutally hurt, maybe destroyed," Dr. Davis replied. "But who—or what—threatens him? I don't know if the District Attorney really cares about such questions—or their possible answers. I know *your* chief concern is whether to treat him as a sick child or a murderer. But maybe the two terms are almost synonymous. Isn't every murderer a sick child?"

Lieutenant Lindsey spoke up. "Look, Doctor, we have a tough job to do in this office. It's going to take more than dirty or sad pictures to convince the boss that this kid was really off his rocker when he pumped two bullets into his father and four into his mother as they lay sleeping. Remember, he pressed the revolver into his father's hand, took some money and the car keys out of his father's pants, and walked out, leaving his folks there, dead or dying. Then he began to worry that they might be damned forever in hell since they had died without receiving final sacraments. That's when he ran to Father Brown.

"Those are hard facts, my friend, and they'll sound cold and brutal when they are presented to a judge. He meant to kill them. He had planned it for some time, at least two months. Tony Damchuck, a neighborhood kid, was his only friend—if you can call him that—and he told us that Vincent showed him the gun about a week before that fatal morning, and said he was going to kill his parents. He even asked Tony whether a bullet fired through the exhaust pipe of the family car would cause carbon monoxide to escape, so that they might die of poisoning. See how bent he was on making their deaths look like suicide? Why? To get away with it, of course. And now maybe he will." The detective shook his head. "I don't know what makes this kid tick. Maybe he's a psychopath, Doctor."

"I'm not ready to pin a label on him yet," the psychiatrist told him. "In the last analysis, the law forces me to do so, I know. But I want a little more time with Vincent before I choose one."

His smile was wry as he got up to leave. "Anyway, there's one person in this office who hasn't made up her mind. She's in charge of the case for the present, and she'll have something to say. I'll send in my reports on a daily basis." He said good-by and walked out of that depressing little room.

His reports flowed in for the next three weeks. Despite his heavy load of daily court appointments Dr. Davis managed to spend long hours with Vincent. In those sessions he used all the skill and delicacy at his command, and as I carefully read every word he wrote I realized that underlying the terse summaries and flat sentences was a solid foundation of a genuine communication between the boy and the doctor. Apparently the fact that Dr. Davis had seen the erotica and knew of the unusual sleeping arrangements slowly eased Vincent into a frank discussion of life in the Danzey home.

He remembered how, even as a shy and sensitive boy of five, he hated the language his parents used when they quarreled; even now he recoiled when the doctor, with studied nonchalance, interjected an occasional obscenity into their conversations. When Vincent was ten, his father took him aside and started to tell him about sex, using gutter words. Vincent ran to the bathroom and vomited.

His mother was irritable, high-strung, and extremely domineering. Vincent's brother, ten years older, was already in the service, and she made the boy help with many household chores. He did the laundry, ironed shirts for himself and his father, even cooked. Meanwhile, his mother would lie on the couch in her slip and read magazines. Often she went out for hours on end; on those days he would return from school to find an empty house and a hastily written list of chores waiting for him.

Had he seen his parents' magazines and pictures? Yes! And he hated them. Especially the pictures of completely nude men and women. He had burned many when no one was around. After a while he became convinced that his mother was not a good woman: she always had piles of money in her purse and he wondered where she got it. Was she really on all-day shopping outings, as she said she was, when she returned with a purchase that should have taken five minutes, not five hours? Women did bad things.

"What bad things?"

"You know what I mean."

But *he* had to be good—all the time. Once he brought home a test that was not graded 100 per cent. His mother hit him so hard in the eye that it blackened. The next day she put make-up covering on it and sent him off to school. How old was he when that happened? Eleven. For several months afterward, he had prayed and received Holy Communion almost every day.

About a year ago, Vincent continued, while he was having a bowel movement, his mother called out to him that he was stinking up the whole house. Holding his fury and resentment—"his slow burn"—inside, as usual, he went into her bedroom to apologize. Before he realized that his parents were having intercourse, he was in the room. His mother laughed as he ran out.

He had seen his mother naked many times when she was bathing or showering, but he had never before seen his parents in the act. That night he dreamed about them, and the whole dream was about intercourse. Night after night, that scene kept coming back in dreams. It was then he began to think about killing his mother.

He found his father's loaded gun and hid it in his room. When he started high school that year he felt under more pressure than ever to excel. In addition to the household chores he now had to struggle with Latin and a very tough English teacher. He pulled through Latin, but he felt certain he would fail English.

He had the sex dream every night. Finally came that terrible night, the ultimate horror. In the dream he replaced his father in his mother's bed. He awoke aghast. Only the lowest animals mate with their sons, he thought. If she continued to live, her evil would destroy him. Resolved as to what he must do, he arose, dressed himself for school, took the weapon from its hiding place, went to his parents' room, and emptied the gun into their prone bodies. He had meant only to kill his mother, but his father also had to die.

"Why, Vincent?"

"Because he was there with her. Because he woke up."

Dr. Davis's last report ended with a short paragraph:

> Now we confront the final question: What more terrible (to him) thing was this terrible deed intended to prevent?

And we knew the answer. With deepened insight into the tormented, half-crazed mind of his patient, the psychiatrist had been able to penetrate to the core of the problem. I put a call through to him at once.

"Dr. Davis, I'm sorry to bother you, but this is important. In your final report on Vincent you omitted a diagnosis. I know you can't answer a question about insanity that is phrased in terms of the McNaughten Rule, but please tell me this before I talk to the D.A. and hear his decision: In your judgment, was this boy responsible for his act of killing? Can we hold him culpable?"

"He isn't psychotic, if that's what you mean," the psychiatrist answered. "Not now—and probably not then, although of course I can't be sure of his condition when he stood in that doorway. He has a deep sense of persecution as well as an abnormal horror of sex. I think we've learned and seen enough to know, at least in part, why he's disturbed. He needs long years of help; he also needs warmth and love and understanding. He's very young. Won't that be an important factor? His religious sense is very, very strong. I think there should be some element of punishment in whatever judgment the court makes. He needs to expiate . . ." His voice trailed off.

The conference with the District Attorney a few days later was brief and conclusive.

"I've read everything in the file," he said. "Danzey had a terrible life—no doubt at all about that. But I would be remiss in my duty to the public if I permitted his case to remain in the juvenile court.

At the hearing tomorrow please advise Judge Hoffman that I am proceeding with a murder indictment."

"He will be one of the youngest murder defendants in the history of this Commonwealth. He's only thirteen years old!" I exclaimed, shaken by this announcement, even though I had prepared myself for it. "Why not follow the procedure set down by your predecessor in the *Chalmers* case? That boy was fifteen when he strangled a little girl. We heard the case in juvenile court and he was committed to a state school until he turned twenty-one."

"I never agreed with the procedure in that case," the District Attorney told me bluntly. "Some of the Common Pleas judges were very upset by the way things were handled. We're going to treat this case differently. If you don't agree, and don't feel you can state my position in court, I'll send in Bob Springer, the First Assistant. In fact, I feel that's the better plan. He'll appear first thing tomorrow and take care of it." He ended the interview by placing the call to Springer.

When Senator Shoreham, who had been appointed Vincent's lawyer by the court, learned of the decision, his well-known temper erupted. Then his eyes filled with tears.

"All right," he said, "if that's the way it has to be. But they won't put him in a penitentiary for life, they won't throw his life away—not if I can help it! You know, when I was in the legislature, I realized for the first time that we had no mental hospitals or even units for children. They were thrown in with adults in those large, locked-up pens we call wards. One of the last things I did before leaving office was to establish a separate section for kids at the Thomasville State Hospital. We have fine doctors there like Davis who specialize in disorders of adolescence, as well as an excellent nursing staff. That's where Vincent should be!"

"How will you manage to keep him out of prison?" I asked him. "In this state the penalty for murder is either death or life imprisonment. In a few minutes my office is going to request that he be certified for indictment by the grand jury on a charge of murder. He's not legally insane at this point, nor is he likely to be when the case comes up for trial."

The stooped but dignified old man looked at me sadly. "We lawyers must find a way to be less barbaric," he said.

After hearing the District Attorney's request, Judge Hoffman asked, "Have you considered all the reports on this boy's home background? His psychiatric studies? There is precedent, you know—good, solid legal precedent in the *Mont* case for holding a boy charged with homicide as a juvenile delinquent. In that case the death was accidental: the boy was shooting at cans with a rifle when the victim stepped into his line of fire. It was manslaughter. True, this killing was not accidental, but weren't there circumstances that exerted such pressure on the boy that he cannot be charged with deliberate malice?"

Senator Shoreham spoke up vigorously. "There are enough extenuating circumstances here to fill this courtroom. I renew my plea that your Honor keep this boy in juvenile court. I've had Vincent examined by my old and eminent friend, Dr. James Horowitz, one of our most distinguished psychiatrists. Would your Honor hear him now?"

"It's an honor to have Dr. Horowitz in this court," replied the judge. "Are you prepared to say, Doctor, that the boy is insane and committable to a mental hospital?"

"Not in those terms, your Honor," the psychiatrist responded. "As you know, I strongly oppose the present formulation of the insanity test on the grounds that it is the ultimate insanity."

Bob Springer came forward. "Our office is perfectly correct on the law, your Honor. The Juvenile Court Act specifically excludes murder from your jurisdiction. These cases of first- and second-degree murder can be tried only in an adult criminal court—as they have always been under Anglo-American law. We find no basis here for saying that this act of homicide did not, on its face, constitute legal murder. All the elements are present: premeditation, *mens rea*, and the like. We'll be glad to hear what Dr. Horowitz has to say about Vincent when we get around to the sentence, since apparently he and Senator Shoreham do not propose to present a plea of insanity as a defense."

Reluctantly, the judge concurred. Vincent stood rigidly at attention, bending his body stiffly to listen to his lawyer's whispered asides. When he heard the judge announce that he would be detained at the Youth Study Center while awaiting trial, he asked that he be allowed to continue his sessions with Dr. Davis and that Father Brown have the same visiting arrangement. The judge granted both requests.

After Vincent's indictment and arraignment, Senator Shoreham's real work began. He shamelessly buttonholed the District Attorney across a luncheon table and reminded him that they both wore the same political button; he placed friendly, discreet calls to each of the three judges who would sit together as a panel to consider the case— a mandatory procedure when a plea of guilty is entered by a defendant in a murder case. He begged City Hall news reporters to play down their stories about Vincent.

"Stop calling him a model boy! That's the whole damned trouble with a kid like this! And it makes the public even more angry, because they can't understand how things like this happen. Well, damn it, I can tell you how they happen," he would add fiercely.

And he achieved the impossible. Pleading no defense—*nolo contendere*—he gently eased Vincent onto the mercy of the three men in black who were to decide his fate. His final summation proved that he was still one of the best word-weavers in the business: he meshed Dr. Davis's simple, firm analysis based on his studies of the boy with Dr. Horowitz's glossier theoretical threads and at the end produced a protective individualized mantle of immunity from criminal responsibility for Vincent which even the most cynical observer would not dare remove.

The court rendered an unprecedented sentence:

> . . . The sentence of the Court is that you be imprisoned for the rest of your natural life, your initial commitment under this sentence being to the ———— State Hospital, to which you will be taken by the Sheriff of Philadelphia County, and at which institution you are to remain until such time as a Medical Board of the ———— State Hospital recommends your transfer to another mental hospital or comparable facilities within the Commonwealth and under the administration of the Department of Public Welfare of the Commonwealth of Pennsylvania and only after such recommendation is approved by this Court . . .

After the President Judge read the sentence, he turned to the spectators and to the press and explained. "The whole purpose of this is that he is not to associate with hardened criminals as he would in a penitentiary or a reform school. Reform schools are just penitentiaries. If we can save him, we ought to do it. We can't throw

him to the dogs. He was always treated at home like Cinderella."
Cinderella, the classic throwaway everybody loves . . .

Shortly after Vincent went to the hospital, I began to correspond
with him. Most of his letters were cheerful; occasionally he sounded
depressed. He developed a great passion for racing automobiles, and
from time to time requested a special magazine or book on the subject. His brother, whom the Red Cross had flown home from Germany to attend his parents' funeral, was granted a special discharge
from the Army. At first he had seemed devoted to Vincent. He had
stood by him throughout the trial, even though he rejected Senator
Shoreham's repeated pleas to testify on behalf of his brother about
the home conditions. But as Vincent's stay at the hospital lengthened
into months, the brother's visits became less frequent.

Two years later, the psychiatrists became concerned that Vincent
was making too little progress in learning to be independent and mature. His attractive appearance and excellent manners had won him
the affection of the nursing staff, and the doctors feared that the
boy's skill at manipulating many of the adults around him prevented
him from facing his own inadequacies and problems. Senator Shoreham, whose health was failing, had not been able to keep up his visits
to the boy, but he received regular progress reports from the doctors.
When the news became disquieting, he invited me to his home, where
he had been confined by his physician, to discuss the situation.

"What was it Dr. Davis said he needed?" he asked. "Years of
help—warmth—love? I think he needs a relationship with a strong
older woman who can become a good mother symbol to him. I know
a remarkable woman who might be just the kind of person I'm
talking about. She is the head of a very fine hospital. It doesn't have
a special adolescent unit similar to the one Vincent is in now, but it
might be an excellent place for him to be in. You see, the whole
hospital is unlocked. There isn't a single key in the whole place. The
atmosphere is like that of a large university campus."

He thought for a moment. "Just the thing. I'll talk to the President Judge about transferring him."

Senator Shoreham died shortly after Vincent was transferred by
court order to the other hospital, and I still regret that he never had
the joy of seeing Vincent Danzey slowly come alive and develop
his potentialities.

Dr. Fredericka Lane, the director of the hospital, is a handsome, magnetic woman with children nearly Vincent's age; she has helped him come to manhood. He is now attractive and articulate, quick and perceptive; he completed not only high school but also an intensive in-service training program as a psychiatric aide. He is especially skilled at soothing and comforting the most troubled and physically crippled patients. When he is on duty with them, says Dr. Lane, everything seems to "swing." With her remarkable insistence upon dignity and respect for all her patients, and her belief in firmness, discipline, and compassion, she has helped Vincent set goals for the future. His plan is to continue working at the hospital and to obtain approval from the President Judge to attend premedicine classes at a nearby college.

Dr. Lane encourages him at every turn. After all, she points out to him, she too started out in psychiatry as an aide.

Smiling, Vincent reminds her that he began one rung lower. "I started out," he says, "as a patient!"

One day I was present during a review of his work. Dr. Lane asked him what experience had been the best during his stay in a particular cottage.

"A finger painting that Mark and I did yesterday of a sports car."

"But Mark is blind!" said Dr. Lane in astonishment.

"I don't think he always was, Dr. Lane. He seems to remember colors, and I guided his finger. The important thing is that he let me touch his hand; don't you agree?"

After Vincent left the room, Dr. Lane explained to me that Mark at age seventeen had gouged out his own eyes with a teaspoon and had maintained a completely withdrawn silence for the past four years. "Vincent doesn't know this," she added.

"Another Oedipus?" I asked. "Is that part of it?"

Dr. Lane nodded. "He believed he sinned, and so he obeyed the Biblical law of an eye for an eye. Don't you think it is wonderful that Vincent is working with him?"

No longer a throwaway, but himself a rescuer of others, he had to kill before anyone realized how desperately he needed help. Born to a throwaway fate, he could endure it no longer, and by a dark and hideous deed put an end to the evil around him, and within him. Miraculously, this end was also his beginning as a vibrant human being.

8

SOME TIME-WORN SOCIAL SLEDGE HAMMERS

Everyone warns that the American family is threatened on all sides. Articles in scholarly periodicals as well as in popular magazines stress constantly that rising divorce rates, changing styles of child-parent relationships, and the "sexual revolution" are undermining the foundations of family life.

After years of involvement with dependent and delinquent children brought to the juvenile court of America's fourth largest city, I am convinced that we dare not dismiss these views as mere alarmist talk, for we have seen, at first hand, the wreckage and its youthful victims. Furthermore, it is not just a phenomenon of the Sensational Sixties; family disruption has been increasing steadily since the end of World War II.

What are these children we have characterized as "throwaways by birth" if not the casualties of family breakdown? True, a small percentage of them—a Vincent Danzey or a Beatrice Rossi for example—suffer because one or both parents are distorted and abnormal, but others are damaged not so much by their parents' aberrations as by the fragmenting of family life, which is commonplace in our society.

How a family shatters into such dangerous slivers and chunks is the work of researchers in the social sciences. *Why* children are permitted by the community to grow up under such perilous hazards is a question for our national conscience to deal with. More directly, as lawyers, community planners, or just plain citizens, we can begin to look at some of the present family law and family welfare systems that are serving as sledge hammers.

For the middle-class family the most common form of breakdown is a legal divorce between the parents, an event that has enormous emotional impact on children and affects how comfortably they live, whether or not they will go on to college, and therefore what career opportunities will be open to them. That they are the ones most severely affected by the legal change in their parents' relationship is an openly accepted fact of life. "It's the kids who suffer" is the chant so frequently heard from teachers, child specialists, judges, and lawyers that nothing less than a total national effort to help these children seems in order. After all, the plight of afflicted young people is logically a prime concern of a humanistically oriented society. We are moved by the sight of a handicapped child on a poster; we give generously to foster research into rare or incurable diseases affecting infants and youth. But to the less visibly crippled young in our midst who do not wear braces or hobble about on crutches, we seem to respond almost not at all.

It may amaze some readers to learn that many of our state laws permit parents to divorce each other—even when children are very young—without convincing a judge that the divorce will not cause their offspring injury. Sometimes parents are not even required to present proof, in the form of a signed agreement, that they intend to cooperate with each other in the upbringing and care of their children.

In Pennsylvania, for example, under the present divorce law, the court weighs two primary issues: is the parent who is seeking the divorce really "innocent and injured," and has he—or she—proved by legal evidence the alleged grounds for divorce? The complaint, the first salvo fired in the suit, does not contain a single place for listing the children born of the marriage. *It is as though the children do not exist, and the only result of the legal surgery is to separate the unhappy bride and groom on the moldering wedding cake.*

One might take it for granted that a society beset by disruptive juvenile behavior would seek to reform laws regulating family relationships, and heed those family and child experts who are urging new policies. One might also assume that court procedures would make use of those professionals who have worked out techniques for dealing with individual family members caught in a crisis.

The exact contrary is the case. Efforts to obtain uniformity between the various states have not been generally welcomed; any success has thus been hard-won. And it has been impossible to gain widespread support for a Federal divorce law. The late U.S. Senator Arthur Capper devoted his entire career to this effort, and failed.

Many current divorce laws are line-for-line copies of statutes adopted by eighteenth- and nineteenth-century lawmakers whose vision, both world-wide and personal, was light-years away from ours. Take the case of Pennsylvania, an important, industrial "keystone" state. Although its present divorce law was approved in 1929, it is an almost total replica of the original divorce law passed in 1785. Before that year, divorces were obtained in Pennsylvania only by petitioning the Governor, or by special acts of Assembly. Actually, even the limited provisions of that colonial law were progressive for the times; in England an absolute divorce law was not adopted until 1857.

Why has the Pennsylvania legislature, like others in many states, refused to update a divorce law reflecting the viewpoint of a colonial society in which women had few legal rights and children had virtually none?

For one thing, lawmakers have been reluctant to tamper with the divorce codes lest, by making legal dissolution of marriage easier to obtain, they would further weaken the family as a social institution. Such reasoning, while well-motivated, flies in the face of irrefutable statistics; far from discouraging men and women from seeking a divorce, the present law merely encourages them to be dishonest. Some even commit perjury in order to obtain marital freedom. By ignoring completely the existence of any children resulting from the union, the present system on the one hand allows the departing parent to neglect his responsibilities and, on the other, forces the remaining spouse who has the total burden of caring for the children to seek aid in the courts. When the absent parent is prevented from continuing a normal relationship with the children, his only recourse is to file suit for visitation rights; the case is often heard in a court unfamiliar with the family's past problems.

Lawyers, often unfairly depicted as efficient managers of divorce mills, are generally unhappy with this state of affairs. Since 1960 the Philadelphia Bar Association through its Family Law Committee has studied proposals for reform. At a meeting in January, 1967, the Pennsylvania Bar Association voted to lend its support to the enactment of a proposed new Divorce Code. After much debate, the Code has received the qualified endorsement of the Philadelphia Bar.

In addition to such controversial innovations as making "living apart" grounds for divorce and establishing a system of alimony, the most vital reform of the proposed Code is to make children's welfare a primary concern of the divorce proceeding. Not only must parents submit to a mandatory "cooling-off" period and to reconciliation procedures modeled along techniques currently used in Ohio, California, Illinois, Wisconsin, Michigan, New Jersey, and Minnesota; the court may also appoint a guardian ad litem, a special protector of the children's interests. The court will grant a divorce only upon his recommendation that the children will not be irreparably harmed and that adequate arrangements have been made not only for their financial support but for their other childhood needs.

Legal reforms of this kind are necessary if we are to begin to check the widespread family erosion that imperils the future of so many seemingly privileged American middle-class children. The divorce system should no longer be allowed to shatter important fragile human relationships. The public should recognize that the divorce procedure must compel parents to behave maturely and responsibly toward their children even though they can no longer endure the bonds of matrimony. After all, as Pennsylvania Judge Chauncey de Puy has observed, an enlightened view of divorce means that society provides a decent funeral for a marriage which is beyond resuscitation. It should not, however, include children in the burial rites.

Children of poor black ghetto-dwellers who cannot afford the luxury of divorce are crushed by another antiquated legal system which antedates divorce procedure by two centuries. These children and their parents are enmeshed in the American public welfare system: a direct outgrowth of the English Poor Laws formulated in the years 1535 to 1601 to cope with the social problems of the Elizabethan era.

Viewing the poor as either inherently lazy or vicious, these laws gave the poor barely enough help to keep them above starvation level, and bestowed, along with these pittances, so much moral censure and stigma that for centuries they have been set apart from "respectable" society.

The first state to create a welfare department was Illinois, in 1917. Until the Great Depression of the thirties, local communities grudgingly administered a system of relief that made fairly long-term residence in a particular locale a prerequisite to relief payments. Many of these early state agencies incorporated in their very titles the idea that the poor were to be punished for their poverty; they were frequently officially termed *boards of public charity and correction.*

The first White House Conference on Children and Youth, held in 1909, urged the humanization of relief laws by making children eligible for help irrespective of their parents' marital status. This plea was shunned because many administrators feared that this plan would foster immorality and vice. When the New Deal Aid to Dependent Children was passed by Congress in 1935, these same guardians of morality dictated the new provision that only children whose fathers were absent from home would be eligible to receive benefits.

Orphans and children deserted by their fathers were in the clear; but what was to happen to youngsters whose fathers did not earn enough to maintain them, yet wanted to live with them? In order for a harassed mother to qualify for relief payments, which amounted to considerably more than the few dollars sporadically earned by the father, she could not have him in the home.

That this has occurred in thousands of family situations is clear when one compares the present percentage of ADC families receiving help because of "desertion" with the ratio of twenty years ago. During the early years of this program, one-third of the children had been deserted by their fathers. Today these "abandoned," fatherless boys and girls make up *two-thirds* of the relief rolls.

I attended a national conference some years ago, and during a session devoted to the reform of welfare systems a Mississippi delegate declared that the problem was not economic but moral, because 99 per cent of the ADC children in Mississippi had been born out of wedlock. When we asked him if children living in conditions of direst poverty could receive state help if their parents were married and together, he shook his head in a firm negative gesture. Since he was a Deputy Attorney General in charge of the welfare program for that state, we accepted his word.

He was right. Despite the fact that in 1962, under the leadership of the Kennedy Administration, amendments to the Social Security Act of 1935 were passed permitting children of unemployed fathers *living at home* to receive ADC benefits, only nineteen states—*not one of them Southern*—modified their own procedures to include these children in welfare programs.

The 1962 amendment made this extension a temporary one, and children were not permanently included in the ADC programs federally until 1967. But Pennsylvania took early advantage of this amendment. One welfare supervisor summed up the operation of the program by saying that "we take families as we find them. We look only at the needs of children. Having a father is as important to a child's growth as having good teeth." When I pointed out to him, however, that the eligibility provisions were still strictly enforced and that individual case workers continued to pressure mothers about their home situations, he had to admit that wide gaps existed between theory and practice.

Recent Federal decisions have found the one-year residence requirement for eligibility to be a denial of "equal protection of the laws." No test cases have yet been brought to compel states to give relief to children whose fathers have not deserted where the laws prohibit such payment to them.

It is a shocking fact that for thousands of American children, getting enough to eat is contingent on growing up without fathers. And this system is supported in the name of morality and decency.

These and other evils of black ghetto family life bestirred an American social economist, Daniel P. Moynihan, then Assistant Secretary of Labor and Director of the Office of Police Planning and Research in the United States Department of Labor, to issue in March, 1965, a controversial report, *The Negro Family, The Case for National Action*, which revealed the confusion of even skilled investigators in this field. (Moynihan himself is the product of a broken home; his childhood was one of great poverty in New York City's Hell's Kitchen. Formerly a university professor and assistant to Governor Averell Harriman of New York, he was selected by President Nixon to be Presidential Assistant for Urban Affairs.)

Moynihan had served on a four-man team (the others: Sargent Shriver, Adam Yarmolinsky, and James Sundquist) who had hammered out the Poverty Program, based in the Office of Economic Opportunity. Disappointed at the emphasis on community action programs which ignored the realities of impoverished family conditions, Moynihan determined to set down the outlines of a new policy that would develop employment opportunities for Negro men and thus allow them to return as breadwinners to homes now run by "matriarchs"—the mothers and grandmothers who must assume full responsibility for the family in order to be eligible for benefits.

Moynihan and the report were severely blasted from many quarters because of his seeming condemnation of Negro family life —particularly his censure of the role of Negro women. Nevertheless, he succeeded in riveting attention on the connection between the welfare aid programs and patterns of family disintegration. Many commentators felt that he had confused cause and effect when he entitled one section of the report "The Breakdown of the Negro Family Has Led to a Startling Increase in Welfare Dependency." They believed that the welfare system itself had given rise to the patterns of family breakdown which the *Report* revealed.

In drawing together his statistics and findings, Moynihan tended to overemphasize the Negro figures and minimize the importance of data on the whites. His 7-to-1 ratio of Negro illegitimate births over white ones, with its seeming implication that white extramarital sexual activity was dramatically lower than that of Negroes, ignored important factors which his critics were quick to point out: selective reporting of white illegitimate births, the prevalence of shotgun marriages among whites, the unreported abortions that white women undergo, and the freer access to contraceptives and birth control information that the white community enjoys. Another "fantastic error" of which Moynihan was accused was that, by his emphasis on the high degree of white family stability in contrast with the Negro pattern he described, he overlooked entirely the fact that white divorce rates skyrocketed almost 800 per cent in less than a hundred years. He also failed to acknowledge that the increase of white illegitimacy—more than 50 per cent in the last twenty-five years—is at a greater rate than the Negro's.*

However, Moynihan's emphasis on a revised government policy which plans for families rather than individuals was well placed, despite any errors and shortcomings in his methodology. The welfare system has failed to secure for poor children even their minimal birthrights as American citizens. Every now and then, an innocent life like Rita Blake's is dramatically snuffed out and a momentary outburst of indignation follows. Yet the system goes unchallenged. Recently, a thirty-nine-year-old widow and her seven children were found living in a terribly deteriorated house in the Philadelphia ghetto. (The newspaper photograph of the family's living quarters was a chilling reminder of the day I went to the Blake apartment.) She said that she had not talked to her "social worker" from the Welfare Department "for some time." Immediately, the welfare "establishment" responded by denying the woman's statement. Yet, after the publication of the photograph and the family's pathetic story, better housing, which the Welfare Department said was non-existent, was quickly found by city officials.

Impatient with American apathy to their plight, Negro parents and children have begun to make articulate demands for changes. The courage and determination these youngsters show in the face of official resistance have been documented in Robert Coles's study of pioneering efforts at school integration in the South: *Children of Crisis.*

After the Negro novelist Kristin Hunter made a poignant study of an unwed adolescent Negro mother, she wrote an article entitled "Pray for Barbara's Baby," which appeared in the August, 1968, issue of *Philadelphia Magazine.* In it she pointed out that the quarrel is not with individual social workers—many of whom are equally revolted by current practices—but with the system itself, which is barbaric, inhuman, and relentless in the blows it deals vulnerable and fragile children.

On October 29, 1965, Dr. Martin Luther King delivered an

* William Ryan, "Savage Discovery: The Moynihan Report," in *The Nation* (November 22, 1965). This article, together with the Moynihan *Report* and other valuable critiques, is reproduced in a valuable anthology by Lee Rainwater and William L. Yancey, *The Moynihan Report and the Politics of Controversy* (1967).

address on the theme, the Dignity of Family Life. He spoke eloquently on the past and present black Americans born throwaways in this land:

> No one in all history had to fight against so many physical and psychological horrors to have a family life. The fight was never lost; victory was always delayed; but the spirit persisted, and the final triumph is as sure as the rising sun.

PART THREE

BRANDED AS THROWAWAYS

PART
THREE

PROLOGUE

A visiting anthropologist from another planet would be sorely vexed to understand why our juvenile justice system labels some children "dependent" and others "delinquent." A dialogue between the visitor and the law enforcement officials and court administrators who decide which label to use might go something like this:

"This boy and that girl have committed outrageous crimes, sir!" the officials explain.

The stranger ponders their words for a moment, then speaks: "Did you not inform me, Gentlemen, in the long briefing session before you permitted me inside your juvenile tribunal, that this court was different and unique? That it was concerned not with individual antisocial acts, but with the personality and growth development of all children who come before you? When you recited the glorious history of the Juvenile Court movement in your country, did you not proudly declare that this court proved that your race was no longer obsessed with punishment, but had moved forward to an enlightened concept of therapy for deviant citizens—at least for the youngest among you?"

(He pauses. No reply.)

"If you are really social doctors, why do you spend so many hours in the legalistic ritual of labeling the symptoms, instead of probing their causes?"

(Papers shuffle. No one speaks.)

"Frankly, Gentlemen, I see little merit in your efforts. There is no difference in the pathology of background between your delinquents and the so-called dependents. What is the purpose of sorting them out this way? So that they can be branded separately? They all come to your attention as part of one huge unresolved youth problem. And what do you do? You carefully divide them into two groups— and then you use virtually the same treatment on both! Displaying the same unscientific attitude that permeates most of your social endeavors, you dispatch them to the same kinds of dreary outposts. Between the modified orphanages you grudgingly maintain for the 'needy' ones and the junior jails to which you consign the 'nasty' ones, I see a difference as large as the eye of a needle through which your proverbial camel cannot pass. Can you explain this?"

(Not a movement; not a sound.)

"Gentlemen, I am aware of—but unimpressed by—the high-sounding goals you mouth to each other. Have you nothing to say to *me?* If not, I must conclude that your juvenile justice system is but an attempt to appease the community, not a genuine effort to establish an effective program of treatment for these children.

"Your 'modern' application of the phrase *juvenile delinquency* seems nothing more than another form of the century-old branding iron used to mark the troublesome for brutalization. What is your justice system but a half-hearted substitute for the whipping post, the stockade, yes, even the gallows you trotted out several centuries ago for these children?

"I respectfully submit, Gentlemen, that though your scientists have devised vehicles to carry you swiftly to the moon—a dull watering-place, I assure you—you are still trillions of light-years behind interplanetary commonwealths in the management of your human affairs. Your treatment of deviant children is a good example of your backwardness. Do you *really* believe it is civilized, or even human, to view them as throwaways to be cast aside like those rumpled tissues you carry about with you?

"I ask, with all due respect, are you planning, as I read in one of your journals recently, to exile your young people to the Moon?"

(He pauses. No reply.)

"Thank you, Gentlemen. This conversation has been most instructive. Good day."

9

THE GANG'S ALL HERE

If we had engaged Central Casting, we could not have found a more perfect team of court bailiffs than Big Jim Pinto, 6 feet 4 inches, hot-tempered and white, and Big Leo Powers, 6 feet 4 inches, soft-spoken and black. Most of the time their duties were purely ceremonial, but their sheer physical bulk provided twin towers of strength when they quietly took their positions at each end of a line-up of one of the juvenile gangs we frequently faced in juvenile court.

Big Jim invariably stood at the left, near the long windows that looked out on a quiet city scene; Big Leo manned the more dangerous end by the exit doors where scuffles and angry interchanges were likely to occur, and where occasional desperate breaks for freedom punctuated the end of a hearing. Since Big Leo lived in the North Philadelphia ghetto, he knew many of the children and parents who came before the judge; his affable, quiet courtesy surfaced whenever one of these families appeared. But he had only contempt for the gang cases, which were dreaded by all the court workers because of the swarming numbers of bodies to be counted, fed, escorted back and forth.

"They should all be sent to prison," he would mutter to no one in particular. "Worthless bums, shooting poor people." And to an accused defendant who appeared in court in battle uniform—a sweaty bandana for headgear or one gold-hooped earring signifying a declaration of war against a rival gang—he would whisper, "Take off that junk, Buster. Don't you know you're in front of the Law?" And when the lawyers would raise technical objections, Leo would shrug his massive shoulders in utter frustration.

One particular oppressive July day, as the hands of the clock at the rear of the courtroom approached twelve and a welcome brief respite for lunch (frequently no more than twenty minutes lest the day's court list drag on interminably), Big Leo came forward and announced to the judge, "Get ready for a big one, your Honor. They're bringing in the Algerians. All twenty of them."

The Algerians. Their very name evoked visions of gleaming knives and pistols, night raids, tortures, and mysterious rituals. To make our task harder, their house counsel was a talented, volatile black activist whose favorite gambit was to place the police department on the defensive by interposing at the outset charges of police brutality. Fireworks at noon: a glum prospect.

"Bring them in," said the judge. "We'll hear the case now. Is Mr. Johns here? Where is your lawyer, boys?" he asked of the first defendants to approach the bar of the court.

"I'm here for Mr. Johns." I recognized the young lawyer as one of the assistants Johns used from time to time. "Jonathan Gray, appearing for Otto Johns," he said distinctly to the stenographer. "Mr. Johns is busy in criminal court on a murder trial."

"Very well," Judge Hoffman said. Turning to the officers who were already spreading out their reports and their exhibits: "I trust this doesn't involve a murder—or does it?" He stared at the sawed-off rifles, pistols, and assorted zip guns pyramiding into a miniature arsenal as these officers of the Gang Control Unit, a cadre of specially trained police within the Juvenile Aid Division, emptied out big paper bags onto the exhibit table.

"Not quite, but very nearly," replied Sergeant Wellston, one of the unit's stalwarts who was in charge of cataloging the permanent exhibit of juvenile weaponry at police headquarters. Wellston could reel off the arms supply of each of the active nineteen or twenty ghetto gangs targeted by the police as sources of trouble. "This is what I mean, your Honor," he said, pointing to a thin mulatto girl in her early teens who stood uneasily on crutches.

"Objection, your Honor!" snapped Mr. Gray. "The sergeant is prejudicing my clients! I ask that his remark be stricken from the record."

"So ordered. Let's proceed, Mrs. Richette."

Until Big Leo announced the case, I had not known it was on the day's list. Since last-minute listings were not unusual and preparation beforehand was a rare luxury, no one was surprised that I buried myself behind carbons of single-spaced police reports, whose format —as well as the syntax—sometimes boggled the mind.

After a few minutes of rapid scanning and underlining I looked up. "All right, Sergeant. Please be sworn in and proceed."

Uneasy shifting and whispering among the twenty defendants brought a sharp rap for order from the bench.

"Mr. Powers," Judge Hoffman said to Big Leo, "are these gentlemen lined up in proper order?" And as the bailiff nodded vigorously, he said, "We'll have order. Mr. Gray, I want silence from all your clients."

Sergeant Wellston began his narrative. "Nearly a month ago, on a Friday afternoon, July sixth to be exact, at about five o'clock, we . . ." The sight of the defense lawyer's pencil poised above the long yellow pad made him stop short; avoiding the fatal pit of hearsay, he went on: "As a result of information received, we went to the corner of Fifteenth and Ash Streets, which is the headquarters for this group," pointing toward the Algerians.

"Objection! Hearsay! Incompetent!" Gray shot out.

"Continue, Sergeant," said the judge. "I know what goes on at Fifteenth and Ash, and so does every citizen who lives within a mile of that trouble center."

Wellston resumed. At the ghetto intersection they found two of the defendants, "Smokey" Green and "Bubbles" MacEvers, dragging a bleeding girl off the sidewalk into the luncheonette known as the Bean Bag. She was severely wounded in the left leg and was almost unconscious. Their story to the police was that she had been "greased"—shot—and left lying on the street. They claimed that they had just come upon her. Her wound was bleeding profusely, the blood reddening her slacks and staining the clothes of the boys who brushed by her. Even the officers who lifted her onto the stretcher of the police ambulance later found blood spots on their uniforms.

Who was she? Just before going into surgery she finally had spoken her name: Veronica Evans, aged fifteen. The gun blast had shattered her left leg beyond repair, and when she came out of the anesthesia, Sergeant Wellston had heard the surgeon tell her that he had been forced to amputate it. Ronnie had turned her head away, and hours later, still in deep shock, had refused to answer any of the sergeant's questions.

Smokey and Bubbles, in custody at the Juvenile Aid headquarters, had been equally uncommunicative at first; but after several hours of interrogation by Gang Control officers, they had told at least part of what they knew.

As Sergeant Wellston pulled out the blue-covered statements of the two boys, defense counsel took a few steps toward the police witness and said, "You can put those down, Sergeant. Your Honor, I object to the reading of these statements. Even though the boys are now in custody as juveniles, there is a possibility that after hearing testimony your Honor may decide to certify some of these boys for trial in adult court. Your Honor has done so in the past in cases of shooting. Now, even though the present rulings do not extend constitutional protections to them while they are in police custody, I believe that in an adult court their confessions would be inadmissible. They were *not* warned of their rights to counsel; they were detained for long periods of time; and above all these statements were taken from them under extreme police coercion and force."

A woman sitting on the front row stood up. "Judge, they done beat them!" she cried. "My boy told me!"

"Who are you, madam?" asked the judge.

"Mrs. MacEvers. Bubbles's mother. He told me."

Bubbles turned around and said, "Shut up, Ma; please shut up."

Sergeant Wellston whispered to me that she had been in the police station and that she was lying now. I turned to the judge. "Your Honor, Sergeant Wellston is testifying. May he continue? Sergeant, was Mrs. MacEvers present when Bubbles gave you his statement?"

"Yes, she was right in the room with him," he replied. "Your Honor, at least twice before we took his statement we called for her to come. When she didn't show up, we took the patrol car and brought her in over her protest that she was tired of coming down to the police station. We knew this case was going to be serious so we were extra careful to have her in the room when we warned him of his rights and took down the statement. Here it is, with his signature and those of two witnesses and his mother."

"I'll allow you to read the statements, Sergeant. I'm overruling your objection, Mr. Gray. Read the statements, Sergeant."

Although interviewed separately, both Bubbles and Smokey had told a similar story. Geronimo, alias Joseph Whitsely, was the fearsome warlord of the Algerians, the arbiter of war and peace. A warlord is a gang's *ad hoc* leader—a combined Secretary of State and Commander-in-Chief whose power is delimited only by the veto of one boy designated as the gang's runner. In the Algerian setup, John MacEvers, alias "Bubbles," currently held this post.

Recently Geronimo had deserted his long-time girl, Cissy Lee, sister of a respected Algerian senior, Terry Lee, who was serving a long prison term for robbery. His new love was Veronica Evans, who had recently moved into the neighborhood.

For some time suspicion had mounted about Veronica's loyalty to Geronimo and to the Algerians. This growing distrust of the pretty newcomer was carefully nurtured by Cissy, who used Smokey, the gang's trigger man, to turn the boys against Veronica. Smokey told Geronimo that Veronica was swinging with the Mountaineers, a hated rival gang, and that she had been seen talking to the Red Baron, Geronimo's counterpart in that group.

At this point the two accounts diverged. Bubbles insisted that Veronica was "shacking up" with the Red Baron and that Geronimo, knowing she was two-timing him, ordered Smokey to kill her. Smokey stated that at a full council meeting of the Algerians they had voted to "get" her. Several boys were named as possible trigger men and a kind of contest was set up to see who got her first. Smokey's statement ended on a note of modesty tinged with arrogance: he wasn't that fast on the draw—but on the other hand, would he have shot her in the *leg?*

Despite the many notes he was taking, Jonathan Gray declined to ask a single question of the sergeant on cross-examination.

"Call Veronica Evans," intoned the crier.

She hobbled forward uncertainly, clumsily off balance, not having yet mastered the new crutches.

"Miss Evans," I began, "please tell the court the circumstances of your injury."

She stood silent, straining forward on the wooden supports. Tiny seed-pearls of perspiration gleamed at her hairline.

"Speak up, Veronica," said Judge Hoffman. "I want to hear how this terrible thing happened to you."

"I don't remember, Judge. I just don't remember."

"I'm going to give you a few minutes to remember, Veronica. I'll declare a five-minute recess."

I followed the girl into a small anteroom where she lowered herself into a chair. My "Hi!" brought forth no response. I offered her a cigarette but she declined. As I lighted mine, the girl said sullenly, "It ain't gonna be no use to talk to me. I'm not gonna tell you one thing. I don't remember. Judge Hoffman can put me away until doomsday. O.K.?"

"What are you afraid of, Veronica? Or should I ask, Who scares you most—Geronimo, Bubbles, or the Red Baron? You know them all, don't you? What about Cissy Lee?"

"That bitch," the girl replied. "I'll get her someday. One leg and all. Anyhow, I want to ask you something. I don't want to go home. I'm going to have a baby, but I don't want my mother to know. Can you send me away?"

"Who is the father of your baby?"

"You gonna bring that up here? Forget it. I'll take that smoke."

I passed her a cigarette and said as she lighted it, "We're not going to bring that up now. Not in front of all these people. Look, Judge Hoffman is a very understanding man. He doesn't like to hurt people, especially children like you—like all of you. But how can he help you if you won't tell the truth? First of all, we have to know who did this horrible thing to you. People who go around shooting at girls on streets shouldn't be roaming around free. O.K.? Now you say you're pregnant. Don't you want your baby to have a father—even at least a name? We're trying to protect you and a lot of other people. That's why it's important to know the truth."

Veronica remained mute, the standard response to this patient adult plea, which I delivered over and over again to children who had clammed up in court.

"O.K. That's it, Veronica. Let the chips fall where they may. Let's go back."

Wheedling and cajoling ghetto children who view the law and all its operations with supreme mistrust was an exercise in futility. I had come to respect the stubborn dignity behind the refusal of these children to accept us as allies in their turbulent struggle for survival and identity. Middle-class children capitulated more easily and accepted adult manipulation.

"Well, Mrs. Richette," said Judge Hoffman when I returned to my desk. "Are we ready to continue?"

"Veronica refuses to testify about the shooting. She makes no accusation against anyone."

"Is that correct, Veronica?" asked the judge.

She whispered, "Uh-huh."

"Yes or No, young lady!" The judge rapped sharply with his pencil.

"No, your Honor, I don't remember. Yes, I can't testify."

She was a bright girl all right, and she treasured her life, even if she would have to live it out on one leg. Could it be also that, like many other young girls in her situation, she felt protective of the new life growing within her?

"All right," Judge Hoffman told her. "I can't compel you to testify, but I'm going to hold you at the Youth Study Center as a material witness." He turned to the Juvenile Division representative, "Is there a delinquency petition filed against Veronica?" Receiving an affirmative reply, he beckoned to Big Leo to escort her out of the courtroom.

"O.K., boys, now we'll get down to business. This little girl is so terrified she won't talk. First, I want to hear from Smokey and Bubbles."

Jonathan Gray moved next to Smokey. "Your name is Ronald Green, also known as Smokey?" he began.

The youth nodded.

"Is the statement you made to the police the complete story of what happened? Suppose you tell me again, Smokey."

"We found Ronnie lying on the street, so Bubbles and me decided to take her into the Bean Bag so we could call the ambulance. Then the fuzz came—I mean the police—and they took us to the district.

Bubbles and I was really messed with, and then they wrote out this statement and made us sign it. Both of us. Bubbles and me. We was really messed with."

"Tell the court what you mean by being messed with."

"You know. They told us they knew we had shot her, that we could get the chair or life for attempted murder. When we laughed at them, they started pushing us around. We was there for eight hours without eating or drinking anything."

"When you signed that statement, did you do it of your own free will and accord?"

He shook his head. "Nope."

"Your Honor," said Jonathan Gray, "these defendants were deprived of their constitutional rights by the very gentlemen who are sworn to uphold the law. Hence their statements are inadmissible, and I move that all charges against these two boys and the others be dropped immediately."

"May I insist upon the Commonwealth's right to cross-examine this witness?" I asked. "Mr. Gray should make this motion after all the testimony has been heard, your Honor."

"I'll make my motions whenever I choose," Gray shot back.

"Counsel—both of you. Let's have no further quarrel. Go ahead, Mrs. Richette, cross-examine."

"Ronald," I began, "how did you happen to be at Fifteenth and Ash Streets just at that moment when Veronica was hurt?"

"Bubbles and I always go home together. We was just passing by."

"Did you hear any shots?"

"No."

"Why did you move her? Don't you know it's dangerous to move a wounded person?"

"Don't know. We was just trying to help," he said impatiently.

"Couldn't you have called for help without moving her?"

"I guess so."

"Now, when you got to the police station, what time was it?"

"Oh—something to seven."

"Weren't you given a sandwich and a Coke at eight-thirty?"

"No, ma'am." Then more emphatically, "No."

"Didn't your mother come at eleven o'clock?"

"I don't know. I was kind of dozing. Must have been closer to two or three in the morning."

"Was your mother in the room when you made your statement to the police?"

"I don't know. I told you I was dozing."

No point in continuing down this dreary alleyway of interrogation. I got to the core.

"Did you shoot Veronica Evans?"

"Nope."

"Do you know of your own knowledge who did?"

"Nope."

"I renew my motion, Judge," interjected Gray.

"Mr. Gray, I'm going to overrule your motion. I believe that this boy was warned of his rights, even though as a juvenile he has no privilege against self-incrimination. You have offered no evidence of physical abuse of these boys by the police. Therefore, on the basis of his statement that he participated in a war council of the Algerians and helped to plot the assault on the girl, I am going to adjudge him delinquent. Where is Bubbles? John MacEvers, that's his name. Do you wish him to testify? I'm going to adjudge him on the same basis. Mr. Gray, we have a terrible problem here.

"The summer is only half begun, and already this makes the sixth—or is it the seventh?—gang shooting before me. The bloodshed in our streets must stop. If these boys want to be heroes according to their gang code, if they aren't going to tell us what they know, then they are going to be committed. Let them be heroes in jail. Look at that lovely little girl. She's going to be a cripple for the rest of her life. Why? Does it make any sense to you? Where are the parents of these boys? Let them come forward."

He paused while the group assembled in front of him.

"Parents—all of you—I don't know what you did, or didn't do, what all of us failed to do for these boys, that has turned them into such killers and brutes. The police have rounded up your sons and brought them in as members of one of the most lawless gangs in our city. Over the past five years I've sent many of its members away for long periods. I've sent away the warlords; three are now in prison at Camp Hill. Whenever we chop off the head of this gang, like some mythical monster it seems to spring a new, tough one. Three years ago, Geronimo was just a junior! Now he is the Lord High Executioner decreeing life and death.

"This isn't a simple problem for the courts or the District Attorney or the police; even getting evidence would require a small section of the Federal Bureau of Investigation working full time. These Gang Control men, this handful of truly dedicated officers, have to do their case investigations and at the same time keep a constant watch on the many active gangs operating in this city. Sergeant Wellston has a superhuman task. All of us do. The police and the courts alone can't clean the filth and corruption that has been glutting our cities.

"Listen, my friends, I know you have hard lives. But these are your sons. Please keep them under control. I'm warning you, boys, and you can send the word out to the Red Baron, to the Mountaineers, to all your buddies and your enemies: You declare war on us; we have to come back at you hard. But unlike you, we believe in justice under law. So I don't send you away just because someone, even a police officer, *tells* me you are in a gang, or are supposed to have had a meeting. But whenever I have evidence—solid evidence—I'm going to act, and all your protests about police brutality and the rest aren't going to affect my thinking. Is that clear, parents? Do you understand, boys? This is for real. Now, Sergeant Wellston, about these weapons—where did they come from?"

"Acting on information received, we went to Cissy Lee's house the day after the assault with a search and seizure warrant obtained from your Honor. In the closet of the room which Cissy shares with her three sisters—ages twelve, seven, and three—we found this sawed-off shotgun, three automatics, and two zip guns. We interrogated Cissy Lee and she stated that she does not know how the guns got there. She said they may have been left there by her brother, Terry, who is now at Camp Hill. We took the weapons out immediately, your Honor. The automatics were loaded. There are quite a number of small children in that house, and any one of them could have been killed. Cissy's eleven-year-old brother, Dicky, was questioned and he said he didn't know how they got there. But the three-year-old girl said, 'Dicky put them there with Cissy. I saw them.' Of course, I know your Honor can't take her word on this."

"Call Mrs. Lee," ordered the judge.

A trim, worried-looking woman in a practical nurse's uniform came up.

"Mrs. Lee, did you know these guns were in your house?"

"No, your Honor. I work an early shift and when I left that

morning, I went to that closet to get out the kids' playclothes for the day. There was no guns in my house then. The baby says they brought them in around lunchtime. Oh, God! My babies could have been killed." She began to weep quietly.

"What do you have to say about Cissy and Dicky? Dicky is on probation for breaking parking meters. Cissy attends a special disciplinary school for truancy and misconduct; there's one remedial for shoplifting."

Mrs. Lee dried her eyes but said nothing.

"O.K. Cissy, come up here and start talking. Did you turn these boys against Veronica?"

"Nope. Why waste my time with her?" she asked scornfully.

"Weren't you Geronimo's girl friend before she came along?"

"I'm still his girl. She never changed anything."

"What about these guns? They didn't just march up to your room by themselves. How did they get there?"

"I don't know. I was out. Dicky was in the house."

"All right, Dicky, come up here. Let's hear your story."

He was a tough, alert little boy, a full-blown street Arab at eleven. The success of the Algerians' recruiting efforts with young boys like Dicky Lee is the direct result of the massive failure of schools and social welfare agencies to understand and help them change their sordid life patterns. These youths are denied the opportunities and incentives all children need to develop solid values. Dicky was the fourth of seven children by five different fathers, uncertain which man had fathered him, tutored by warlord brother and camp-follower sister. Now he had but one thought, one dream of self-fulfillment: to sign the blood-pact with the Algerians.

To be admitted to the brotherhood he would have to show by at least one act of self-sacrifice that he possessed "heart"—that blend of daring, subjugation to the will of the gang, and defiance of the Man (at that moment, the judge) that marks the full-fledged gang brother. Dicky was now about to initiate himself into the Algerians by committing perjury so that the other seventeen boys could walk jauntily out of the courtroom. He would be remanded, along with Smokey and Bubbles, to the Youth Study Center until a "suitable" facility was found. This would not be the first time that a boy's performance in juvenile court proved to be the crucial test for gang membership.

The irony of it! Here was a court dedicated to rehabilitation unwittingly providing the initiation rites that enabled an eleven-year-old boy to enter the inner councils of a gang! If only he could be stopped . . .

"Dicky," said Judge Hoffman patiently, "you're not going to tell me that you found these guns in the sewer or in an empty house, are you? You don't think this old judge is going to believe that, do you? Or that somebody came running up to you and said, 'Here, take them'? That's the current story this year, isn't it?"

Dicky just stared at him defiantly.

Judge Hoffman turned to the lawyers and said, "You wouldn't believe how that story originated. Mrs. Richette remembers. Thunderbird—one of our regulars—was brought in with three stolen suits which he was calmly carrying away when the police found him in the subway concourse. He didn't quite know how he got them, he said, but an unknown man dashed past him and threw them into his arms with the words, 'For you, Thunderbird!' So I wouldn't be a bit surprised to hear that some total stranger rushed up to Dicky and without breaking gait flung the guns at him and vanished forever. Is that how it happened?"

The boy nodded, unsmiling.

"Mr. Gray, he will never tell us the truth, and I don't think anyone should force him. His life wouldn't be worth a plugged nickel if he did. This is guerrilla warfare, and traitors are dealt with summarily. What's his school report?"

The Board of Public Education representative who had been sitting at a desk behind the bench began a depressing litany: "'Absent for over half the school term. Fights with and curses teachers. Makes absolutely no progress. At eleven is reading on a second-grade level.'"

Apart from the child's name, the report was indistinguishable from those of most of the senior Algerians—as well as hundreds of other throwaway children who pass repeatedly through the doors of the juvenile court.

"Hold Cissy Lee at the Youth Study Center for a plan. And keep her away from Veronica Evans," added the judge, "even at mealtimes."

"All boys already on probation will remain so. I want a report on them in thirty days. All others mark 'Discharged as to offense.'

Remember my warning. And get the word out: I won't tolerate this senseless violence!"

As the boys filed out, Big Leo turned to no one in particular and said, "Isn't that something? A group of kids run wild, and our hands are tied!"

I reflected bitterly that tomorrow's news coverage of the Algerians' hearing would perhaps trigger another angry editorial in which the courts would be assailed for mollycoddling gang members.

The community-versus-gang pattern is all too familiar. With the advent of warm weather, the gangs awake from their winter hibernation and take to the streets. At the first sound of gunfire, the community is also aroused from its torpor, demanding its pound of flesh while the juvenile court is aiming at rehabilitation. If we in court agreed that the community was right in its demand—which we do not—we would allow the mere suspicion of gang participation to result in long confinement. Despite severe criticism from some of the press, we have refused to pervert due process of law by making the court a star chamber for inquisition.

Furthermore, we do not need more clinical studies or sociological dissertations to understand why the Dickys, the Geronimos, the Bubbles, and the Smokeys declare hostilities against each other. They are really at war with society, but are powerless to challenge their invisible enemy, who have consigned them to the ghettos, taken away their fathers, ignored their mothers, and poisoned their childhood. Unsophisticated, not trained to reason things out, often nonverbal or inarticulate in their responses, they give vent to their anger at life by assaulting each other.

This misdirected rebellion must be quelled. These gangs stab, club, and shoot rival gang members who invade their "turf"—the trash-littered alleys and streets they are sworn to protect—or who, as in the case of the Algerians, steal their women. Occasionally one of these girls becomes the target for destruction. During the twenty years of its existence, the Gang Control Unit has accumulated records on some fifty-six terrorist ghetto gangs in Philadelphia.

But when I asked members of this unit about more affluent antisocial white gangs based in middle-class neighborhoods, they merely shrugged their shoulders and said, "That's none of our business." By insisting on this myopic view that gang-control work does not include supervising adolescent groups outside the ghetto, the police department reflects a prevailing social attitude. So the names of "nice" kids who wreck and pillage mansions, burglarize homes, shatter windows at coming-out parties, steal cars, or go on drinking and drug sprees are not to be found in the official police files.

The omission, together with the constant emphasis on ghetto violence, fosters the erroneous impression that gang activity is the special forte of Negro youth. So the community is shielded from the painful truth that antisocial adolescent groups are found at every social stratum.

Many so-called "experts" who sort and classify crimes see these affluent delinquent gang members as isolated instances of "good" children who have somehow gone bad. The juvenile justice system itself permits the parents of many of these children to buy their way out of a mess: to solve the immediate problem by paying the damages without looking beyond to underlying causes. And since their attitudes reinforce the community's assumption that the middle-class delinquency is "different," the true situation is concealed.

But why should one boy receive a jail term and another be given a minimal probation or an outright discharge, often at the request or through the influence of parents and important community leaders who at the same time press for sterner measures against "delinquents"?

Is it because the child-processing bureaucracy is dominated by middle-class professionals who share class and status values with the parents of the affluent delinquents? Is it because the American white middle class cannot admit that its own children feel the same tensions and angers more freely vented by ghetto children? Is it because we ourselves refuse to face the violence within us, denying it vehemently while we continue, young and old, to lap up scenes of violence on television and movie screens?

Even though many of us continue to cling to the myth that people with white skin are "different," less violent, and hence superior, anyone who spends more than a few days in the Juvenile Court of Philadelphia knows better. I can cite instance after instance of white middle-class gang activity that matches, horror for horror, the wildest depredations of the so-called Jungle groups.

For instance, one spring morning in the early sixties Big Jim Pinto was visibly shaken as he prepared to call the first case on the day's list. Looking out at the budding trees beyond the courthouse, I felt a faint premonition, knowing that it is in this beautiful nascent season that, like bright green weeds through the cracks in the city streets, the first stirrings of youthful violence crop up.

As the bailiffs started to call the names of the parents, Big Jim spread his hands on the bar railing, murmuring, "I can't believe it. Sergeant Sweeney's son, charged with murder! And the four other kids—my neighbors! It's absolutely sickening!"

Sergeant Raymond Sweeney of the Philadelphia Police Department led his fortyish, handsome, and red-eyed wife to her seat. Accustomed to standing at the bar of the court waiting to give testimony, he seemed dazed to find himself sitting in the parents' section. Murder, conspiracy, aggravated assault and battery, and robbery were the charges facing his seventeen-year-old son John and four of the boy's best buddies: Roger Earle, also seventeen, and Anthony James, Edward O'Leary, and James Casey, all sixteen years of age.

The boys filed in and lined up in front of the bench. Standing solicitously behind them was one of Philadelphia's noted criminal lawyers, Barton Bailey (known affectionately in legal circles as "Weeping Willow" Bailey for his ability to punctuate his eloquent summations and pleas with tears, which he allowed to flow unabashedly down his ruddy cheeks). Bailey opened with an understated flourish.

"Your Honor," he said softly, "this is one of the most distressing matters I have ever encountered in my years at the bar. Were it not for the tender age of these boys, I would waive a preliminary hearing, but I am hopeful that your Honor will retain jurisdiction and treat this as a case of unlawful homicide, rather than murder, and give these children the benefit of the wise protections of this juvenile court."

While Mr. Bailey was speaking, my secretary came and handed me a telephoned message from my boss asking that the case be certified for a murder indictment in adult court. I spoke up and told the judge what my instructions were, and stated that I would have to oppose any move to keep this case in juvenile court. Unruffled by my statement, Bailey smiled affably and renewed his plea to Judge Hoffman to reach a contrary decision.

The mention of a murder indictment in adult court produced muted sobs among the parents. Mr. Bailey, one of the best lawyers around, turned and gave them reassuring nods and an encouraging smile before settling down to business.

The principal police witness was Homicide Detective Jerry Brill, another seasoned police "regular." Now his hands trembled slightly as he opened his report. He had known Sergeant Sweeney for years.

"At ten-thirty Sunday morning—yesterday, your Honor—a Mr. Stanley Kramer while walking with his two young children through Fairmount Park came upon a man, clad only in undershorts, lying bleeding by the creek in the middle of the park. The man was unconscious; he had been badly beaten about the head and torso. Mr. Kramer contacted a park guard who in turn summoned the police. The man was taken to the nearest hospital, where he died an hour and a half later without ever regaining consciousness."

"Who was he?" asked the judge.

"Investigation proved that the victim was one Edward Stewart, white, aged forty, who lived nearby. He was an unemployed teacher."

"I don't mean to interrupt Detective Brill unduly," said Mr. Bailey courteously. "I am sure Mrs. Richette will prove these facts by competent evidence, so I will not object to this hearsay testimony—at this time." Bailey never relaxed, even for a moment.

I nodded, and Detective Brill resumed.

"From our investigation of the neighborhood, we learned that five defendants, Earle, Sweeney, James, O'Leary, and Casey, had been in the park drinking beer and wine. Victor O'Connor and Simon Cassidy, who are not charged with homicide, are here as Commonwealth witnesses because they were also in the drinking party, bringing the total number of boys to seven. We questioned them all in the presence of their parents and five admitted beating up the victim. We have signed confessions from them taken in the presence of Mr. Bailey, who was summoned to the station house by Sergeant Sweeney almost at once."

"A beating is very different from a murder," remarked the judge. "Mr. Bailey, do you have copies of these signed confessions?"

"I do."

"Then in order to proceed efficiently, have you any objection to Detective Brill's testifying if he summarizes the contents of these confessions? It's much faster and less laborious than the question-and-answer method. Since you have the confessions, you are able to check the accuracy of the detective's testimony."

"No objection whatever, Judge."

Brill began his narrative. He was no Homer, but the way he blended police terminology with his own stilted paraphrasing of teen-age talk made his tale peculiarly horrifying.

"About seven o'clock this past Saturday night, Victor O'Connor started to collect the liquor for the weekly Saturday night drinking bout of this group of boys.

"He secured two cases of beer from a David De Santo, aged fifteen, who in turn had received it from his uncle, a beer distributor named Gerald De Santo. From a Miss Jacqueline Grant, aged twenty-one, he received a quart of whisky and a gallon of wine. Hiding the liquor in the car trunk, he picked up his friend Simon at the Cassidy home. The two of them drove to a dairy bar on Fairmount Avenue, their usual meeting-place, where the five boys before your Honor were waiting. They all drove off to the park."

I was struck by Victor's resourcefulness, even though I knew many of the devious techniques teen-agers use to circumvent the section of Pennsylvania law that prohibits the purchase of liquor by persons under twenty-one years.

"What about this regular Saturday night drinking?" asked Judge Hoffman. "How long has it been going on? Are these boys in a gang?"

"Your Honor, all these boys stated that they have been drinking in the park on week ends for about a year. We have had many complaints from residents about numerous neighborhood boys drinking there. Apparently no one wanted to tell Sergeant Sweeney that his boy was one of them. According to our records, no formal complaint had ever been lodged against these specific boys."

"I am all too aware of what boys and girls do in that and other parks in so-called nice neighborhoods," said the judge. "By the way, where are the two people who provided the liquor? I suppose they have been arrested?"

Detective Brill gave an affirmative nod and continued, "It was about eight-thirty when they arrived in the park. They decided to chill the beer by placing the two cases in a creek although they were actually sitting some distance away in a grove near where the victim was found the next morning. Other boys joined the party from time to time. A few girls came by, but they had dates and went on their way. It was, if I may say, a big, open-air party for at least three hours.

"By about eleven-thirty, only the original seven remained. Simon Cassidy saw something white moving through the trees near the bank of the creek. Thinking it might be a girl, he went up to investigate. He returned a few minutes later, saying, 'Hey, I've got me a real queer! He's a winner!'"

During his interrogation Simon had explained that "winner" meant a great talker, someone who wouldn't let you go—like a drunk.

"At this point, John Sweeney got up and said he wanted to meet this winner, and off he went. When he didn't return after about fifteen minutes, the rest of the group decided to investigate. As they got close, they saw the deceased, Edward Stewart, on his knees, performing an unnatural sex act on the Sweeney boy. When the group approached, Sweeney broke away and pulled up his pants."

It was painful to see the Sweeneys' response to these words. The father sat rigidly in his chair, eyes staring forward; his wife's head was buried in her hands. She seemed about to faint. A court nurse moved close to her, smelling salts in hand.

"Roger Earle took over the situation at once. According to the boys, he is more or less the leader. He walked over to the deceased and asked him for money. The deceased said he had only small change, and gave Earle about thirty cents. Earle said they wanted more—much, much more. He told the deceased that faggots like him should be well-heeled if they wanted to do tricks with boys. The deceased said he would go home and get money, but Earle, who was a little drunk, thought Stewart might call the police. He grabbed the man by the shirt collar and started to punch him.

"The deceased was slightly built; Earle was at least four inches taller and about twenty-five pounds heavier. He knocked Stewart to the ground and called the other boys over. Earle, Sweeney, James, O'Leary, and Casey started to undress him. At that point both O'Connor and Cassidy, who wanted them to stop, decided to leave, so James, O'Leary, and Casey followed to make sure they didn't walk off with the remaining half-case of beer still cooling in the stream. They dragged it back nearer to the action and then rejoined

Earle and Sweeney, who were quarreling about what to do next. Earle was all for killing the man; Sweeney was not so sure. The man, semiconscious after the beating, kept moaning 'Help! Help!' "

In Earle's signed confession was the statement that he had wanted to kill the man from the start. At the age of eleven, he said, he had been molested by a homosexual, and ever since then had wanted to kill all of them. All the boys stated that while he was beating Stewart, he was in a fury, calling him vile names.

The detective paused for a few seconds and swallowed hard.

"Sweeney suggested that the five boys take a vote. They had three choices: (*a*) to continue beating him for a little while, (*b*) to let him go home to get the money, which was a safe thing because no faggot would call the police, especially after he had 'blown' a minor, or (*c*) to kill him. They voted; the poll was three-two in favor of death. O'Leary and Casey, the dissenters, said they wanted no part of killing and would take a couple of beers back to the grove and wait until the others returned so that they could all leave the park together. They intended to ask Victor O'Connor to wait around with his father's car, unaware that he and Cassidy had already gone. Earle, Sweeney, and James said O.K., and O'Leary and Casey left. It was then about midnight.

"For the next two hours," Detective Brill continued, "the three boys took turns beating Stewart. Roger Earle forced the man's legs apart and kicked him repeatedly in the groin; Sweeney and James punched him. When Earle began to look around for large rocks, the other two also collected a few stones. Between beatings, they sat down and drank beer. Sweeney kept saying, 'I never killed a guy before. I guess I'll find out what it feels like.' Earle kept leaping up to attack. 'Look, the s.o.b. is moving around. I'm going to give it to him right in his goddamn balls!' Finally, after the last bottle was drained, Earle said, 'I guess we've finished the job, but let me just give him one more.' He picked up the largest stone he could find and hurled it at the supine man, hitting him on the left side.

"It was the *coup de grâce*. The boys left Stewart, bleeding and unconscious, for dead.

"Rejoining O'Leary and Casey, they all walked out of the park and went to their homes to sleep off their beer-whisky-wine hangovers. When they woke up early Sunday afternoon, they heard the neighborhood rumors about the dead man found in the park. Later that evening they were rounded up together with a dozen other boys the neighbors said also frequented the park on weekends."

"I've heard enough, Detective Brill. Do you have an autopsy report?"

"Yes, your Honor. The autopsy shows the following: two fractures of the skull, brain contusions, fractured ribs, abdominal bruises, several deep cuts over the left eye. Because of the many beer bottles littering the area, our first theory was that he had been drunk and had fallen in the creek. But it didn't square with the heavy bruises around the groin or his seminudity."

"Mr. Bailey, any questions?"

"Not at this time. If I may speak, your Honor, these boys were in a heavily intoxicated condition. By the detective's testimony, they had consumed two cases of beer, wine, and whisky. The deceased had solicited at least one of them to commit sodomy, and performed the act. These are all mitigating circumstances, which I submit, your Honor, make the case different, and not suitable for adult criminal court. I'm not suggesting that these boys go unpunished. No; far from it. But I think they ought to be given a boy's punishment, not the penalties we reserve for men."

"Mr. Bailey, I thank you for your remarks. However, I think I know all that can be said in mitigation on behalf of the boys. They haven't been arrested before, but this doesn't mean that they haven't broken the law before. By their own admission they have been drinking for a year. Why didn't the parents check their sons' activities more carefully? How could a boy come home week end after week end reeking of liquor and go unnoticed? The parents were in bed asleep or out partying themselves. You see, Mr. Bailey, *they* treated their children like adults. Boys their age are not supposed to drink until two in the morning, are they? I'm sorry, but I think this was a wanton, terrible, vicious killing, and I am going to hold all five of them without bail for the action of the grand jury. I'll let another judge and jury decide whether or not O'Leary and Casey were accessories to the death of that unfortunate man."

Sergeant Sweeney stood up and nodded gravely at the judge. It was the right decision. He would have recommended no less for any other arrested defendant.

Within two months the five boys were tried separately on varying charges. Roger Earle, convicted of homicide, robbery, conspiracy, and aggravated assault and battery received a sentence of five to fifteen years in a maximum-security prison. Shortly after his arrival there, his behavior became bizarre and his homosexual drive overt; he was then transferred to a prison where he could receive closer psychiatric supervision.

John Sweeney and Anthony James, convicted of the same charges, were sentenced to serve two to ten years in a prison for young felons. Both had good records there and earned their parole at the expiration of the minimum sentences. Edward O'Leary and James Casey, whose convictions of aggravated assault and battery carried prison sentences of eleven and one-half to twenty-three months, served their time in county prison.

Victor O'Connor, who had collected the liquor and transported it to the park, served an eighteen-month sentence in the same county jail. Simon Cassidy was put on probation.

The twenty-one-year-old girl who purchased the wine and whisky for O'Connor was placed on probation on charges of contributing to the delinquency of minors and violating the Liquor Control Code. Similar probation was decreed for the uncle and nephew who had provided the two cases of beer.

For some time afterward, according to Big Jim Pinto, the park was quiet on week ends. Park guard reinforcements made better patrolling possible, and the gangs stayed away. But the drinking parties went on, the furtive meetings continued; behind the picture windows and within paneled dens the cry rang out, "The gang's all here!"

Of course the gang is here. It is an integral part of growing up in contemporary America. But what is the meaning and importance of the gang to adolescent boys—the poor as well as the affluent? For both groups the gang serves to fill the emotional void created by neglectful, disinterested, or apathetic parents. Ghetto children from matriarchal families lacking firm masculine controls have as their nearest male models the successful petty-underworld figures. They strive to imitate these unsavory characters in their crude aggressions and defiance of authority.

More privileged youngsters find through their peer associations the solidarity and the sense of belonging that are glaringly missing in their homes. Often their fathers are physically present but emotionally absent. Immersed in their own strivings for status, such men renounce an active and responsible paternal role, content to let their wives handle all matters of supervision and discipline. The mothers, in turn, are unable to control the boys. Studies of these affluent teen-agers show that the youngsters themselves believe the parents set too lenient standards and are too casual about enforcing them. When asked to devise their own codes of behavior, these adolescents invariably impose upon themselves far stricter regulations than those their parents customarily invoke.

Questioning the complexities of life in the difficult contemporary scene, these children get few satisfactory answers from adults. According to the Report of the President's Commission on Law Enforcement and the Administration of Justice, they accuse "those ahead of them of phoniness and of failure to define how to live both honorably and successfully in a world that is changing too rapidly for anyone to comprehend." Such youths become dangerously detached from their families and other adults who might have provided controls. Their rootlessness thrusts them into dependence on their own peers, some of whom will be neurotic and even psychopathic leader-types who will lure them into illicit acts. There is a marked similarity between middle-class and ghetto adolescents in the group-association pattern that both follow.

Yet, differences between the two classes are real enough. In contrast to the more affluent group who tend more often to destroy property, the less privileged teen-age boys vent their destructive urges on each other. With such a bleak future in store for them, the gang gives them *some* security, even though it brings them daily into conflict with the rest of society.

The belief that these ghetto youngsters will respond positively to alternatives that society might offer them is more than just an act of faith. In Philadelphia, members of one of the most notorious gangs were recruited by a Temple University staff member to work out some socially acceptable expression of "what they were all about." The boys themselves decided to make their own film, directing, writing, photographing, and acting in it. The result was a powerful and eloquent documentary entitled simply *The Jungle*. After its successful reception by many community groups, the boys decided to form a corporation to conduct other artistic and business activities. They now finance new projects by showing the film to various organizations and groups. At the end of each viewing, these enterprising young people frankly answer the searching questions that members of the audience pose.

In the summer of 1968, after violent outbreaks of warfare in the Philadelphia ghetto areas, District Attorney Arlen Specter asked the leaders of two rival neighborhood gangs to serve as special consultants in his office. They agreed to do so. Shortly afterward, one of these gangs, the Moroccans, responded to the efforts of local adult leaders and decided to publish their own newspaper and "tell it like it really is." Soliciting advertising revenue, they started from scratch, worked hard, and soon began to bring out weekly editions of *Dig This*, producing a series of creditable, moving articles and selling issues for a nominal price. When the staff expressed the hope of being able to stay in the publishing business, a small group of poverty-program leaders and neighborhood readers began seeking funds to keep the newspaper alive and flourishing.

The resiliency of youthful ghetto dwellers is evident in the fact that many of them *do* survive tragic and ugly childhood and adolescent experiences and become respected members of society. The roster of these men and women is an impressive one. Many of them have become successful leaders in business, politics, various professions, and the arts. Those who, like Gordon Parks, the noted photographer-novelist, remember poignantly their own early years and do not turn their backs on children who so desperately need help and care now, make a special contribution to the future of this country.

The gang is all here, yes—but mainly because *we* are not *there*.

10

RAPE
IS A
FOUR-LETTER WORD

Matthew Brady, aged sixteen, charged with rape."

At the sound of his name an intensely black, powerful boy straightened to his full height. He was well over six feet tall; except for his beardless countenance and the eyes of a frightened child he looked totally out of place standing at the bar of juvenile court. The question flashed through my mind: Who had committed this deed—the man or the boy?

"Where is the complaining witness?" Judge Hoffman asked. "I won't hear the case without her. Who is that woman back there? Come forward, please."

A disheveled crone slouched in the back row slowly moved forward; her uncertain gait was that of an invalid or an alcoholic. As she came closer, we could see that she was prematurely withered and gray; she was somewhere in her early or mid-forties. When she came up behind the boy she reached out to touch him, then withdrew her hand. The boy seemed to sense her gesture. He glanced at her for an instant, then turned away.

"Who are you?" repeated the judge.

"This boy's mama, Judge. I ain't the lady he messed with."

"Where is his father? Or uncle or some male relative?"

"His poppa died in North Carolina before he was born. I came up here with him and his sister when he was six years old. Ain't got no family up here at all, Judge. Just the boy and me and my friend Mr. Lee."

"Yes, I see," he replied, reading the thick blue court record beside him. "Where is his sister?"

"I sent her home to North Carolina two summers ago, and she never come back. Got into trouble, they say, and got put in the County Home."

As his mother rambled on, the boy became restless. He shifted from one foot to the other and tugged at the rope that served as a makeshift belt, his trousers were hopelessly stained and torn.

"Why are his clothes in such a deplorable condition?" asked the judge. "Are the arresting officers here?"

"No, your Honor. I'm Detective Green. This is just about the way he looked when he was brought in last night. Of course, we interrogated him for a good while in the district station house, and then we had to hold him until morning because there was no room for him at the Youth Study Center, and we thought it would be foolish to take him on an hour's ride all the way up to the House of Correction when he had to be down here again at nine o'clock this morning."

"Your boy is in serious trouble, Mrs. Brady," the judge said sympathetically. "He needs a lawyer. Can you get him one soon?"

"Ain't got no money for a lawyer, Judge," she replied. "Mr. Lee don't want no parts of Matt. He wouldn't even give me carfare to come down here. I walked on down. Can you get him a lawyer, please?"

"We'll try our best. Did you say that you walked in this heat?"

He reached under the robes and pulled out a bill.

"Here, Jim," he said to a court officer. "See that she uses this to get home."

Judge Hoffman's dispensing of funds from his own pocket for routine items such as carfare, food, shoes, and the like had become part of the everyday scene. A compassionate judge who took on the burdensome task of giving some immediate practical assistance to thousands of poor black and white children or their families needed a full coin purse underneath the black silk folds of his robe. A penniless youngster may need carfare to look for a job. He may need a nourishing meal before reporting for his first day's work—if he is lucky enough to find employment. Therefore, Judge Hoffman had established an informal crisis fund over the objections of social workers who frowned on such informal help. But none of them offered an alternative to the judge's extended hand, because there was none. Aid to children is indirect and veiled in bureaucratic regulation; services, not money, is the slogan, regardless of the circumstances or the need.

Mrs. Brady tucked the money into a pocket of her dress. "Thank you, Judge. I've been coming down to court a lot with Matt. Ever since he was eleven years old."

"Detective Green." The judge resumed the immediate task. "I suppose I must continue this case. Where is the victim? I also note that there are two other defendants, Thaddeus Early, aged twenty-one, and Donald Beasley, seventeen. But I see only Matthew. Where are the codefendants?"

"Early and Beasley are fugitives at this point. Early is in New Jersey and will probably have to be extradited," Green told him. "Beasley's mother did not report him as a runaway, but she thinks she knows where he can be found.

"As for Miss Martha Malvern, the victim, she's in the hospital with a broken pelvis. Nobody knows when she will be able to appear in court, your Honor."

"A broken pelvis may require months of hospitalization. This doesn't sound like a friendly rape."

The anomalous concept of an amicable forced sexual act was devised by a court deluged with so-called "rape" charges by and against adolescents. It had proved useful in weeding out those situations in which the element of force was clearly an afterthought on the girl's part, either because she was embarrassed at having been found in the act by the police or a parent, or because she wanted, for her own reasons, revenge on the man. But injuries like Miss Malvern's were not part of these pseudo rapes. The charge against Matthew *was* serious.

The judge instructed me to call the Juvenile Committee of the Junior Bar Association to see if they could provide counsel for Matthew.

"On second thought," he added, "this boy may need an experienced criminal defense lawyer. There is a possibility that the District Attorney may want him to be tried as an adult. Call our friends at the Voluntary Defender Association first."

The year was 1958: nine years before the United States Supreme Court ruled that a boy in Matthew Brady's position must have a lawyer at his side when he faced serious charges in juvenile court. Despite the then-prevailing view of child-care experts that juvenile hearings should be informal and free of legal "clutter," Judge Hoffman insisted that children accused of crimes carrying serious penalties in the adult criminal code should be represented by lawyers. Since many of these young accused were penniless, the lawyers often served without a fee.

"Tell the lawyer that Brady may face a possible murder charge in the near future," Detective Green said to me quietly as he gathered up his reports. "We have his signed confession, which connects him with Early and Beasley in another rape the week before this one. The victim was a seventy-eight-year-old woman who was found dead in her rooms just two blocks away from Miss Malvern's place. An elderly gentlemen, Alonzo James, was in Miss Malvern's apartment when the boys came in. He has already identified Matthew as one of the group. We'll have him in court when the case is listed again. Now we have to find Early and Beasley. I may be back before long and so will Matthew. That boy frightens me," he added just before he left the courtroom.

Within a week Detective Green informed me of three developments. First, Beasley had been picked up in the attempted burglary of a grocery store and had confessed to being involved in the attacks on both Miss Malvern and the old woman. Second, he was absolutely sure that Matthew had been there during both rapes, and a full partner in all their plans. Third, Early's relatives in Trenton who had been shielding him finally told the police where he could be found; after a brief shoot-out he had surrendered and agreed to return to Philadelphia without any extradition formalities to stand trial for both murder and rape.

"We're ready to go on the murder pinch," was Detective Green's conclusion. "Who's going to be in court for Matthew—Perry Mason?"

"Not quite," was my rejoinder. "The Voluntary Defender has no one to assign at this time, so the Junior Bar Association is sending over a lawyer who has been at the bar just a short time."

Early was arraigned in juvenile court because his two codefendants were minors, but the judge made it clear at the outset that his role would be that of a committing magistrate hearing testimony at this preliminary proceeding. As the three took their places at the bar, Brady, the youngest, towered over his two buddies. Beasley was a thin, tense-looking lad with a severe acne condition that gave his yellow-brown skin a mottled effect. Early was short, squat, and hard as a bullet. Dark wet circles of sweat spread down the sides of the brown prison shirts the three wore.

"Is counsel present?" asked the judge.

"Ready to proceed, your Honor," said a bookish young man who could have just emerged from the stacks of a university library. "I'm Fred Van Clyde, a member of the Juvenile Defense Panel of the Bar Association. It seems that Beasley and Early have no counsel at this time. Will your Honor permit me to appear for all of them, although my specific appointment was to Matthew Brady?"

The judge inclined his head Yes, and Van Clyde, motioning the trio to step back a bit, carefully placed himself as the apex of a small triangle. His neat seersucker suit and regimental tie were already beginning to wilt in the late July heat. He stood there, the ubiquitous yellow pad in hand, as Green, the original investigator, began to testify.

"On July second, in answer to a reported suspicious death in the North Five Hundred block of —— Street, police from the district went to the apartment—really a room—of one Vera Lacey, colored and seventy-eight years old. There they found Mrs. Lacey's body in a severe state of decomposition."

He paused and I asked: "Was it possible to fix the date of death? Where is the Medical Examiner's report?"

"Yes," he replied. "I have it right here. Mrs. Lacey had been dead for about three days when the body was found; she must have died on the preceding Saturday or Sunday. The body was rotting, as I say. Thousands of maggots were crawling everywhere——"

Van Clyde stopped writing and looked up aghast. "Why was that, sir?"

"The place had one window, which was closed. The room was filled with garbage and other refuse. This is a pretty rough neighborhood, Counsel, and Mrs. Lacey lived alone and kept mainly to herself. The police were called because one neighbor thought the smell was getting to be too much, even for that house. You have no idea what a slum place can smell like in hot weather . . . Well, anyway, the body was taken to the morgue, and an autopsy conducted. The examination showed semen in the vagina, and bruises and discolorations as signs of possible rape."

"Did you say *possible* rape?" asked Van Clyde without lifting his pencil from the pad.

"I mean rape," said the detective firmly.

Judge Hoffman interjected. "What was the ultimate cause of death according to that report?"

"Suffocation, your Honor, Mrs. Lacey wore a long flannel petticoat. Apparently a strip from the bottom of it—please excuse me a moment, I want to check that."

He reached down into a paper shopping bag and pulled out what seemed to be a huge gray rag, looked at it briefly, and nodded.

"Yes, a strip was cut off the bottom of this petticoat and used as a gag. It was still around her mouth when she was found. Whoever tied it did a very good job. It pressed so hard against her gums that both her dental plates, top and bottom, slipped. Mrs. Lacey was on public assistance, your Honor, and the records show that the Welfare Department got her those plates last year. I may say that sometimes they don't fit as well as they could. That's what happened here. The plates fell back into her throat, and she couldn't breathe. According to the statements made by Brady and Beasley, the old woman began to scream when they forced the door open. Early punched her and applied the gag. Brady and Beasley stood by the door to see if anyone had heard her scream. No one came."

"How did the police connect these boys and this man to Mrs. Lacey's death?" I asked.

"When Matthew Brady was being questioned about the rape of Miss Malvern, he mentioned that he heard that Tad Early had raped an old woman on North —— Street. We continued to question him, and he told us the whole story. It was one of those good breaks that we don't get too often in these cases."

"Any questions, Mr. Van Clyde?" said the judge. "This is clearly a case of murder—first degree—and I am bound to turn the juveniles over to the District Attorney for indictment and trial as adults. It's clear from the testimony that Mrs. Lacey died during the course of rape. You may ask any questions you like, of course, but I want you to know now that little can be accomplished at this stage."

This kind of judicial admonition flashes a red light to a defense lawyer: the less said here, the better for your client. Inexperienced as he was, Van Clyde got the message.

"No questions."

"Very well, I'm holding all three without bail on a charge of murder. You know, Counsel, they are involved in another case yet to be heard: the victim is hospitalized right now. That matter remains in the juvenile court as far as Matthew Brady and Donald Beasley are concerned. I hope you will represent them both. Each of the three will have lawyers appointed to them on the murder charge by the judges who will ultimately hear those cases. Perhaps you will be on Matthew's defense team along with a senior member of the bar. Since each of them is entitled to two lawyers on a murder defense, you may very likely be on this case for a long time, if you choose to."

"There is one thing, your Honor," said the young lawyer. "I would like to read Brady's statement to the police and his signed confession."

"I would be glad to let Mr. Van Clyde see them if he will come to my office later in the day," I said.

"By the way, where is Mrs. Brady?" asked the judge. "I don't see her in the court."

Matthew was being led out of the courtroom, but he wheeled around. "She's sick again, Judge. She sent me a note."

"What's the matter with her, Matthew?"

"Stomach trouble. She's had operations—she's got over a hundred stitches in her. It's that booze is eating her up."

So that was it. Mrs. Brady's infirm step and pained movements were those of an invalid *and* a drunk. The judge nodded understandingly.

"I know, Matthew. I've been reading about your life."

Then in the brief pause before the next case was called, Judge Hoffman said to me:

"I think that boy's juvenile court file should be studied by everyone connected with this case—prosecutors and defense counsel alike. I'm ordering that these records be made available to the lawyers on both sides, and I hope to heaven they read every word in this hideous file."

Late that afternoon, Van Clyde walked into the small quarters that served as a base for the assistant district attorneys then assigned to the juvenile court.

"Welcome to Kubla Khan and its marble splendors!" I greeted him. "It's a touch removed from M., J., and N., but just as real," I added, alluding to an old, aristocratic law firm for which Van Clyde worked.

"Wrong," said Van Clyde. "It's *more* real. I'm really getting very involved in this case. Matthew Brady is on my mind all the time. I was never very interested in criminal law, but I volunteered for the Juvenile Committee out of curiosity and because it seemed the right thing to do. How do you stand looking at those kids all day? I don't know about you—you're a Yale Law graduate, aren't you? I'm Harvard—but law school never prepared me for a client like Matthew Brady. What can be done for him? I'll bet he gets the chair. Did you read the editorial in one of the papers the other day? It called him and the others three wild beasts roaming the jungle. It sounded almost sorry the police weren't allowed to shoot them and bring in their pelts." He paused a moment, looking at an open file in front of me. "Are you reading Brady's record?"

"Yes. I'm almost at the end. I've reached the point when Matthew was last in court, two months ago. Here, read his confession while I finish."

Van Clyde poured over the nine-page signed confession.

"I don't believe it," he said finally. "Have you ever spoken to Matthew?"

"I don't think so. Certainly not at great length. I rarely have time to interview children in the morning before the session opens. You must realize that he is just one of several hundred kids we see every week."

"Did you know that he is practically illiterate? How many sixteen-year-old boys can there be who can't read or write? Matthew

Brady can spell dog, cat, and boy, but three-letter words are his limit. He can write his name, but who the devil can read it? What school does he attend? Where has he been all his life?"

I tried to explain, knowing that Van Clyde, like many men and women from privileged backgrounds, found the conditions of poor children hard to believe. "Look. There *are* hundreds of children in our high schools who are functionally illiterate. Try reading Paul Goodman's book, *Growing Up Absurd*, sometime and you'll see. Matthew is another wasted resource; it happens all the time. He attends the Boone School, a special disciplinary school, but he's not there because he's a behavior problem—he has always been docile. He was sent there because it was the only school with a flexible enough program to let a boy just sit around all day without irritating anyone. In this court file, there's a note from Boone that Matthew wouldn't even play checkers. You see, they have a checker game going all the time for boys who can't or won't read or work."

"Checkers requires concentration," my visitor murmured, "and I guess Matthew isn't capable of concentrating. Boone School—as in Daniel? When he said it, it came out sounding like 'Boom'! And he didn't know how to *spell* it either. He also didn't know the address, but said he could show me where it was."

"Mr. Van Clyde, he doesn't even know his home address. He went to school only three times last year, so you can hardly expect much. We have, for whatever it's worth, an I.Q. of sixty-three on him."

"All right, then—read this confession. It has words in it like 'force,' 'attack,' and 'rape.' Rape! That's a four-letter word. He can't even spell it! A three-year-old nephew of mine has a better vocabulary than Matthew, who's sixteen! These couldn't be his words, and he certainly wasn't able to read it, much less understand it, despite the printed capital letters above his signature that state he's done both. It seems the police questioned him for quite a while."

"It's hard to tell; he stayed at the district all night because there were no free beds at the Youth Study Center, so I suppose they could have talked to him all night. Let's say twelve hours! Are you implying that he was coerced in some way? You've talked with him —wouldn't he have told you, or somebody, if he had been strong-armed?"

"Maybe yes, maybe no. I didn't ask him. Nevertheless, it's an outrageous situation these kids are in!"

"Careful, Mr. Van Clyde. You show definite symptoms of a bleeding heart. That will never do. You might stain the Oriental rugs in your plush law offices!" I teased him. "No, seriously, I agree with you, of course. All we can hope is that the boy gets an extremely sharp and sensitive senior lawyer. I hope you'll be there, too. Of course, *we'll* send our top talent in. The public watches very carefully to see what happens to defendants charged with rape and murder. The boss will press hard. He's up for re-election next year."

Van Clyde shook his head disbelievingly. "I guess I just don't get it. It will be interesting to see what happens. Let's keep in touch and let each other know if anything pops on this case."

About a month later, as I was hurrying along a busy corridor in City Hall, a soft-spoken, balding, cherubic-faced man put out his arm to stop me.

"I was just about to call you. I've been appointed counsel for Matthew Brady, with Fred Van Clyde. I want to see the juvenile court records. I have permission to go through the boy's file."

"Oh, that's great, Mr. Schatzberg," I replied, pleased because Jerry Schatzberg was one of the most able lawyers in town. "A very good thing for Matthew to have you and Van Clyde. Just call me and I'll be glad to arrange for you to see Matthew's records."

Gracious and erudite, he was more than an ornament to the bar; Jerry Schatzberg was an asset in many unusual ways. Although he had an extensive civil practice, criminal law remained his passion. For affluent clients his fees were handsome, to say the least; but he did not hesitate to accept many court appointments every year to defend indigent men and women charged with capital offenses. Utterly meticulous in all his trial preparations, softly deferential to judge and jury, he chose his weapons subtly but unerringly well; and to rich and poor alike he gave the same devoted thoroughness, skill, sophistication, and determination to win.

Thus I was not surprised when he stopped in my office a day or so later and extracted from his briefcase a mass of stapled notes. "I read over the Brady file, and I'd like to check out a few things with you, if you have a moment," he said.

I motioned to him to sit down, thinking how like him it was to have begun working on the case so quickly.

"I went to visit Matthew's mother yesterday. I had forgotten that people actually lived in that area. It's just beyond Skid Row, as you know, and at first glance it just seems like a jumble of deserted factories and warehouses. But if you look closely, and peer around corners, there are all those crumbling tenements, awful little stores, and the usual assortment of tattered-looking kids playing in the alleyways. Mrs. Brady has lived in a succession of apartments within that four-block area ever since she came from North Carolina.

"Right now she has a second-floor front apartment: two rooms, a bedroom, and a kitchen; they share a common bathroom with the other tenants on the floor. And she pays thirteen dollars and fifty cents a week for it—that's fifty-five dollars a month! I estimated how much the landlord collects from that miserable house: there are three floors with two apartments on each one; he gets fifty-five dollars for the front apartments, forty-five dollars for the rear—making a grand total of two hundred ninety dollars every month! He hasn't spent a penny on the place in years. Peeling paint, rotting door jams and sills—the whole thing is one big housing-code violation. Mrs. Brady's apartment isn't too bad, though. Very little furniture, but fairly orderly."

Schatzberg was a remarkable man, I thought. This was what more lawyers needed to do: get out of their offices and see and touch the rough surface of their clients' lives.

"She couldn't tell me too much about the boy. I don't think she knows him at all, even though he is her son. She says he's no trouble to her, that he tries to help out by working, but that her boyfriend, Mr. Lee, and the boy don't get along. While she was in the hospital last time, they had a big row, and it was Mr. Lee who made her take Matthew down to court when she came home."

"I thought something like that was behind that incorrigibility petition she filed," I told him. "The probation officer who investigated her complaint said he suspected the mother of trying to accommodate the paramour, but Mrs. Brady denied it. By the way, did you read what the boy said that time at the Youth Study Center? I have it here:

" 'I think I am kind. I try to help her. I didn't go to school for three months because I was trying to find a job. Mama needed medicine and she didn't have any money. Anyway, I really didn't have clothes to go to school, or to find a job.' "

"But he did find one," observed Schatzberg. "On an ice wagon, for about two dollars a day. I didn't think there were any ice wagons left! Or people with iceboxes!"

"The Youth Center referee dismissed the mother's complaint and added this comment for the record: 'It's the mother who actually needs chastising in this situation. The boy has been utterly neglected. He has had no religious training, and he has developed no interests, no hobbies, no organized recreation. *Nobody pays any attention to him.* He hangs around on street corners with unsuitable companions. Despite this, he has been working, and buying a few clothes for himself and his mother.'"

"Mr. Lee is also a drunkard," Schatzberg added. "And no great breadwinner—he earns about forty dollars a week, just enough to keep them both in booze and pay the rent. Matthew was hungry most of the time, I think. That's why he broke those parking meters: he used the change to buy himself a hot platter at a nearby diner. Imagine! And he was only eleven years old at the time."

"I'm sure he was often hungry. What a way to start life."

"Yes, and that was his first brush with the law. The next two arrests at age twelve involve stealing food, both times from Skid Row characters coming out of the Mission." Schatzberg paused, troubled. "It sounds awful to say that a kid stole doughnuts from helpless old drunks. Why didn't *he* go to the Mission himself, I wonder?"

"The place is run by a charity that wants to reform Skid-Row men. To get a hot bun, you have to look drunk and you have to take the pledge. Hungry kids are not allowed in!"

"I see." Schatzberg scribbled a note to himself. "This is the kind of information I want. Frankly, when I read the boy's background it was like reading a Dickens novel. I know every word in that file is true, but I don't want to use just *my* words to describe this background for the jury; they may think I'm being maudlin or sentimental. I want the hard testimony of people who know these things first hand. You know: social workers, teachers, all the psychologists and psychiatrists who examined Matthew every time he came to court. That poor kid was just about examined to death, with the same dreary diagnosis every time—home situation deplorable; mother an ineffectual alcoholic; youngster is very slow and very limited, not really educable, can't read or write; and on and on and on.

"It makes me angry every time I think about it. Why the hell didn't somebody try to change some part of it? Why didn't somebody do something?"

"You're right to rage," I told him. "I do it all the time. Dylan Thomas put it so well: 'Rage, rage, against the dying of the light.' That's exactly what childhood is for too many of these kids; a slow, sad blacking-out of the future and of whatever was shining and good inside them. And who notices that it's happening? Almost no one. Until Matthew broke the law, nobody noticed him. I'll bet just about every child in his grammar school faced the same grim problems he did. And the situation hasn't changed."

"Well," said Schatzberg, "at least there's one psychiatrist I can call who lays it right on the line: that psychiatrist for the County Court, Dr. Stephenson, and I quote: 'Even a more intelligent youngster could not cope with this boy's environment!'"

As Matthew's trial for murder unfolded several months later, his lawyers felt almost as gagged as the old woman, Mrs. Lacey. The presiding judge would not permit any of the sociological evidence that Schatzberg had so painstakingly collected.

Granting the motion of the District Attorney to exclude this mass of material, the judge told Schatzberg sternly, "You're an experienced lawyer, sir. You know that this testimony is irrelevant to the question of guilt or innocence. You haven't entered any special plea of insanity—and even then, strictly speaking, it could not be allowed. Get on with your case properly, sir."

Schatzberg studied the jurors uneasily. The solitary Negro he had been permitted to include on the jury avoided his glance. The other jurors had looked grimly at the photographs of the victim's body and listened sternly to the testimony about the dentures, the gag, the maggots, the semen. The lawyer sensed that they had steeled themselves against his plea for mercy. He was right. After five hours of deliberation the jury foreman stood up and read out the verdict: First-degree murder. Death by electrocution.

Schatzberg seemed more upset than the boy as the sentence was repeated. And not because it ended his unbroken record of never having a client go to the chair. Much more importantly, the boy had not had a full and fair hearing. The detectives, for example, had referred several times to the fact that the boy had given his confession after his arrest for Miss Malvern's rape. Schatzberg's objections, swiftly fired from the defense table, had not been fast enough to drown out the fatal words "prior rape." The jury heard them. Although he had stressed the boy's background in his summation, they had had only one bit of human evidence as an exhibit: Matthew's mother. Mrs. Brady had been permitted to testify that the boy had come home on the night of the murder and had not seemed unusual to her in any way. She had managed to clean herself up a little for the occasion, but there was nothing especially poignant about her. In answer to a question on the stand, she said she was a day worker, and a few of the white women-jurors nodded. Perhaps they themselves employed a woman like Mrs. Brady. Didn't all those domestics look alike anyway?

Almost immediately, Schatzberg began to study the trial transcript night after night, slowly constructing the framework for his appeal seeking a new trial. He went to see Matthew regularly in the small, bare prison office whose only adornment was a wall calendar.

"Today is Wednesday, November second, isn't it?" Matthew asked him one day.

"That's right."

"Mr. Schatzberg, I made up my mind. I'm going to learn to read and write. That word is Wednesday, isn't it?" he asked, pointing to the calendar. "They have a class here for inmates like me who can't read. I'm not the only one. Even if I get the chair, I won't die a dumbbell."

Shortly afterward, Miss Malvern left the hospital and went to a nursing home, outfitted with crutches and special shoes provided by the Department of Public Assistance. She would be crippled in her movements for a long time, but she was able to testify in Juvenile Court on the unresolved rape charge against Matthew and Beasley.

Young Beasley, who was Matthew's age but about 30 I.Q. points ahead of him, had been a principal Commonwealth witness against Matthew. After pleading guilty to second-degree murder (by prearrangement between his court-appointed lawyers and the prosecutor), he received the comparatively light sentence of seven and a half to fifteen years.

Tad Early, the adult, was not tried for murder until several years later. The District Attorney's office decided, in his case, to press first the rape charge lodged by Miss Malvern, on the theory that his conviction would compel him to enter a plea which would forestall a full trial. The strategy worked. Early ultimately received a sentence of life imprisonment for his part in causing Vera Lacey's death.

Finally, in juvenile court, Schatzberg was able to paint the full portrait of Matthew that he had not been permitted to present at the murder trial. The juvenile court, with its broad mandate from the legislature to inquire fully into the total life of a child, was free to take a long, searching look into the boy's past and present condition. With Matthew and Van Clyde standing next to him at the bar of the court, Schatzberg began:

"I have joined Mr. Van Clyde at his request. In the preparation of Matthew's murder defense we came upon extensive evidence which we feel the juvenile court should hear. Even though he has received the capital penalty in another court, we request that your Honor keep jurisdiction over the boy in this matter. We have filed motions for a new trial; the proceedings here may well have a bearing on what happens to our appeals."

"You may take all the time you need, Mr. Schatzberg. I realize that the compensation for the murder defense does not cover your appearance here. Nor is Mr. Van Clyde receiving a fee. I commend you both on your dedication and your interest in this boy," the judge said quietly.

Martha Malvern, the Commonwealth's chief witness, limped to the bar of the court. It was hard to believe she was thirty-eight. Once attractive, perhaps even pretty, her alcohol-ravaged countenance was expressionless throughout her testimony. She had been drinking beer with Alonzo James, her elderly "common-law husband," when Early, Beasley, and Brady broke in. She knew all three from the neighborhood, and had even gone out with Early several years ago. Yes, she turned a trick now and then; yes, with Early, too. The last time was about two years ago.

She thought they were paying a friendly call until Early and Beasley pushed Alonzo out of the room. A little high on the beer, she even joked and laughed with them at first. Matthew? What was he doing? Well, he kind of stood off to one side, like he was a little stupid or something. Then Early pushed her onto the floor, pulled down her panties, and had intercourse with her. Beasley kept telling him to hurry up, that the old man was pounding on the door. He took his turn next, and when he was finished, he and Early pushed Matthew down on top of her. When the boy hesitated a bit—"looked like he couldn't make up his mind"—she seized her advantage. Flinging him off, she ran screaming to the open window. Early and Beasley tried to pull her down; she lost her hold and fell out, crashing onto the sidewalk two stories below.

"Was Matthew exposed?" I asked.

"Uh-huh."

"Did he enter you?"

"Not much, just a little bit."

But even the slightest penetration is sufficient for a conviction of rape. Beasley had testified at the murder trial that Matthew had been on top of the gagged, dying Lacey woman for "a couple of seconds."

Schatzberg skillfully established by his questions that Martha Malvern earned her living as a prostitute, that she had a vast experience with men and boys, and that in her own mind she made a distinction between Matthew's role and Early's and Beasley's. As she put it:

"I don't think he knew why he was there. Like a big, scared baby, he was."

Then came the remarkable background testimony by the reputable middle-class people who had seen Matthew the child at first hand.

A court doctor who had given the boy a physical examination five years earlier explained that he could not answer any of the usual questions put to children—queries about weight, height, illnesses. Eleven-year-old Matthew was probably the most backward child he had ever examined; he therefore remembered him vividly.

A teacher from the grammar school that Matthew attended for eight years had counted five different men living with his mother over a three-year period. When she asked the mother about this situation, Mrs. Brady said she would stay with any man who fed her and the boy. In class, the teacher said, Matthew seemed to be sleeping most of the time. His clothes were so threadbare that she and another teacher gave him some garments they collected from friends with children his age.

The attendance officer from the Boone School stated simply that the boy did not go to school because he was really the main support of the family. Even though he explained to Matthew that, like the other teen-age boys at the school, he could be excused from afternoon sessions to go to work, the boy had come to school only three days.

Dr. Stephenson, who had made the most recent studies of Matthew, listened to this testimony. When his turn came he summarized his position in one terse statement:

"I don't believe the boy is basically vicious. He is without goals, without affection. He doesn't know how to have a relationship with anyone, so he will go along with anything in order to be accepted. A boy like Early or Beasley could lead him anywhere, especially since he has very poorly developed ideas of social responsibility." He paused before adding, "How could he have developed them? Society has shown no sense of responsibility for him."

Who could deny the truth of that? Forced to steal in order to eat, obliged to crisscross the city streets with his ice wagon, Matthew had been a throwaway for years. At last, society was about to act—but it was to brand him rapist, murderer, delinquent. For all concerned, I thought, the price of waiting too long is destructively high in more ways than one. And I asked myself then as now: *How much longer can society afford to wait?*

Schatzberg's final witness was the boy's first grade teacher. She recalled that during the whole time Matthew had been in her classroom he had not spoken a single word.

Judge Hoffman stood up.

"Mr. Schatzberg and Mr. Van Clyde. You have presented more than an appeal for mercy; the testimony here is an appeal to the conscience of this community. I hope"—he glanced significantly at the reporters whom Schatzberg had invited to attend the hearing—"that the press prints every word that has been said here today."

He ruled that until the appeals on the murder case had been completed he would impose no sentence on the boy, but would remand him to prison.

"I'd like the notes of testimony transcribed, please," asked Schatzberg as he collected his file.

"We have no funds for transcripts to indigent defendants," the judge pointed out. "However, I don't want you to pay for them yourself. We'll verifax the official set—as many copies as you need."

With indefatigable zeal Schatzberg filed appeal after appeal, undaunted by the refusals of the state supreme court and the Federal district court to order the case reopened. After I resigned my post I continued to follow closely the developments in the case. Almost seven years elapsed in the process. In that time Matthew's prison education had been so effective that he was able to read some of the simpler documents Schatzberg brought to him for his signature.

Meanwhile the Pennsylvania Legislature had declared a year's moratorium on the death penalty while senators and representatives heatedly debated its pros and cons. Seizing upon this changed climate of opinion, and armed with excellent reports on Matthew's progress from the prison social worker and psychiatrist, Schatzberg made one desperate last foray. He and Van Clyde appealed to the trial judge who had so adamantly resisted their earlier entreaties. A miracle! The seasoned jurist had had second thoughts about the plight of a boy like Matthew; in the interim he had been shocked by several cases in which some police officers had coerced dazed, illiterate suspects into making confessions.

Then, too, there was the *Miranda* case in 1966, the United States Supreme Court decision requiring that persons in custody be advised of their right to counsel before the police interrogated them about crimes carrying severe penalties. Schatzberg calmly accepted the news of a new trial for Matthew. He and Van Clyde went back to Schatzberg's office and toasted each other with a drink; then they went to work.

As Schatzberg chose Matthew's jury the second time, he was very careful to question potential jurors about their views on race and to find out whether they agreed that sex crimes could be committed as a result of social conditioning. He also made sure that better than half the jurors were black. Even though they were all middle class and respectable, they would accept more readily the truly desperate life situation the boy had been forced to endure.

Schatzberg's summation dwelled in detail on the boy's undeveloped thought processes and power of judgment, on the lack of any socializing forces—religion, love, the need for goals, guidance—during his vital years of development. He concluded by noting that many Americans—children and adults—lived as Matthew had, under the very eyes of a complacent, cruel society which ignored its basic human commitments.

"Ladies and gentlemen of the jury, of course we cannot eliminate all the conditions which drive men—and boys—to crime and to evil. But in a civilized society we should try to satisfy at least the basic needs of every child so that he doesn't have to be superhuman or heroic to resist the all-surrounding temptations to crime and anti-social conduct. We don't really try. That's why Matthew Brady is before you today begging you for his life, for which we cared so little."

Schatzberg knew even before the foreman announced the verdict that the boy would live. The verdict: Guilty of *second-degree* murder.

Before the judge imposed sentence, Schatzberg outlined the boy's wonderful progress in prison. Matthew had learned to read and to write and had become interested in sports. His superb physical strength and natural agility had convinced the athletic director that the boy should have special training. Matthew had become the prison's boxing champion.

"Isn't it pathetic," he concluded, "that only in prison did all this talent and skill begin to flower? Isn't it a tragic irony that sometimes society helps its outcasts only by condemning them to prison to get rid of them?"

As I listened, I thought of Jean Genêt, who had written his first novel on brown wrapping paper under the dim light of a prison cell.

Brady received a sentence of from six years and nine months to twenty years in prison, to become effective as of the date of his first conviction, thus putting him well past his minimum term.

"I'm placing a minimum review date of two years, however," the judge stated. "I want to be sure he continues to progress."

Matthew Brady will shortly be released. Schatzberg is confident that he will never get into difficulty again. The young man wants to teach boxing and athletics to slum children, and hopes that a settlement house or an antipoverty project will hire him, despite his parolee status.

One bizarre coda will never find its way into the written score.

It seems more than a coincidence that both of the women involved in the two cases were not teen-age girls; one was old enough to be Brady's grandmother; the other was a few years younger than his mother. Was he seeking through physical contact some womanly warmth that had been denied him all his young life? Whenever anyone asked him why he had gone along with Early and Beasley, Matthew said simply, " 'Cause I didn't have a girlfriend."

From the outset, Schatzberg was aware that Matthew had never known a woman's love. So he was astonished to receive a long-distance call one day from a soft-spoken woman who wanted to discuss the boy's case. It came while one of his appeals was pending. Her purpose in calling, she said, was to retain him so that he could get Matthew a new trial that would establish his innocence and set him free.

Schatzberg explained that since the court had already appointed him Matthew's lawyer because the boy was indigent, he, Schatzberg, was duty-bound to advise the court if someone came forward with money to pay for a lawyer. He would then be discharged. Of course, he could continue with the case in a private capacity, but then he would have to charge her at least five thousand dollars. (For eight years of continuous legal work in Matthew's behalf, he was eventually paid by the court the sum of twenty-one hundred dollars.)

There was a long pause at the other end; no, she had nothing like that in mind, she could afford only a few hundred dollars at most . . . Her seemingly genuine interest in Matthew quickened Schatzberg's curiosity and he invited her to come to Philadelphia to discuss the matter further. They made an appointment for the next morning at eight-thirty.

When she failed to appear that rainy, cold morning, Schatzberg was neither surprised nor upset. Strangers make and break appointments with lawyers all the time. His schedule was full and he went about his business without giving the matter further thought.

At day's end he dismissed his secretary, but remained in the office to do some work while waiting for his partner to finish with a client, so they could have their usual daily conference. Some time later, when the outer office door clicked, Schatzberg looked up and saw a tall, stunning brown-skinned woman walk into the reception area. She was wearing a beautiful black silk raincoat—imported and expensive, he thought—with a matching turban. From her arm swung a magnificent alligator handbag; her high-heeled shoes were of the same reptile skin.

"I'm looking for Mr. Schatzberg," she said softly. "I want to see him about Matthew Brady."

"I am he. Come in, please."

He was struck by the complete femininity and sex appeal she emanated. Judging her to be about twenty-four years of age, he found her quite seductive. She kept smoothing her sheer stockings as though to call attention to her shapely legs. After accepting a light for a cigarette held between well-manicured fingers, she began to speak quietly and rapidly.

Mr. Schatzberg was doing a good job for Matthew, she knew, but she wanted him to be set free. She loved Matthew deeply and wanted to marry him. She had a good secretarial job in New York and could support him; she worked for a politician who was a generous man.

Now Schatzberg interrupted. "Who is your employer?"

His intuition told him something was amiss here, but he was saving the big questions until he was more certain of his ground. When she said she wasn't free to give out that information, his suspicions were confirmed. She was playing a game, all right; maybe one that would jeopardize Matthew's fragile chances.

Schatzberg stood up abruptly. His voice was harsh.

"Look, I've had enough of this. You are not telling me the truth; I won't continue this interview. What are you up to? Who sent you here? Either tell me the truth or I'll call the police." Although he had no reason to summon them, he hoped that his words would shake her up and make her level with him. As she hesitated, he put his hand on the telephone.

"All right," she sighed. "You win. I don't work for a politician and I'm not a secretary—but I do live in New York."

"Who are you?" demanded Schatzberg. "How do you know Matthew Brady?"

"I met him at ——— Prison."

"Just what do you mean by that? You weren't working there, I'm sure. Wait a minute . . . Maybe I should ask you, 'What are you?' instead of 'Who are you?' Answer me."

She laughed girlishly. "I almost fooled you, didn't I? I was a prisoner there, on an assault and battery rap."

With those words she pulled off the turban. The contoured masculine haircut was so becoming that Schatzberg had a moment of final doubt.

"You had better drop all talk of marrying that boy," he said sharply. "I'll say this much for you: you are the best damned female impersonator I've ever seen. You should be in the Mummers' Parade —you'd win first prize as a drag-queen. Now what is this all about?"

She-he smiled.

"I love that boy with all my heart. He never knew I was alive the whole time we were in prison. You know he's very strong—the boxing champ—so everyone obeyed him. It's not easy for someone like me in prison. In fact, it's damned tough. Nobody leaves you alone. One day when a particularly obnoxious fag was hassling me, Matthew walked over and without even looking at me told him to leave me alone. That was absolutely all there was between us. Now I just want to help him."

"I see." The lawyer nodded. "But if you really want to help Matthew Brady, you'll stay out of this case. Completely out. O.K.?"

As they both stood up, he glanced into his partner's office and saw that the client had left. "Would you be willing to do me one small favor before you go? When we get to the foyer, would you sit down for a minute and do that stocking routine of yours? I want my partner to see us."

The heavily made-up eyes widened. "I'd be delighted."

They played their little charade, and then Schatzberg said good-by.

A moment later his partner appeared in the doorway. "Who was *that?*"

"Oh," replied Schatzberg casually, "some dame who's madly in love with Matthew Brady and wants to marry him."

"Matthew Brady!" his partner exclaimed. "Well, there goes your theory of feminine deprivation right out the window. That kid has himself a real woman."

"No," replied Schatzberg. "He doesn't have a real woman yet. But maybe someday . . ."

11

GIRLHOOD
IS A SWAMP

Thursday, agree all the standard dictionary references, is thunderday, named in honor of the old Teutonic god of the angry skies, Donar. To us at juvenile court, Thursday meant literally a time of turbulent upheaval, for it was the day set aside for the "older girls" list. On that day we heard—and judged—wayward adolescent girls between the ages of sixteen and eighteen. On that day we descended into a veritable swampland.

Unlike the behavior of their younger counterparts and their male contemporaries, whose more conventional lashing out against society betokened their rage to live, to survive, these girls' transgressions— less spectacular, directed mainly against themselves—symbolized their will to die. Behind their cosmetic masks, occasionally applied with the elegant expertise of an artist but more often daubed on in gaudy imitation of a favorite actress, lay a sinister determination to resist all efforts to change them. The mask had to remain, even as a deathmask. These girls were our superthrowaways: they had decided to lend society a helping hand to speed up the process. Their total life energies were concentrated on pursuing that dizzying, spiraling, down-hill course.

As though to symbolize this difference, these girls had for many years been segregated from the other court-bound children, both while in detention and at the hearing itself. This apartheid, however, had come about for practical rather than philosophical reasons. Although welfare and correctional officials did occasionally suggest, in defense of the status quo, that these girls should be kept away from other delinquent children lest they contaminate them, they could not have been seriously expounding a "germ theory" of delinquency, since they made no effort to close down as public health hazards the "rehabilitation" and "training" centers which exposed hundreds of children to the most virulent strains of the illness.

From 1908 until 1952, all of Philadelphia's delinquent children—except the older girls—were detained in a cheerless late Victorian building on the western perimeter of the tenderloin district. Much of the history of the city's juvenile court is bound up with that building. Its miniscule dimensions and small detention quarters, now housing at most twenty-five or so girls, attest to the modest number of juvenile delinquents requiring detention both prior to and during World War II and a half-dozen post-war years.

Until 1952, when the new and immediately inadequate Youth Study Center opened its doors, the older girls were housed in an ancient, ugly school building a few miles from the City Morgue. After the younger children being kept in custody were transferred into the new facility, the older girls were herded into the vacated old graystone building, very much like poor relatives amid the second-hand furniture and various relics of the past. So pervasive is the official cynicism toward the rehabilitation of these girls, they are still hidden away in juvenile court attics and basements like the monstrous siblings in Gothic novels.

Every Thursday, twenty-five to thirty girls came out of hiding and into full view as they walked through the shabby doors of our makeshift courtroom. Daughters of doctors and college professors rubbed shoulders with the children of slum slatterns. As confused middle-class mothers and fathers stumbled into a courtroom for the first time in their lives, expensive fragrances mingled with the stale smells of body sweat entrapped in the airless room during the week.

Mrs. Matthews, the sensitive, compassionate supervisor of the

Older Girls' Division, was present at these sessions. Even in this pinched, dim setting, she generated warmth and reassurance. Her comprehensive summaries on the girls ended frequently on a note of optimism: "if only somehow the right plan could be worked out, a good home arrangement found . . ." Even when we were limp with frustration and disillusionment, Mrs. Matthews' reassuring "We'll keep trying" got us through the day.

Thus, it was with considerable shock that we heard her say, before court opened:

"I'm at a complete loss about Ava Sinclair, Judge Hoffman. I honestly don't know how to proceed: she's a very difficult girl, and isn't even a Pennsylvania resident. And she is involved with at least *fifteen* men. We know because she kept a score card. Would you like to see it?" Rarely had I seen Mrs. Matthews so anxious.

She handed the judge a piece of cheap stationery with gaudy garlands bordering all four sides. Handwritten at the top, in an equally elaborate script (characterized by circles instead of dots above the i's), was the heading: *Amours of Ava Sinclair—February to March*. Below that were four carefully divided columns. The first was full of the names of men, including nicknames and surnames; then came three columns headed *Straight Intercourse, Sodomy,* and *Other*. Beside the names, large, bold check-marks appeared under the appropriate heading.

"This is just an outline," Mrs. Matthews explained. "She's very literary, and has written a complete account while she's been here— it is really something, your Honor. She's the first girl on this morning's list."

After several years in the criminal courts, we had few illusions left about the physical beauty of the average whore. Many of the Thursday girls who made their bodies available to scores of men were pathetically unattractive. So there was a sharp intake of breath on all sides when Ava Sinclair walked into the courtroom. She was truly beautiful. Tall, voluptuous, her scrubbed unmade-up face as exquisite as a cameo, her sensuality unconcealed by the drab denim detention clothes, she stood before us without a trace of embarrassment or guilt.

"Good morning, your Honor," she said, smiling coquettishly at the judge.

"Are your parents here?" asked the judge.

"They were due in this morning from Florida," Mrs. Matthews answered for her. "Perhaps they have gone to the main courthouse instead of coming here. We'll check on it right away."

"Very well. We'll come back to this case later."

"Judge," said the girl in a soft, provocative voice. "May I talk to you before my parents arrive?"

The judge nodded and beckoned to the matron to escort Ava to a small, sparsely furnished anteroom that served as his once-a-week chambers. The ugly glass and wood bookcase was empty; not one lawbook was to be found in the entire building. The scattering of dusty, unmatched chairs intensified the neglected, decaying look of the room. We sat facing Ava who had slithered into one of those chairs and now draped herself gracefully against the scuffed leather back.

I received barely a passing glance but she turned her full gaze on the judge. "I was hoping we could talk alone, your Honor." Again her voice was intimate, excluding me entirely.

"Well, Ava," the judge said firmly, "this young lady is part of the court staff and is often present when I interview children. But if you would feel better seeing me alone, I'm sure she understands."

The judge later told us what happened after I left. Ava sprang out of the chair and moved over to the bookcase. After posing there for a moment, she wheeled around to face Judge Hoffman.

"Not a single book! That's funny. You know, I feel like that bookcase right now. Absolutely empty. Absolutely unloved."

She crossed her arms over her shoulders in a gesture that was half a huddle and half an embrace. "Oh, I wish I had someone to love. I could make someone very happy. I haven't been with anyone for days and days. Do you understand . . . ?"

The judge stood up. Unbelievable as it seemed to him, Ava had selected him as the next entry on her score card!

She quickly moved to his side. "Don't call the matron yet, please, Judge. I have a lot I want to say. I know I'm very mixed up. My parents are absolutely no help, and never were. I don't want to go back with them, even when the trials are over. Do you know that I have to testify against nine men? I was with six others, too—sailors, they were—but they can't find them. I don't think they gave me their real names—the creeps. They've arrested the ones they could find— even my beautiful Johnny. They've lumped them all together, all those pigs and my sweetheart. He wasn't even with me for my Sweet Sixteen birthday party last Saturday. How ironic that Ava Sinclair celebrated her sixteenth birthday in a medieval dungeon. It's like a Dumas novel, isn't it?"

As she spoke she glided sinuously around the room in a kind of pavanne so that when she asked the last question she was directly in front of the judge. She gazed at him with wide, velvet-soft eyes, waiting for his reply.

"No, Ava, it's not like a novel at all. You're a bright, beautiful girl, but you *are* all twisted inside. God knows how we can ever straighten you out, but we mean to try."

She gave a low, mocking laugh. "Oh, I've got lots of things inside of me. I even have a bye-bye baby inside. And who the daddy is we'll never know. Poor bye-bye baby." She laughed again.

The judge opened the door and Mrs. Matthews and I walked in.

"Ava, your parents have just come in," the supervisor announced. "They have a lawyer for you. They want to see you before the case is called."

"Hell's bells!" the girl exclaimed. "If Daddy thinks he can get me out of this mess, he's even goofier than I thought."

As she left the room, the judge looked at me. "Would you believe she even tried to seduce me? And do you know she thinks she's pregnant?"

Before returning to the courtroom, he again checked the hearing sheets for the day. In addition to Ava's own hearing on a delinquency petition, filed by the juvenile division of the court, there were, just as she had said, the cases of nine arrested men—seven police officers and two sailors—whose preliminary hearings were also scheduled that day. Ava had been involved in sex acts with each one; the charges against the men included prostitution, sodomy, fornication, and corrupting the morals of a minor.

Attached to these arrest sheets was the file on Ava Sinclair. The judge scanned the papers inside the folder. Under Mrs. Matthews's watchful eye, the probation officer had been unusually thorough in compiling the many events of Ava's crowded young life into a narrative the impact of which was accentuated by the clinical references interspersed throughout the record.

The Sinclairs had moved to Florida from New England when Ava was three years old. Her father had been a professor of physics at a small northern college, but he had accepted a better teaching position offered by a larger university. It was on the outskirts of a small semitropical resort town where the family settled. Ambitious to earn more money, Dr. Sinclair ventured into business with an electronics company that rapidly became successful, employing about fifty workers. After the birth of Ava's younger brother, the family moved to an elegant, spacious villa complete with swimming pool, tennis court, and a domestic staff of two: a cook and a gardener. Ava attended a private school. She was a beautiful and happy child with a great passion for water sports and dancing. She saw little of her father, but adored her mother.

The years passed without event until she was about twelve. One day she began to menstruate, and she ran to her mother with a happy announcement of her ripening womanhood. To her horror, Mrs. Sinclair burst into tears and locked herself in her room for hours. It was the cook who gave her a box of sanitary napkins and an aspirin for her cramps. When Mrs. Sinclair finally came out of her room, red-eyed and depressed, Ava ran up to embrace her. Her mother pushed her aside, saying that she was unclean, that now Ava's life would be wrecked because men would be after her all the time, that she would have to hide her body very carefully, because there were Peeping Toms everywhere. And she must *not* tell her father what had happened to her. Above all, she must never be alone with a boy or she would surely be raped. She told Ava that she had been raped when she was fifteen and that she had bled for days and days. That night the young girl went to bed unhappy, shivering, and afraid. Perhaps she had been raped, too—whatever that meant. That must be why she ached and bled.

When Ava finally spoke to one of her friends at school about her mother's warning, she found herself the object of ridicule. Boys, said everyone, were fun and wonderful. Sex didn't hurt, said a thirteen-year-old who had been sleeping with a boy for six months. Only a little bit at first, but what did that matter? And if boys made out with you, they called you up all the time for dates and you became very popular. Ava's mother was clearly a bit goofy, they concluded.

But Ava believed that her mother was right. Sex *was* dirty and ugly; men really wanted only to hurt you. For two years she shut herself off from the world; her life was walled in behind the gates of her house and the doors of her school. She excelled in her studies, and was a straight honor student. She read Sir Walter Scott, Shakespeare, Dickens, and books of religious mysticism. Her favorite novel was *The Razor's Edge* and she dreamed one day of meeting a striking man who was steeped in the wisdom of India and looked like Tyrone Power. This secret dream was locked inside of her, away from her mother's prying eyes and listening ears. Even when her friends telephoned her about a homework assignment, she could hear her mother breathing on an extension phone. She knew her drawers were carefully examined; her books held in mid-air to disgorge hidden filth. Slowly, Ava began to burn inside. Why didn't her mother "knock it off"?

Shortly after her fourteenth birthday she began to have fantasies about great love affairs; she no longer closed her ears to her schoolfriends' conversations about sex. She also began to invent excuses for staying at school later than usual, but her mother continued to drive up in her big Cadillac convertible every day at the regular closing hour and wait for her. One day Mrs. Sinclair could not drive to school because she was due at an important business meeting with her husband. Instead of taking the cab that had been dispatched for her, Ava left by another exit with a friend and went to a drive-in down the road for a Coke. When a boy came up behind her and whispered, "Hi, Baby!" in her ear, she began to tremble, but she turned to look. He was handsome and flashily dressed. He asked if he could sit down with them; her friend said she had to leave, but Ava stayed and soon she and the boy were talking intently. She felt she had known Mike a long time, but when he asked her for a date, she said No. He pressed her, and she finally agreed to meet him on Friday evening near the drive-in.

All the way home, she alternately hated herself for having agreed and planned how she would slip away. She had to make up some excuse about not coming home in the cab, and for once the mother accepted Ava's explanation without question. For the next few days she could not concentrate on her school work; by the time Friday came, she was so keyed up that she could not eat.

After supper her mother went to her room to lie down and her father went back to the plant. Leaving her brother in front of the television set, she slipped out of the house. In her purse was a hundred-dollar bill, the only money she could find in her father's desk. The boy was waiting for her in front of the drive-in. He was with another youth whose date had not appeared. His friend had a souped-up jalopy into which they all climbed. Ava felt frightened and free. She didn't want another girl along, so she suggested that they had waited long enough. They went off in the direction of a neighboring county. Mike began to caress her and she responded. It happened just as she had imagined it would; she could excite any man she wanted to. The driver glanced sidelong at the passionate couple. Soon he pulled into a motel, one of those anonymous, squalid establishments named "Flossie's" or "Josie's" that blister the countryside. They pooled their money; with Ava's hundred dollars they could have afforded to stay for ten days. When they asked for two adjoining suites, the caretaker barely glanced at them.

The Sinclairs sent out a three-county alarm for her, and she and the boys were picked up on Sunday. Ava's account of the weekend, lucid in every sexual detail, was labeled as fantastic by the juvenile court officer who interviewed her that evening.

When her parents arrived at the detention home, her mother wanted the boys charged with forcible rape. Dr. Sinclair hid his face in a handkerchief as Ava told her mother that she had not been raped, that she had gone willingly and would go again and again, no matter what happened to her. "Filthy little bitch!" her mother declared. "You will never set foot in our house again."

Ava's father appeared alone at her Florida juvenile court hearing. When the judge asked him what he recommended, he handed over a beautifully typed-out letter on his business stationery. The gist of it was that he and his wife wanted the girl put away indefinitely. Ava looked at him coldly. The judge was more upset at her indifference than at her father's refusal to talk to her. After scolding her for her hardness of heart, he signed an order which stated:

> The Court, having determined that the said child failed to return to her home and that she has endangered her health, welfare, and safety by having unlawful sexual intercourse, and the said child's acts and conduct being more hostile to herself than to others, and the Court finding the said child's need and condition such that she should be committed to the Florida School for Girls where she may have sufficient supervision and opportunity for sufficient work, recreation and education, and the said child again being assured of the Court's interest in her; it is therefore ORDERED and DECREED that the said child is hereby committed to the Florida

School for Girls until she shall have reached the age of twenty-
one years, unless sooner lawfully released . . .

Ava listened to the droning voice of the clerk reading the order
aloud. Six years' imprisonment. Her mother would be disappointed.
A life sentence, at least, was called for!

Ava had decided that the last phrase, "unless sooner lawfully
released," was the most important part of that order. At the school
she began immediately to talk about sex, and only sex, to anyone who
would listen: staff, girls, the help. After three weeks the superintendent and the social worker gave up, and within a month she was
back in court for a second psychiatric evaluation. The training
school, the only court facility available, vowed she could never
return.

The doctor who spoke with her overcame his initial shock when
Ava opened the interview by asking, "Don't you think sodomy is a
superior sexual practice?" He tuned out all the patter and the fantasies
and tried to hear Ava's deeper, unspoken message. In his report he
noted that the girl's mother appeared to be suffering from a severe
emotional illness, undiscerned by the father, and that many of the
girl's problems stemmed from the mother-daughter relationship. He
recommended long-term, extensive psychiatric therapy.

Dr. Sinclair denied emphatically that his wife was ill, and asked
for a list of out-of-state psychiatrically oriented schools to which
Ava could be sent. After looking it over, he selected an institution
near Philadelphia because it was "far enough away." The eight-
thousand-dollar annual tuition fee would place a small strain on his
finances, but he was willing to sign immediate commitment papers
under the Mental Health Act, or take whatever other measures were
necessary to get rid of his troublesome daughter. Ava was flown up
to Philadelphia with a matron-guard and placed in the school within
a matter of days.

The Antonin School, nestling quietly in a wooded grove in one
of Philadelphia's expensive suburbs, is for the disturbed children
of the wealthy and the near-wealthy. Many parents hustle their
youngsters off to it when they face juvenile court commitment. Ava
now met the throwaways with tiaras and T-Birds who, like her,
hated Mommy and Daddy and their surrogates at the school—the
"shrinks" and the social workers who stood in a four-to-one ratio to

the children. Ava made several runaway attempts before she finally succeeded, during a group tour of the Philadelphia Art Museum. It was exactly three months after her arrival in Pennsylvania. She headed down the Parkway, past the Youth Study Center and the courthouse, straight to the honky-tonk district on Market Street where sailors and street-women hooked up for the night.

Within a few hours, Ava struck pay dirt. A swinging sailor she met took her to a rooming house near the Society Hill district and paid her month's rent. During the next twenty-nine days he returned frequently with his best buddy, and Ava was happy with her *ménage-à-trois* arrangement. During the long spring afternoons she went for solitary walks. She was soon spotted by the police who patrolled the area. She escaped arrest easily, however, by using her ability to "turn men on," as she modestly put it. In fact, she turned on seven police officers in various locales: alleys, her room, a police car, and a ramshackle hotel checked frequently by police. Shortly after the beginning of her interlude with these older men— all married—she began her serious sexual bookkeeping. The idyll ended when an alert police lieutenant overheard snickering comments about Ava's energetic performances and decided to investigate for himself. He found her in bed with her two sailor friends. As the men were dressing she whispered to the new arrival that they would be leaving soon and she would be ready to make him very happy. When the lieutenant said they were all under arrest, she dressed in utter disbelief and went with him and the sailors to the police district.

When he came to the end of Ava's file, Judge Hoffman returned to the courtroom where the grave-faced lieutenant sat with a deputy commissioner and a police stenographer. Her interview with her parents and their lawyer had ended unsatisfactorily. Her mother, I learned, had cursed her hysterically, her father had wrung his hands, and Mr. Thornton, a corporation lawyer recommended by Dr. Sinclair's Florida law firm, confided to me that the girl was a phenomenon beyond his ken. "I guess the state prison for women is a definite possibility, isn't it?" he asked in bewilderment.

After the judge's decision to hear the cases of the nine men first, Ava came forward as the principal Commonwealth witness. Her testimony was very short and very sweet; occasionally she smiled at the defendants as she recalled their various trysts. The judge held them in moderate bail for indictment on all charges. Regardless of

Ava's background and her promiscuity, they were, after all, police officers whose sworn duty was to protect a sixteen-year-old girl—if necessary, from herself. Instead, they had exploited her many times, despite the fact that they knew her age.

Several of the more stouthearted wives of the accused officers were in the courtroom. After fixing bail, the judge addressed these baffled, hurt women:

"It would be foolish to let this destroy your marriages," he told them gently. "This girl has a lovable and sweet way about her, and it would take a very strong-willed man indeed to resist her blatant invitations. She has the mentality and the physical equipment to sway most men."

Ava giggled and shot a triumphant look at her parents.

"Dr. and Mrs. Sinclair, step forward, please."

Patiently the judge explained that the girl had to remain in Philadelphia because she would have to appear in criminal court as a witness against the nine men. The Antonin School had immediately informed the Court that she could not return; therefore, unless the parents had another alternative in mind, the girl would remain in detention until the trials were over—as long as four or five months, perhaps. Mrs. Sinclair spoke first. Her lovely face, a more mature replica of Ava's, contorted to spit out the words:

"As far as my husband and I are concerned, your Honor, she can rot here. We've had it! Now we hear she may be pregnant. I've no doubt she is! Surely *you* have places that handle this kind of thing—can't she have the baby somewhere and then be put away in an institution?"

"Yes, Mrs. Sinclair, we have hospitals and shelters for unmarried pregnant girls—the Salvation Army hospital and a maternity home run by the Catholic Church. But they are probably filled to capacity. After all, Ava is not a Pennsylvania resident, and we must give priority to girls from this area. If she *is* pregnant, and you refuse to take care of her, I'm afraid I'll have to send her to Pennypack House, which is a wing of the House of Correction. It's a prison, Mrs. Sinclair." The judge looked steadily at the woman for a long moment, but she made no comment. "If she's still there by the time she is ready to deliver, she can have her baby at our city hospital, Philadelphia General.

"But Ava cannot stay here indefinitely. She is a Florida resident

—and also your daughter. You simply have to face that and work out some plan for her. You just can't pass her along like a crate of oranges, F.O.B., to the state of Pennsylvania."

Then he turned to Mr. Thornton: "Counsel, please talk with these parents and try to come up with a workable solution for that young girl. I can see from their attitude that they have written her off. I think they did so a long time ago. But the juvenile court has a responsibility, even to a nonresident of this state, and I'll say here and now that I don't like to think of her, or any other child, spending all those months at Pennypack, but it's all we have at the moment. Please let us know what the family decides to do."

When I checked with Mr. Thornton about a week later, his news was discouraging. Dr. and Mrs. Sinclair had sent him a check for his fee, but the note of thanks they enclosed contained not a word about future arrangements for Ava.

After another hiatus of several weeks, the judge asked me to telephone the parents in Florida. Dr. Sinclair was pleasant but aloof when I told him that Ava was definitely pregnant. I also reminded him that, without other instructions from him, she would have to go to the House of Correction soon.

"I have my wife and my family to think about, Mrs. Richette. You seemed so kind, and Ava liked you. Why don't you break the news to her that she has to stay in Pennypack until she has the baby? She can place it for adoption—we'll sign whatever has to be signed. We'll come for her when it's all over. Maybe by that time my wife will feel better."

"But Dr. Sinclair," I pointed out, "your *wife* may feel better, but how do you think your daughter will feel? She's sixteen years old! If you do this, you're deserting her when she desperately needs you, and her bitterness toward you now will grow into a hate that can destroy her. Do you really want that to happen?" I waited for him to answer, but when he did not, I went on: "Wouldn't it be better to take her home as soon as you can? I'm sure we can get early listings in the adult trials, so that she can leave Pennsylvania quickly after testifying."

"Out of the question. My wife won't hear of it; she won't even fly up to visit her."

"Why don't you come up alone? I'm sure the judge would give

you permission to see Ava, perhaps even take her out for a few hours. It's hard being locked up, Dr. Sinclair."

There was a pause. Then he sighed audibly and carefully measured out his words: "I don't think so . . . I don't know if you understand, but I can't be alone with her. Ava is capable of anything; you've seen proof of that. She may be my daughter, but in my opinion she's a mighty dangerous girl for any man to be with—alone."

Dr. Sinclair meant every word he said; Ava sat in Pennypack House for the next few months with no visits from her family to ease her sense of aloneness. As she grew larger and her body became awkward and heavy, her surface merriness and her pride in her Messalina exploits vanished and darker moods took their place. When she had to ride downtown to court she would weep all through the preceding night. Red-eyed, unkempt, she looked at least ten years older than her sixteen years as she sat in the witness chair.

Ava's baby girl, born in the city hospital, was left there; arrangements for adoption were turned over to a local agency on whose board Mr. Thornton served. Ava returned to Pennypack House and began writing frantic notes to the judge, begging him to release her. Finally, her father arrived with a private detective. Before meeting the girl in the sheriff's cell room he stopped in to thank the judge for his concern. When asked what the family intended to do next, Dr. Sinclair replied, "We have a good private mental hospital lined up. Here are the commitment papers."

"She won't last a week!"

The father shrugged and answered laconically, "It's either that or jail, I guess."

It was only three weeks later that I received a call from a sheriff in a small Florida Keys community. I recognized the name of the town immediately: it was the site of the hospital to which Ava had been committed. She and a male patient had run away, the sheriff announced. Since she had been in Philadelphia for many months, he thought perhaps she had headed for her old haunts. Would I please alert the police department and the court workers?

But Ava vanished from sight. If she did return to Philadelphia, she went effectively underground.

Many swamp girls become extremely adept at hiding. No one hears of them again until perhaps twenty years later, when they face the new crisis of middle age. Then, haglike, dissipated, unable to turn enough tricks even to keep themselves in liquor, they reappear in court as vagrants, disorderly streetwalkers, and the like. This troupe of misdemeanant women parade through the magistrates' courts in cities all over America. They are twentieth-century Hogarth etchings come to life. This time it isn't Daddy and Mommy who turn their backs, but the whole community. The usual treatment is to give these women a cursory physical examination for venereal disease and, if they pass this test, enough carfare to get to whatever they call "home." Until the next arrest, or perhaps an early death in a city hospital . . .

Sad Thursday, as we came to call our weekly sessions in the Older Girls' Division, had its successes as well as its failures. Many of the girls we saw were highly receptive to the kindly ministrations of the probation staff and the cultivated, attractive woman physician who was regularly on duty. Many girls left the old building never to come back again except to pay a social call to Mrs. Matthews or Dr. Fay.

But there was that nucleus of less resilient girls for whom our available services were inadequate, sometimes even destructive. Take, for example, an impulsive, quick-tempered girl prone to violence. Those small, cell-like rooms and the absence of an outdoor exercise or recreation area triggered off a claustrophobic reaction that often culminated in a chair-smashing, dish-throwing spree. If several kindred-spirited girls happened to be in detention at that moment, a near-riot ensued. These periodic melees may have relieved the inmates' tensions, but they produced little improvement in the appearance of the place. Inevitably, the smashed furniture was replaced by identical pieces, fetched from some city warehouse that presumably contained an endless supply of dust-gathering pre-Depression furniture.

Perhaps the most dedicated and energetic of these interior re-decorators was Penny Walden, a lithe, muscular, brown-skinned girl whose court records were so thick that they were divided into two volumes, Part I for her exploits up to the age of fifteen and Part II for her police and court contacts thereafter. Penny enjoyed the unique distinction of having so bad a record in the disciplinary school for girls maintained by the Philadelphia Board of Public Education that at fourteen she had been officially dropped as uneducable. Referred to the court as an incorrigible, she was sent to a farm-type school near Philadelphia where after two months of pandemonium, the staff voted unanimously to return her to court. Her next step was a state training school in the western part of the state. She lasted somewhat longer there: six months. After an assault upon a matron which fractured a jaw and split a nose, Penny was back in detention again.

"What am I going to do with you now?" asked the judge.

"I don't want to be locked up any more. I can't stand it, your Honor," she said gruffly.

Penny's mother stood nearby. "Why are you so bad, girl?" she asked.

The girl remained silent.

As the judge riffled through Part I of her record, he noted that Penny had been officially labeled "bad" since she first began school. Mrs. Walden was a widow; her husband had died in a railroad accident when the youngest of their six children was only a few months old. Mrs. Walden supplemented her Social Security benefits with meager earnings as a day worker. Although Penny was the oldest child, she was never left in charge of the home on the days when Mrs. Walden went to her suburban employer's home. The next sibling, Jack, took over; it was evident he was both the most responsible and, in her own words, the best child she had. Penny and Jack fought constantly. When her fists could not beat him down, she reached for the nearest weapon at hand—a kitchen knife, a fork, scissors, a table lamp. In her early years, much of Penny's violence was arrowed directly at her family. When her mother tried to intervene, Penny lashed out at her. When she began to punch and maul her mother, Mrs. Walden herself agreed that for the sake of the younger children Penny had to go away. Later, her fury began to erupt everywhere.

"I've run out of institutions, Penny," said the judge wearily. "Now the court's recommendation is that you go to the Women's Prison at Muncy. You will probably be the youngest girl in the whole state ever to be sent there: another first for you."

Under Pennsylvania law, although both unmanageable boys and girls in their late teens may be committed to prisons from juvenile court, there is a difference in their respective situations. Camp Hill, the male prison, has a program geared to handle young offenders up to the age of twenty-five. Muncy, however, is the maximum-security prison for all women convicted of offenses ranging from malicious mischief to murder.

"I am most reluctant to commit you to Muncy, Penny," the judge continued. "Why did you attack the matron at the training school?"

"She was picking on me all the time, Judge. I just couldn't take it any more."

"Do you have any suggestions?" The judge turned to Mrs. Matthews and me.

"I know the psychiatrists don't agree, your Honor," the supervisor replied, "but I am convinced that this girl can be handled in a hospital better than in a prison. However, I realize that she has been declared nonpsychotic and that no state hospital will take her under the present state of the record."

If only we had had a good psychiatrically oriented residential school to send her to when she was nine or ten, I thought to myself, not for the first time. One had finally been opened after fifteen years of planning by the State Department of Welfare, but almost a whole generation of children missed their chance owing to the delays caused by political wrangling over funds.

"I want to make a statement for the record," the judge declared. "I want to note that this girl has been known to the court since she was eight years of age, that she was violent and antisocial even then. She has been on probation and she has been committed to various institutions. Now, at seventeen, she has committed a serious assault, and the only available facility is the State Prison for Women. I believe it is wrong, unconscionable, to subject a girl with her background and life experience to a prison for mature women offenders. She is likely to be victimized sexually. She may become even more defiant and aggressive. Yet I cannot return her to her mother and to this community. I am forced to sign this commitment order, but I do so reluctantly and sadly. I feel that the community and this court, which is devoted to the well-being of children, should do better than this. We haven't moved very far away from the eighteenth century if all we can do for our Penny Waldens is send them to jail."

Although these older girls make up less than a quarter of the juvenile court population (the 1967 Philadelphia Juvenile Court

Report places their number at 16 per cent, or 1,955 out of 12,180) they require more intensive, personalized, and long-range supervision than many of the younger children whose numbers are more overwhelming. The truth is that "delinquent" girls are more baffling, less amenable to conventional court approaches which rely on the youngster's flexibility and will to change.

As the extreme cases of Ava and Penny show, there is an intense mother-daughter conflict which colors the girl's view of herself and the life choices available to her. Peter Blos and other psychoanalytically directed therapists conclude that the mother-daughter relationship is a "sadomasochistic bond" which results in the girl's hostile dependency on the mother. (See his paper, "Delinquency," in *Adolescents: Psychoanalytic Approach to Problems and Therapy,* Lorand and Schneer, eds., 1965.) Whether or not we agree with this conclusion the fact of the matter is that, for this court group of youngsters, the long-term "insight therapy" that the psychiatrists advocate remains a Utopian dream. When seriously ill, identifiably "schizophrenic" children crowd our detention centers because there is no room for them in mental hospitals, it is both irresponsible and cruel to suggest as an immediate measure that these masked, self-destructive girls should also participate in the waiting game.

In the psychiatrists' view, adolescent delinquent behavior is an "action-screen" behind which hides, not the arrogant, defiant, seemingly omnipotent rebel, but a cowering, angry, and dependent child who is afraid of life. The greater the fear, the more flamboyant the boy's strut, the more impenetrable the girl's mask.

Just as such boys lack a worthy masculine figure to emulate, when these girls reject their mothers—responding in kind to a real or imaginary maternal hostility—they are left with no acceptable figure to pattern themselves upon as they approach womanhood.

Determined to temper some of the harsh realities of our heartbreaking Thursdays, Judge Hoffman and I decided in the fall of 1960 to call together a handful of volunteer women who had expressed their concern and willingness to help throwaway children, to see what they could do for our superthrowaways. We could certainly use some subprofessional assistance to relieve the overburdened probation officers, we told them.

For years the Big Brother Association of America had used a one-to-one volunteer approach in their program for delinquent boys.

If a "Big Brother" could assume some part of the missing father's role in a boy's day-to-day process of growing up, why couldn't a volunteer woman, after a brief training course, be subtly introduced into the life of a troubled girl and become her friendly counselor and, if necessary, a much-needed prop? Especially in the case of first offenders whose disturbed behavior was not yet acute, couldn't that "sadomasochistic bond" be altered by the creation of a healthy warm friendship between the volunteer and the girl? There were no guarantees that our idea would work, but it was worth a very good try.

We christened the new organization "Teen-Aid." Any allusion to the volunteer as a Big Sister was unsatisfactory because (a) it carried a religious connotation and (b) it ran counter to our belief —confirmed over many years of experience with these girls—that this new relationship had to be kept distinct and separate in everybody's mind from a *family* relationship. In less than six months of concentrated effort, we realized that our idea *was* working. We had not attempted to play psychiatrist by viewing a girl's delinquency as a neurotic act and treating it as such; yet we found that we were able to help her break old patterns and to forge new and better ones.

Fully briefed in weekly sessions with a gifted clinical psychiatrist, who had also offered his time, each volunteer woman was made aware of her delicate and vital role as a potential new model for the girl. She was encouraged to combine her new perceptiveness with a genuine human affection. By the end of the first year, we saw progress in the cases and growth in the girls. Simply to go on waiting for the millennium would have led nowhere, whereas our realistic and active response to the problem we faced on Thursdays created some breakthrough.

We knew, of course, that the one-to-one counseling approach, though effective, was not enough. Housing, employment opportunities, job training, and scholarships for higher education loomed high as top-priority needs for these girls—and still do. To date, Teen-Aid has found partial answers to all but the first and primary need: a place to live away from home, unsatisfactory home. For many of these girls home is a battleground where constant, futile mother-daughter skirmishes erupt, like campaigns in the Hundred Years' War. Or a wasteland so barren that not even a girl's most minimal needs can be met.

Institutions alone, even those as imaginatively and sensitively run as those of the Good Shepherd nuns, are not a satisfactory alternative. What is needed is a constellation of halfway houses, residences in which a girl can breathe freely, rest, work, and find her way slowly to what she could be if she were allowed to try. But everywhere in the community there is still the fear, hostility, and unwillingness to risk sponsorship of such residences that we encountered in the early sixties. Recently, several middle-class women's service organizations have evinced interest, and one group of socially elite young matrons, spearheaded by the wife of a psychiatrist who is affiliated with the court's diagnostic facility for these girls, is starting to make serious plans for such a project.

We know of no American community that has this kind of halfway-house program for these girls. There are hotels for the respectable working girl, as well as "Y" type of residences—but not for delinquents, thank you. Once branded, a girl finds that these doors have been closed to her. In other countries, experimental programs in group living have worked well. Why can't one of the large women's service organizations, with branches in many major American cities and the membership of thousands of educated, mature women who have raised their own children successfully, take on the task of establishing a fine residential hotel like New York's Barbizon Plaza—but for throwaway girls? And why can't one of the multimillion-dollar cosmetics or women's fashion business—any one of which can thank women consumers for their success—undertake to subsidize such a project?

No one need be daunted by the masks these throwaways wear. Behind each one is a girl who doesn't fit anywhere—not with her family, her school, or the world. And because she does not understand why, she is frightened and lonely.

I vividly recall the words of a sixteen-year-old girl from Brooklyn who was picked up by the Philadelphia police as an amnesiac. After she had been helped by the court psychiatrist to remember who she was and why she had run away from home, she wrote:

> There are no stars in the sky
> Not one.
> I looked up to see—
> I wonder why?

There is no laughter or beauty—
Not that I hear or see.
I wonder why?
I wonder why?
Life here is like no life.
No stars—no laughter or beauty—
No hate or crying or rain.
Just existence without reality.
A dream with a beginning
An existence not existing at all.
I wonder why?

Why? It is a question for all of us. And one that our silence has already answered.

12

THE
BEDROOM
THROWAWAYS

Sexual urges tug at even very young children. "It is my conviction that no child—none at least who is mentally sound, still less one who is mentally gifted, can avoid being occupied with sexual problems in the years before puberty." So spoke Sigmund Freud in *The Sexual Enlightenment of Children*, published less than a century ago. It is almost inconceivable to grasp today, when enlightened parents on every side are demanding early childhood sex education programs, why he suffered scornful abuse by colleagues and society alike for expressing this view.

Freud stumbled upon childhood sexuality through his work with mentally ill women who had been sexually victimized at an early age. Backtracking, he scrutinized the meaning and consequences of these assaults. He was the first observer of those children I call "the bedroom throwaways": children who are exploited sexually by parents and relatives, trusted friends and strangers. Seven decades later, scientific investigators acknowledge the importance of Freud's work by continuing to study and report on the fundamental issue of sex and sexuality. Society is still doing as little for and about *these* throwaways as it does for or about its other junk-heap children.

Perverted adults find it amazingly easy to exploit the latent sexuality of children, although they take a calculated risk when they make their first advances. The cases discussed in this chapter may be shocking and distasteful to read. Nevertheless, they exemplify the degradation and horror to which many innocent children are subjected; and it is important to bring this material out into the open, just as it is vital that parents report immediately these offenses to the police. It is a disservice to society as well as to their own and other children to try to bury the problem.

These cases have not been selected for their shock value but because they show that the overt physical acts in which a child participates need not be permanently scarring. If parents are sympathetic to the child's plight and honestly try to find answers to why their youngster was drawn into the situation in the first place, the whole experience can bring about a more positive family relationship.

We saw *our* bedroom throwaways by a happenstance arrangement, devised by the police and the courts, whereby adults charged with sex offenses against children received preliminary hearings in juvenile court rather than in the more public, less sophisticated magistrates' courts, which are usually filled with gaping spectators, functionaries, and reporters. Though our court's task was not to be their ultimate judges, these pathetic men and women defendants, appearing at the end of the day, evoked both revulsion and pity. All we were required to do was determine whether or not there was sufficient evidence against them to warrant indictment by the grand jury and subsequent trial in criminal court. But the task is not as simple as it may sound.

It is extremely difficult in the traditional courtroom setting to question young children about their sexual experiences while adhering to the legal rules of evidence necessary to protect the rights of the accused. True, we are permitted to lead a child by asking more suggestive questions than are usually allowed; but then we must legitimately ask, To what extent is the child saying what he or she thinks the adults around him—parents, prosecutor, police, judge— want to hear? Fantasies and distortions are so often mingled with reality in a child's mind that even highly experienced interrogators and judges have difficulty sorting out truth from fiction.

The traditional credentials which lawyers use to establish that a child will not lie in court are the youngster's own assurances that he understands the meaning of the oath he takes to tell the truth. Since the word "perjury" has no meaning to most children, we ask rather what he thinks will happen to him if he lies.

"I'll burn in hell forever!"

"The devil will come and get me!"

"My daddy will give me a whipping."

One unforgettable child, in a lovely paraphrase of James Joyce's famous definition of conscience as the agenbite of inwit, replied, "My mind will hurt!"

Sometimes a child was too young to talk. Then, handicapped by the same legal rules that prevented us from prosecuting adults charged with physical assault upon babies, we had no alternative but to discharge the defendant for lack of evidence.

Legal critics have urged that courts shift the burden of proof in these cases to the adult defendants themselves. In other words, when it seems evident that only someone in close proximity to the child could have inflicted such physical injury, the accused should be compelled to explain why he should not be tried or found guilty. This principle, known by the Latin phrase *res ipsa loquitur*, is now used in negligence cases if the injuries are such that they could only have been caused by palpable, reckless, or malicious neglect.

I can recall only one situation in which the Commonwealth was able to hold an adult for trial and convict him without having the child utter a single word of testimony. The victim in that case was an eleven-month-old baby who obviously could not tell us that his father had committed many acts of oral sodomy upon his tiny penis. (Even a six-year-old boy sometimes has trouble describing such things.) However, by practicing an even more unique perversion, the defendant had sealed his own fate: he had photographed his acts in color, using an elaborate time-exposure camera setup. The wife's discovery of these snapshots during a spring housecleaning operation provided the evidence needed to remove the pathological father from the home and thus give the infant a chance for a normal childhood.

These special preliminary hearings served as a grim final punctuation mark to the day in court. As the Juvenile Division representative wearily collected the thick files of the children who had appeared on charges of delinquency, Sam Roselli, the cheerful and dapper Men's Division probation officer who compiled the special list from Morals Squad arrest reports, would stand by. Fatigued and emotionally drained by the scores of throwaways who had just passed before us, none of us was exactly in the mood for levity. Nevertheless, the judge often managed to exchange a pleasantry or two with Roselli before he nodded to the bailiff to begin calling the list. From time to time when a habitual offender was about to reappear, Roselli would issue a friendly alert.

"Our friend in the white Cadillac is back!"

"Not again!" Judge Hoffman groaned. "I thought he went to a mental hospital just recently! How long has it been?" (The gentleman in question was a successful merchant who periodically climbed into his gleaming, customized Eldorado and drove around poor Negro neighborhoods, looking for a suitable place to park near a grammar school. At the afternoon dismissal hour, he would open the car door and expose himself to the homeward-bound children. Even without looking into that man's tortured eyes, it was clear to us that he wanted to be found out and punished.)

Or: "A music professor this time. He claims he never touches a girl unless he's absolutely sure she's of legal age. He doesn't know how she did it, but this fourteen-year-old fooled him with a forged I.D. card!"

Or: "Would you believe a school dentist with his office just a few feet away from the principal? Unless the little girls let him have a good feel and look, he really gives them the business with his dental drill!"

But Roselli's determined effort to relieve the depressing side of his daily work backfired on that unforgettable afternoon in 1961 when he called out the names of Michael and Ethel Sayre.

"Talk about going to the dogs!" he quipped in an undertone as a robust, mannishly dressed blonde in her late thirties strode in with a small, tense, tweedy man about the same age. Only afterward did we realize how terrifyingly appropriate had been his pun.

As Mr. and Mrs. Sayre took their places in the usual position of accused defendants, two smiling, ruddy-cheeked little girls darted into the courtroom, rushed up to the bar of the court, and looked up quizzically at the judge. The taller of the two said, "Hi, Ethel!" to Mrs. Sayre. In a reverse acknowledgment of the greeting, the woman turned coldly away.

"Where are your parents, girls?" I asked.

Again the larger child seized the initiative.

"My mother's here. Oh, here she comes. Leslie's mother couldn't make it. She had to go to work—right, Leslie? Her dad's here, though."

"So you are June Crozier, age twelve?" A pencil ticked off the name on the arrest report. "And this is Leslie Fanton, age eleven? Where is the Morals Squad officer?"

"Sergeant Brent, number five-oh-two." He was paunchy, middle-aged, an everybody's-uncle type, and therefore a wonderful interrogator of children.

"Mr. and Mrs. Sayre, have you retained counsel?" I asked.

"I just called Mr. Bartlett's office. He's on his way," the woman snapped. She turned around and seeing a youngish, curly-headed man dash in added, "Here he is now."

"Have you had an opportunity to consult with your clients, Mr. Bartlett?" asked the judge.

"I have, your Honor, and I have decided not to waive a preliminary hearing. I might add that I represent Mrs. Sayre's employer in a business capacity and that I am here at that client's request. May I see your Honor and the Assistant District Attorney at side-bar?"

When Bartlett and I approached the bench, Judge Hoffman said softly, "What is this case all about?"

"I've just glanced over the girls' statements, your Honor," I told him. "The charge is sodomy, with corrupting the morals of a minor as a secondary item. From what I read, these defendants seem to have violated every section of the sodomy statute; that is, they seem to be guilty of every permutation the legislature has possibly thought of."*

---

* Many states have very explicit sodomy statutes which describe prohibited sexual practices with animals, including barnyard fowl. They evoke satirical amusement in law students, and are scorned by criminal law professors seeking to reform the criminal code. Rarely invoked, the bestiality sections hark back to an era in which legislators, inspired by the Bible, adopted codes straight out of Leviticus. Many proponents of change now advance Kinsey as a point of reference.

"Do you mean that there's even an element of bestiality here?"
The judge looked incredulous.

I nodded. "So the children say. I'll try to bring it out, your
Honor."

Bartlett flushed. "I'm going to object violently, your Honor. My
clients have never been arrested before. Mr. Sayre is employed as a
consulting psychologist with a large industrial firm, and Mrs. Sayre
is a top-flight cosmetics consultant to a beauty-supply firm. I believe
these children are lying, your Honor, and I demand that they receive
psychiatric examinations before we proceed with the case."

"Judge Hoffman," I interjected, "if Mr. Bartlett is going to argue on the basis of past reputation, then I want to point out that it's
a two-edged sword. Neither June Crozier nor Leslie Fanton has
prior juvenile court records, and I see no reason why they should
be treated differently than usual. I oppose Mr. Bartlett's request for
their examination before we take testimony from them."

"I'm going to go ahead with the testimony, Mr. Bartlett," the
judge said, settling back to his chair. "Call the first witness."

Detective Brent began to recount the circumstances behind the
ultimate arrest of the Sayres.

"Mrs. Crozier reported to the Juvenile Aid authorities that she
was having great difficulty with her child, June, now aged twelve.
The girl refused to sleep at home and said that she was moving in
with the Sayres. The mother objected to this and came to us for
help. She made no statement against the Sayres. In fact, she said they
were very nice people, and her own friends for over a year. When
the Juvenile Aid officers began to question the little girl, they became
suspicious and called me into the investigation. As a result of what
I learned from the child, I placed the Sayres under arrest."

"No questions of this officer," Bartlett said, and added quickly,
"if the Commonwealth is now going to call June Crozier, I renew
my motion for a full psychiatric investigation of both children prior
to hearing their testimony."

"I am going to deny that motion," the judge replied. "Call June
Crozier."

The girl held up her right hand demurely. "The truth, the whole
truth," she repeated quietly.

"June," I said in a friendly voice, "tell this court how you came
to know Mr. and Mrs. Sayre."

"I met her in a grocery store about a year ago. She asked me if I would come to her house at night and wash dishes for her and clean up. Sort of like a mother's helper. I told her I would have to ask my mother."

"You said a mother's helper. Do Mr. and Mrs. Sayre have children?"

"No, but they have three boxers. Big dogs."

Suddenly she caught Leslie's glance, and both girls began to giggle.

"Look, children," the judge said sharply, "there is nothing to laugh about. Leslie, go and sit down with your father. June, this is a serious matter. Stop this nonsense and answer the District Attorney's questions."

Swallowing a last bubble of laughter, the child nodded, and I resumed. "Did your mother agree to this arrangement?"

The child nodded. "Oh yes. So I began to work there after supper in the evenings. Mrs. Sayre—Ethel—was very nice to me. She paid me a dollar for doing the dishes, sweeping, and all."

"*When* did something first happen between you and the Sayres?"

"Objection! Leading question!" shouted Bartlett.

"Well," the judge said quietly, "I agree, but with children of this age, a certain amount of leading is necessary if we are to get on with the case. The Assistant District Attorney will be careful about this, I'm sure."

"All right, June, answer me."

"For the first three or four evenings that I went over, nothing at all happened. Then Ethel asked me if I would come and help her on Saturday morning. I said all right. When I got there, about eleven-thirty or so, the front door was unlocked. They live in a two-story house a couple of blocks away from me. No one was downstairs so I went upstairs. Ethel and Mike were in the front bedroom lying on the bed—on top of the covers. They both had bathrobes on. I stood in the doorway and Ethel said, 'Come on in. Sit on the bed with us . . .'" The child paused uncertainly.

"Continue, June. It's all right to tell us."

"Well . . . so I sat there, and Ethel said how nice it was not to have any clothes on. She untied her bathrobe, and then I saw that Mike's robe was loose, too. They were both naked underneath. All of a sudden she grabbed me and started to kiss me. After she kissed me a lot, she took off my blouse and skirt, then my underwear. She put me in the middle of the bed and started to kiss me down here."

A small, nail-bitten hand pointed low on the rough woolen skirt.

"Then she said it was Mike's turn, and she would show me what I had to do to him, and what he would do to me."

"What was that, June?" I prodded her.

"Well . . ." The child hesitated. "His thing—he told me to call it his prick—she put it into her mouth, and then he took it out, and put it inside her."

"And did you do this to him too?" I asked, trying to be as casual as possible in order to keep the child calm. I wanted her to get through the ordeal without breaking down.

The child nodded.

"Answer Yes or No, my dear," the judge interjected.

"Yes."

"He also put his thing into you?"

"Yes. Well . . . not all the way, at first. It hurt, and I began to cry. Ethel laughed and said that's what happens with little girls. Then she said that was enough for today and that we would all get up and go shopping. So we went to some stores and she bought me a skirt and a pocketbook."

"Did you tell your mother about what happened with the Sayres?"

"No. I showed her my new things and she said it was very nice of Ethel to buy them for me. I never told my mother about anything the Sayres did; but she knew them, too, and used to go out with them."

"When was the next time you went to the Sayres'?"

"Oh, in a couple of days, I guess. I used to go three or four nights a week to clean up the kitchen. After the first time, Ethel and Mike always asked me to go upstairs with them. They had a bedroom where we stayed a lot, and also a library with a couch and a big mirror. They liked that room too—on account of the mirror. They would ask me to look and watch what was happening. After a couple of times, Mike put his thing all the way in. I cried, and Ethel said just for that I would have to do it with him every day for a month, and twice on Sundays. I did, too."

"Was Ethel always there when Mike did it to you?"

"Yes. But she always did things to me first. Then Mike took his turn with me."

"Did they know Leslie?"

"No. Leslie was my friend. One time last summer they asked me if I would like to go to New York with them for the week end. That was after my mother stayed at their house overnight."

"Did you say that *your mother* went to that house?" the judge asked. His look was one of frank disbelief.

Mrs. Crozier stood up. "May I explain why I was there, your Honor?" she asked tearfully.

"Please sit down now. We'll hear from you later."

June eagerly went on with her narrative, chatting away now as though she wanted to finish her story before the recess-bell rang. "So they asked me if I had a little friend to take to New York with us. They wanted a nice girl who would get along with them and do the same things I did. I had shown Leslie all the clothes and things Ethel bought me, and she was dying to meet them. So my mother talked to Leslie's mother, and she got permission to come with us. We stayed in a hotel. Mike didn't do anything to Leslie though. Just Ethel did—and then Ethel made me do those same things to Leslie. I had to do them whenever Ethel said. Even in the car on the way home. So then Ethel always wanted me to bring Leslie on Saturdays."

"Was anyone else ever there besides the four of you?"

"No, only the three dogs, if you want to count them."

"What about them, June?"

"Well, they weren't ordinary—they were real smart. Ethel and Mike had trained them to do things. They were all boy-dogs, and they had real names: Ralph, Billy, and John."

"What were these dogs trained to do?"

"Well, lots of things. If you were lying down, they would jump on you and lick you down there. They would also suck your titties."

"What was that last word?" asked Mr. Bartlett, who had been jotting down notes furiously as June told her story. "I'm sorry, your Honor, I missed that. This is just too fantastic for words!"

The stenographer pulled up the perforated role of paper. "Titties—do you want me to spell it, Counsel?"

"Breasts, I mean. But Ethel always called them titties."

"Thank you, June," I said quietly. "Did the dogs do anything else—besides the things you've mentioned, I mean?"

"Oh sure. They can do everything that Mike does—all three of them. They did the same things to Leslie and me that he did. It didn't hurt. Ethel and Mike loved to watch us and the dogs—they said they were really good for . . ." Finally the girl arrived at a barrier.

"Go on," I said. "Good for what, June?"

She looked down at the floor a moment before answering. "It's a dirty word and I don't like to say it. But you know the one I mean. They used that word a lot and asked Leslie and me to use it all the time too."

I saw no reason to press the child further. We all had heard the word often enough in that courtroom.

Now began the dreary litany, a necessary part of the Commonwealth's case. How many times with Ethel? How many times with Mike? How many times with Leslie? How many times with the dogs?

Lots and lots of times. Over a year's worth of times. And after each time, clothes, candy, a trip to the movies or the seashore. So many times that June began to feel tired and sore. It was hard to get up and get dressed to go home. Then Ethel said, "Why not come to live with us? Then we can do it whenever we want to, and we don't have to rush so you won't be late. And there are so many other things we can try."

When June asked her mother if she could go to live with the Sayres, she became upset. The child went anyway, and stayed for three days. When she went home to get more clothes, her mother took her to the police. June didn't want to do anything to hurt Ethel or Mike. Especially Ethel.

The child looked pleadingly at the muscular, impassive woman.

"I really love Ethel," she said whimperingly. "I hope nothing happens to her."

Bartlett looked at her sternly. He hesitated, unsure of where or how to begin his cross-examination, then dove in, reaching quickly for a lifeline: "You said your mother stayed at the Sayres'. Where did she sleep?"

"In the big round bed in the bedroom. We all did. It's big enough for four people."

"How did your mother come to spend the night there?"

"She had been drinking with Ethel and Mike, and she got a little sleepy—well, drunk, I guess. So she just stayed."

"What, if anything, happened that night?" Bartlett, like the rest of us, could not let go.

"Well, I was sleeping, but I woke up. I saw my mother sitting on top of Mike, the way I used to. I don't know what else happened. I turned over and started to play with Ethel's titties. But she was sleeping, so I stopped and went to sleep too."

"No further questions." The lawyer's face was flushed and angry.

"In the interests of time as well as our own feelings, your Honor," I stated, "I will simply ask Leslie Fanton one general question. Her testimony would be cumulative anyway."

"All right," agreed the judge. "We've heard enough."

"Leslie, you have heard June's story. Is it true or is it false?"

The girl nodded affirmatively. "True. All of it."

"Detective Brent," the judge asked, "where are those boxers at this point?"

"Judge," he said, "we confiscated them and took them to the S.P.C.A. shelter yesterday. As far as I know, they are still there."

"Good," replied the judge. "I have an idea. We'll take a short recess."

He went into his chambers alone.

While he was out of the room, I walked over to Mrs. Crozier. A heavy, unkempt, crumpled woman, she was weeping silently.

"Do you have a drinking problem?" I asked.

She nodded Yes silently.

"Do you believe June?"

A vigorous double nod. Then she croaked hoarsely, "When my husband finds out, he'll kill us all. Those two should rot in jail for the rest of their lives."

"Don't talk like that, Mommy," whispered June, who was now sitting beside her mother. "You'll hurt Ethel's feelings if she hears you!"

"Order in the court! Court is now in session!" intoned the bailiff.

The judge returned to the bench. "I want to see the District Attorney and defense counsel. Come up, please."

He spoke to us in a low undertone. "I just checked with the S.P.C.A. and talked to their chief veterinarian. It's true about these dogs, all right. Since they have been at the shelter, they have been in a state of sexual frenzy and have tried to mount every human who came into contact with them. The vet has given them tranquilizers, but he believes that ultimately they will have to be destroyed. They have been so well conditioned to many signals, he said, that it is impossible to try to undo any of it. Apparently they are very intelligent pedigreed dogs. I wanted to check out that part of the child's fantastic story to test her credibility. She knows what she is talking about, no doubt of that!

"Mr. Bartlett, I don't want to tell you what to do, but maybe you ought to consider carefully whether or not to plead these people guilty and ask for a complete psychiatric appraisal. Right now, I can only hold them in five thousand dollars' bail each for the action of the grand jury. I know the District Attorney has a policy of listing these cases quickly for trial, which is why I ask you to discuss the matter with your clients. If they are not going to enter a plea, then I will not order the dogs destroyed at this time. The District Attorney may need them as evidence. As for the girls, I am ordering that delinquency petitions be filed against them, and I will have them both examined by a psychiatrist. You are free to see their reports, Mr. Bartlett, but I don't think they will help you very much."

The lawyer nodded and said, "Thank you. It's a difficult case, I'm afraid. Well, I'll talk to my clients."

"I'll bet Mrs. Sayre calls the shots," observed the judge.

She did. Bartlett could not persuade her to make a legal admission of her guilt, so the cases were tried before a jury. Mr. Sayre received a sentence of from five to ten years, which he is serving in a penitentiary. Under the special provisions then governing the sentencing of women, Mrs. Sayre went to the state reformatory for women on an indefinite sentence. Living in such close quarters with other women did not seem to have the sexually stimulating effect on her that it often has on Lesbians. In fact, she created such a good record that she was discharged after serving time for not quite four years. Despite her refusal to seek psychiatric aid, her probation officer was satisfied with her adjustment to prison and to the community after her release. She never again saw the three dogs; they were destroyed by court order after the trials. Nor, as far as anyone knows, did she ever see or talk to June or Leslie after they testified against her.

Both girls received regular psychiatric therapy at a hospital clinic while they were on probation to the juvenile court. June's reports showed that her home life was very disordered. Her mother's alcoholism was one contributing factor; another was her father's rejection of his parental role. His seizing upon the Sayre involvement as a reason for deserting his family was but a convenient pretext; he had been on the verge of leaving for a long time. After months of treatment, the psychiatrist concluded that very little, if anything, had changed in the child's personality patterns. Regretfully he marked the case closed. Undoubtedly the year's intense, apparently genuine relationship between Ethel and June had left an ineradicable scar. Using the traditional medical term that connotes pessimism of outlook, he marked her prognosis *Guarded.*

Leslie, on the other hand, was less affected than June; fortunately, she had not become as involved with Ethel. In fact, her sexual experience with the older woman was but one strand in the fabric of her friendship with June. Even more fortunately, her parents stood by her throughout the court trials and during her therapy sessions. Her father became especially protective toward her, yet was careful to include her younger sister and his wife in the many family activities he arranged. As she, too, was discharged from probation the psychiatrist's comment reflected his optimism that she would have a more normal adolescence than June.

The difference between the two little girls may not have been apparent by just looking at them; but it was there, just below the surface. June's family background, seemingly placid, was shot through with pathological elements. Behind the lace-curtained windows a relentless family tragedy had been played out from the child's earliest years on. Her parents gave her very little affection, being too caught up in their own strife—caused by Mrs. Crozier's drinking and her husband's inability to hold down a job for a sustained period—to be sensitive to their child's need. The mother was oppressed by her responsibility for her daughter and became even less adequate as June grew older and eagerly sought love and attention. Mrs. Crozier responded halfheartedly at times; at other times, not at all.

The Fantons, on the other hand, were not beset by such problems. And unlike Mrs. Crozier, whose sense of guilt compelled her to denounce constantly the Sayres (and by implication, June), both parents reserved comment about the child's seducers. They wisely elected to view the whole episode as an unfortunate accident, the more quickly forgotten, the better. One child, deserted by an indifferent father, dependent on an alcoholic, inadequate mother, found herself branded as "bad" after the story came out; the other youngster, enveloped in her parents' love and warmth, which they expressed even more after they learned what had happened, thought of the experience as nothing more serious than a bad fall.

Emotionally starved and frustrated long before she met Ethel, June found a relationship that satisfied her deep need, shared by all children, for a loving parent figure. She personifies the bedroom throwaway: precisely the child, all the researchers agree, most likely to become a sexual "victim" and never recover fully afterward. These professionals point out that even though the offending adult is whisked out of the child's life, the hunger for the comfort and warmth of the relationship lingers on. It is not surprising, therefore, to learn that early childhood seductions are inevitably part of the case histories of adolescent and young adult sexual psychopaths.

How devastating a throwaway background can become in the sexual development of children is not truly conveyed by statistics, even when they are culled by sensitive investigators. It takes a child like Virginia Mitchell to make us shudder and begin to comprehend.

Virginia was the teen-age daughter of *Miss* Lucy Mitchell (the form of address she insisted upon). At age thirty-two Miss Lucy had a brood of seven bastard children. Joan was the oldest at eighteen; then came Virginia, thirteen; Joseph, eleven; Donald, nine; Charles, seven; Anthony, five; and John, three.

Tall, emaciated, her henna-red hair wreathing her pale white skin, Miss Lucy looked like a long-discarded Christmas tree on which the top ornamentation had somehow been overlooked. She managed to muster up a bit of maternal dignity as she approached the bench. She asked the judge for permission to talk to me before her brother, Harvey Mitchell, arrived from prison where he had been detained awaiting the preliminary hearing, which was about to begin.

"Harvey's charged with incest," Roselli added helpfully as he saw the judge glance down at the day's list of cases to find Mitchell's name. "The complainants are two of Miss Mitchell's children: Virginia and Joseph." He looked at the woman beside him. "Did you bring them with you?" Roselli asked worriedly.

"Yeah, they're both here." She turned again to the judge. "I think there is something wrong with Virginia. Could she see the head-doctor while she is here today?"

"Mrs. Richette, go out and talk to the girl," Judge Hoffman said. "See if she's able to testify. If necessary, arrange for an appointment with the Neuropsychiatric Department."

The girl was sitting alone in the almost empty waiting room when I appeared with her mother. Two rows behind her sat a thin, dirt-encrusted boy wearing a sweater that was both full of holes and about two sizes too small for him. This would be brother Joseph, I thought to myself. It was clear that Miss Mitchell gave as little attention to her children's appearance as she did to her own. Virginia was a much paler replica of her mother, except her face, which was aflame with acne. She looked like a pointillist portrait seen under a magnifying glass.

Virginia pressed her hands against her flat, hard tummy where the tattered skirt was held to her blouse by a safety pin. "Those babies are really kicking me hard." Then, laughing uncontrollably, she added, "The girls kick harder than the boys. I have two of each. Almost like my mother—only she had three girls, but one died, and four boys. Why did Angela die? Why? Oh, I hope my babies don't die."

"Who is Angela?" I asked, puzzled by the girl's entire speech.

"Angela was my baby, my youngest. She just died last week in the hospital. She had brain fever. Virginia is real upset about it," said Miss Mitchell, flatly. "Stop this crazy talk, Virginia. I don't care *what* Harvey did to you; you ain't got four babies."

"Yes, I do!" screamed the girl. "I've got four and plenty more where they came from. Joseph gave me his babies, and the man who flies in the sky gave me his, and I've got everybody's baby inside of me. Even that old skeleton in the cellar at school, he was with me early in the morning. Oh, my sweet little babies!" She rocked to and fro on the chair and started to hum.

Tears flowed down her dirty, infected cheeks, but she made no effort to brush them away.

"How long has this been going on?" I asked tensely. "This child is sick. I'm going to call our Medical Department."

After I asked a court attendant to call Dr. Anderson, Miss Mitchell answered my question: "Oh, she takes these spells a lot. About six months ago the police picked her up. I had to leave a really good party to go get her. I took her home, and she went to school the next day—she was O.K. Virginia's always a little queer."

"Queer?" the girl shrieked. "Queer? I'll tell you who's queer. Uncle Harvey and Joseph and Donald and even little Charley. All my brothers are queer! Remember Donald's sore ass? That's 'cause he's queer. Not me! I have babies, four of them, right inside of me!"

Again she hummed the soothing lullaby, stroking herself in rhythm. She was still continuing her lament for the babies when Dr. Anderson arrived a few minutes later. He just stood quietly, observing her.

"She certainly seems delusional. As soon as the nurse comes, we'll take her up to the office and arrange for an emergency admission to Philadelphia General. I'll go into court and report to the judge. Here's the nurse now. Let's both go in; have the mother present too."

"Do you recommend a ninety-day commitment?" the judge asked after Anderson finished his brief statement.

"At least, your Honor. If she doesn't improve in that time, she will be transferred to a state institution. Do we have anything more on her background? Why is she in court this morning?"

I spoke up. "She came in to testify against her uncle on an incest charge. Her younger brother, Joseph, is also involved. Mr. Roselli says that five years ago a complaint was filed against the family by the Society for Protection of Children, but no court action was taken. We have the court record here," I added. "I'll make further investigations. Maybe the school authorities can be helpful."

"Good. See what you can find out," the doctor replied. "The hospital's social service department will put together a background report, but that may take months."

"What are you going to do about Harvey, Judge?" Miss Mitchell asked. "He's the one needs to be put away. Joseph is waiting around outside. He'll tell what happened. I should never have let Joey go live with him."

"We'll hear Harvey's case in a few minutes," Judge Hoffman reassured her. "Just wait outside until we call you."

Then, motioning to the sheriff not to call the case immediately, he picked up the old court file and read it intently.

"Append this information to Virginia's commitment order," he dictated to the stenographer. "The court record shows that Miss Mitchell had her first child when she was fourteen years old. She said she was raped, but refused to name her assailant. That child, Joan, would be eighteen years old today. We do not know her whereabouts. Then she had the other six children, naming different men as the fathers. All of them denied paternity. One man demanded a blood test and was absolutely cleared. She has mostly lived with her parents except when she was arrested a couple of years ago for prostitution and when she left home for short periods of time. The Society received several complaints about the condition of the children, but each time, the maternal grandmother promised to take better care of them. The family has been on and off relief over the years. Their mainstay, it seems, has been the grandfather, who has supported them after a fashion. This is Virginia's background. There's probably a lot more that we don't know about, but it's the kind of chaotic home situation that breeds mental illness, incest, and every other social sickness you can name."

He flung the record down. "Are we ready to hear about Uncle Harvey? Bring him in."

Harvey Mitchell had the uncouth, hulking appearance of a mountaineer, despite the fact that he had lived all his life in a Philadelphia slum. The arrest report listed his occupation as a truck driver, his age as thirty, and his status as a single man.

A uniformed police officer approached the bar and identified himself.

"Did you make the arrest, Officer?"

"Yes, I did, your Honor. While I was patrolling my beat, I saw the defendant leave a parked car. His pants and his undershorts were open, and he was wiping his penis with a cloth. This was at five o'clock in the afternoon. I stopped him and went to look in the car, where I saw a boy and a girl—later identified as his niece, Virginia, thirteen, and his nephew, Joseph, aged eleven. Their clothing was also disarrayed, and I learned from questioning them that each had had sexual relations with the uncle as well as with each other. I placed all three under arrest and brought them into the district. Morals Squad conducted a further investigation; that report is right there before you, your Honor."

"Call Joseph Mitchell," ordered the judge.

The boy was red-maned, like his sister, but much smaller in frame. His whole body shook as he stood before us. He quickly affirmed the police report and told the court he had been living with his uncle for two years, ever since his mother went to jail. Shortly after he arrived, several women who used to stay overnight at Harvey's apartment stopped coming, and the uncle told him he would have to take their place in bed. Harvey, the court learned from the boy himself, had been engaging in unnatural sex with his nephew almost every night ever since. But that was not the end of the horror story.

Soon Harvey persuaded Joseph to bring Virginia over on week ends. After the girl had watched them have sex, Harvey asked her to have intercourse with him. He warned her she might have a baby, which she said was okay. Then Harvey told Joey to give her a baby, too, since she was so crazy about them. So Joey did it too. Harvey liked to do it all the time—even in the park or in his car or truck. That's how they got caught.

"Have you ever done these things with anybody other than Harvey or Virginia?" the judge asked the trembling boy.

"Once my brother Donald—he's nine—and I went downtown and there was a man in a washroom. He paid us each a dollar. That was the only other time."

"Donald?" asked the judge. "How old was he then? I want to be sure—this case is like a Chinese puzzle. Every time you think you've solved it, you find another locked box. Where is Donald?"

"He's probably at school. He stays with my grandmother most of the time."

"Miss Mitchell, come forward," the judge thundered. "Have you been listening to Joseph's testimony? Did you hear what he said? What about Donald? You don't know anything about your own children, do you?"

"Wait a minute, Judge. My father takes charge of them all. He and my mother, although she's very sickly. She has a bad heart and sugar in her blood. I didn't know Harvey was doing these things. He offered to take care of Joey while I was in jail, so my father let him. I guess he thought it was one less child to feed."

"I want all these children picked up and taken to the welfare shelter right away. Where's Joan?" he asked the mother.

"Joan got married and left town two years ago. We don't hear from her. And the baby, Angela, she died a few days ago. All the rest is with my father and mother. Please don't take them away from us, Judge. I couldn't help it! Please. It will kill my father. Oh, Daddy!" she sobbed.

The judge, ignoring this last outcry, dictated his order. "Commit Harvey Mitchell to Philadelphia State Hospital for ninety days, for complete observation. Joseph, Anthony, Donald, and Charles Mitchell are to be placed as dependent children in the city's Department of Public Welfare Shelter, and petitions are to be filed forthwith. I'll hear the children's cases whenever they are ready."

Several weeks later, the Department's social worker accompanied the four boys to court. Miss Mitchell looked even more unkempt and skeletal than before; an unshaven, middle-aged man held her arm as she found a seat in the courtroom.

"You have our report, your Honor," the social worker said crisply. "The children will remain at the shelter, as you instructed. The senior Mitchell's home is entirely unsuitable for these children, and we are recommending placement. We have arranged for Charles and John—the youngest—to go to the Catholic Home.

"Anthony," she went on, "who is next to the youngest, is a special problem. He has palsy, and we have to make a special plan for him. He's five years old and has never received any medical attention for his condition. In fact, none of the children has ever had a single visit with a doctor or dentist. The hospital reports that the baby Angela died of meningitis, but that she could probably have been saved if the mother and the grandparents had not been so neglectful.

"Joseph and Donald are being considered by St. Vincent's School in upstate Pennsylvania. We think they will be accepted. They are hesitating about Donald, Judge, because of his nervous condition. It's in the report."

About a year earlier, the police had found Donald sleeping in an alleyway. When he arrived at the district, he had gone into severe convulsions and had remained at the city hospital for three weeks. Although no brain irregularities had been found at that time, complete electroencephalograms were needed now to rule out epilepsy.

"Finally," the social worker concluded, "there's Virginia——"

"Yes, I know about Virginia," the judge interrupted wearily, rubbing his brow in a gesture of pain. "She's much worse and the psychiatrists want to transfer her to a state hospital for a longer period of treatment."

He looked up resolutely. "I want to be sure that these children never return to that environment, but under our child-care system, these placements may be only short-term. Maybe the younger ones —Charley, Anthony, and John—will be lucky enough to go to a good foster home. But the only recommendation for the older boys is a boarding school where they will stay for a few years at most. Then what? It's so cruel to send them back just when they are on the threshold of a new life. Can't you try to find a foster home for Joseph and Donald so that they can be together? Even separately, can't you place them?"

The social worker shook her head negatively. "Not with their kind of sexual acting out, your Honor. We just can't ask our foster parents to take them. As it is, we had to beg the training school to try them. It's a risk."

"And yet we force defenseless children to take every risk," the judge replied. "Here, Mrs. Richette, read this."

He handed me a letter written by the principal of the school Virginia sporadically attended. It was addressed to the Philadelphia Juvenile Court and it read:

> I am very pleased that finally some action has been taken about Virginia. She has worried me for years. This very peculiar girl who talks incessantly claims that she gets up at three and four in the morning because she is afraid to stay with the mother and grandfather. (She won't explain why.) She wanders the streets until seven o'clock in the morning when she arrives at school and stays in the cellar with the custodian. Her clothes are ragged, dirty, and inappropriate. Her face and hands are always filthy and her hair uncombed. On a bitter cold day she wore a very full dirty white organdy skirt, no petticoat, and the black top of a jersey bathing suit. She had no jacket, sweater, or cover over her shoulders. She stopped me to ask me, "How do you like my dress?" . . .

I passed the letter back. "I know that school well, your Honor. A number of kids arrive every morning in dishevelled condition . . . But why, I wonder, was Virginia afraid to stay with her mother and grandfather?"

There was a brief silence as Judge Hoffman stared intently at the much-handled record. Suddenly he called out in a loud voice, "Mr. Mitchell? You are Mr. Mitchell, aren't you?"

The shabby old man next to Miss Lucy nodded, not meeting the judge's stare.

"I've a hunch the apple didn't fall far from the tree. What do you think, Mr. Mitchell? You say you are the grandfather of all these children—isn't that what you say?"

Again the old man nodded.

"But there's more to tell, isn't there, Mr. Mitchell?" the judge insisted.

Head bowed, shoulders hunched forward, the man mumbled something incoherent and covered his unshaven face with grimy hands.

Judge Hoffman pressed on. "I know what you are. I can't prove it, but your daughter knows. Stay away from her, if you can, Mr. Mitchell. Give her and those children a chance—the chance you stole from her when she was fourteen."

He nodded his head, and shuffled out of the courtroom. Lucy Mitchell stood up and asked if she could leave. The judge dismissed her. As the door closed behind her, he said, "Poor wretch. Why didn't she tell the court about him when she was here the first time? Maybe no one took enough time to let her tell. And now we have another generation repeating the pattern."

Even a dispassionate researcher like Kinsey was astonished at the high incidence of sexual experiences involving adults and children. The extent of it first came to light in his study, *Sexual Behavior in the Human Female*. Almost one fourth of the women interviewed by Kinsey's team revealed that sometime between the ages of ten and twelve, they had had genital sex contacts with grown men. Most of the women reporting these experiences had grown up in poverty pockets in American cities. With a sample that included more poor women, Kinsey rightly believed that his figure of 24 per cent would have been considerably higher. He also commented on the lack of revulsion accompanying these memories:

> In most instances the reported fright was nearer the level that children show when they see insects, spiders, or other objects against which they have been adversely conditioned. If a child was not culturally conditioned it is doubtful if it would be disturbed by sexual approaches of the sort which had usually been involved in these stories.

The many European studies of sexually victimized children show repeatedly that disordered family and especially parental relationships drive the youngsters to participate passively, or as eagerly as June Crozier did, in perverse sex acts. Professor T. C. N. Gibbens, of the London Institute of Psychiatry, after thirty years of researching these child victims, concludes that "nice" children with secure home backgrounds who are molested by strangers—a possibility that devoted parents fear most—recover more easily from sexual assault than the children with troubled home backgrounds—the "bedroom" throwaways.

This is not quite the paradox it might seem. These throwaways are not as tough or insensitive as they sometimes appear to be. In fact, their grip on life is tenuous and constantly under threat. Lindy Burton's book *Vulnerable Children* (1968) surveys the substantial research on the motivation of these children. What they seek, as the eminent British sociologist, Dr. Stott, documents in his work *Unsettled Children and Their Families* (1956), is *not* sexual gratification, the easiest available source of joy for the poor. Rather, they yearn for a parental warmth and security they have never had, and it is this unfilled need that leads them into alleys, empty lots, vacant buildings, parked cars, bedrooms—and ultimately, in many instances, into police stations and juvenile and criminal courts.

Thereafter, more isolated and troubled than ever, watched as potential sex delinquents—or perhaps even so branded—these children are denied the one thing they sought. They cannot know it, but from the start their quest was doomed to fail.

13 ═══

THE
PAPER
LABYRINTH

Throwaways, like other children in this world, go to school. From ages six to sixteen, many of them spend nearly fifteen thousand hours in the company of teachers—adults whose sole purpose is to pass on to their charges the skills and techniques that are vital to functioning in the adult world. And yet during this prolonged and close contact with these so-called expert outsiders, children often experience precisely the same rejection and dehumanizing treatment they get at home and on the city streets where they wander in search of play. Instead of providing them with even a minimal survival kit, the school often accelerates their destruction.

In recent years, a spate of compellingly honest books by principals and teachers in ghetto schools—where the largest concentration of throwaways occurs—have dramatically informed readers that the present educational bureaucracies of large cities effectively snuff out any spark of interest or willingness to learn within these children.

Jonathan Kozol's gripping *Death at an Early Age* recounts his struggle, as an idealistic teacher of ghetto children, to buck the

Boston public school system's throwaway philosophy. Kozol's book is a sobering antidote to the celluloid euphoria created by the movie *To Sir with Love*, where a single gifted teacher was allowed to work miracles with a classroom of London slum children. *Who Can Be Educated?*, a recent book by Milton Schwebel, Dean of the Rutgers University Graduate School, asserts that American school programs prevent millions of children from receiving even a bare-bones education. And Edgar Z. Friedenberg, another perceptive observer, has long pointed out that while our schools do help some children to move up in life by preparing them for status careers, they keep much larger numbers off the ladder by branding them, from the early grades on, as ineducable or troublemakers or both.

Armed with this evidence, some educators and concerned parents are beginning to challenge the expenditure of millions of dollars on a failure-ridden system of public education. In *How Children Learn*, his sequel to the provocative *How Children Fail*, John Holt asserts that schools, as we now run them, disrupt the learning process in all children, whether they are throwaways or not. So, near the start of the eighth decade of the twentieth century, Americans have become newly aware that justice and equal opportunity are not available to masses of citizens, and now perceive that public free education is another one of the tragic contradictions in our present society.

Survival itself seems accomplishment enough for throwaway children, who live under such incredibly impossible conditions, yet society makes further demands: "Learn. Please the teacher. Fit into the system." The alternative is clear. "If you don't, we'll push you out." Failure is built into the process from the outset.

What many adults do not comprehend is a basic fact that most children grasp intuitively: the schoolroom is a courtroom, a place where trials are held and judgments made. Reward is often hard earned and punishment readily meted out; the teacher-judge has a potential of awesome power more absolute than anything envisioned in Kafka's nightmares. And individual authority is backed up by a huge law-enforcement process with *its* own rules and regulations, *its* own techniques for punishment, and *its* own correctional institutions. Children are fed into this apparatus with little or no intervention from outside agencies and, until recently, with little challenge from anyone acting in their behalf.

From the day a child enters first grade he is catalogued, tested, watched—and judged. In the egg-carton line-up of students in the average classroom, it is easy to spot a troublesome child who doesn't fit into the neat rows or won't stay put once he has been wedged into place. The harried, overwhelmed teacher may become hostile to such a youngster or may simply be too preoccupied with his other charges to do more than follow the established procedure of filing a report against the "troublemaker." Yet this report, by its very nature an indictment of the student as "different," "special," "non-conforming," has the same effect on his educational future as an official police record may carry in other areas.

In the Philadelphia school system, this Disciplinary Referral Report is an innocuous-looking four-page questionnaire, Form EH 21, known more simply as the Form. Once it has been completed by a teacher, it remains forever in the child's school dossier to warn the world that this youngster spells trouble. If a principal, after reading the Form, decides to put the child out of his school, he corroborates the teacher's charges and sends the report to the district superintendent. That official has a series of "conferences" with parents and other officials, and he may then lower the boom all the way by expelling the child or transferring him to a special "remedial-disciplinary" school or even sending him to juvenile court as an incorrigible. This "procedure," clearly retaliatory, clearly designed to punish troublesome children, is disguised by school personnel as a "counseling" or "handling" device—the latter a much-used "neutral" term which correctly, if inadvertently, implies the manipulating of a balky horse.

Another way for school officials to mask their punitive attitudes is to use the self-serving jargon of social workers. For example, the Form provides a space where the teacher can recommend what should be done to the child; however, the heading under which he writes reads *Special Needs of the Child*. A frequent suggestion is "Juvenile court." After listening to hundreds of cases where the Board of Education filed delinquency petitions based on the Form, I am prompted to ask, *Whose* special needs does this referral really satisfy? The child's? Or the school system's? Is its main purpose to unburden itself of all responsibility and obligation to troublesome, nonconforming children?

Many of the delinquency petitions filed by the school authorities charge a child with truancy. If in fact the schoolroom is a kind of courtroom where the child hears daily pronouncements of his guilt or his failures, he has only one way to protect himself: to stay as far away as possible. A school system that further alienates the already alienated child cannot reasonably demand—or expect—regular attendance. And, with fewer than half of Philadelphia's one hundred and eighty-five elementary schools offering counseling services, no coherent effort is being made to give these children special help. Furthermore, even in those fortunate schools that have such a service, there are five hundred children to each counselor. Only the most difficult and obviously troubled children receive attention; the quiet, withdrawn child is generally overlooked. Then one day, when someone counts up his absences and decides that something must be done, it's "Off to juvenile court!"

Loretta Reeves, aged fifteen, black and a ghetto-dweller, had been lost in the paper labyrinth of the public school system for nine years. Both her I.Q. scores and her marks were just respectable enough to allow her to pass from grade to grade without anyone's paying her any special mind. When she entered junior high school, she began to stay away with increasing frequency, and in her sophomore year she never went to school after the first day.

"Your Honor," said the school representative, "Loretta has one hundred and forty days of absence this year! The school never sees her at all. Her mother has been fined for encouraging her truancy in magistrate's court, but since she is receiving welfare funds, the fine cannot be collected. We are asking that this youngster be committed to a correctional institution."

I scanned the court summary of Loretta's background: two-bedroom apartment, third floor rear. Youngest of three children fathered by two, possibly three, different paramours. Mother single, completed seventh grade, works occasionally at factory and unskilled jobs. Had hysterectomy few months ago, is still recuperating. Older sisters also live with mother.

"What kind of course is Loretta taking in school?" Judge Hoffman asked the representative.

"General Studies."

A big nothing, I thought, an insipid pablum of unchallenging material placed in feeding troughs before hundreds of children: take it or leave it.

I looked at Loretta. Her eyes were bright and intelligent; there was an inner refinement and dignity about her that set her apart from the other truant children we were accustomed to seeing.

"Your Honor," I asked Judge Hoffman, "would it be possible to retest Loretta and do some intensive studies before you make your decision? She might be a wonderful candidate for Teen-Aid. After all, she hasn't committed any offense other than staying away from school; there's no pattern of antisocial conduct anywhere in her record. A training school for girls should be our *last* resort, not our first step."

"Agreed," said the judge. "I was thinking along those exact lines myself. I will arrange for comprehensive testing, and we will relist the case in three weeks. Meanwhile, please do refer her to Teen-Aid. Is her mother here?"

"Yes, Judge, here I am." A tall, attractive woman in her early thirties came forward. "I don't know why the school is making such a fuss. Loretta is a good girl. She just doesn't want to go to school. She stays at home and helps me and her sisters and the babies."

The judge was pleasantly interested. "Babies? Whose babies?"

"Her two sisters'. We have four little babies, and there's a lot of work to be done at home."

"I see," he replied. Then, turning to me, he said firmly, "Be sure someone finds out what that is all about."

Loretta and her mother met me at the end of the court session in the Teen-Aid office on the mezzanine floor of the courthouse. Judge Hoffman and I had founded the organization only a few months earlier and already it was flooded with referrals from the juvenile court judges and probation officers.

With the lack of community interest in delinquent girls, short of committing them to correctional schools, we had had only conventional probation to fall back on, and judging by their return appearances in court, it did not appear to work terribly well. So more and more of the girls (who constituted 20 per cent of the total number of delinquents) were being sent away to a handful of these schools, most of them far from Philadelphia.

Today, Teen-Aid is a thriving, viable organization, but when Loretta and her mother sat down for their interview that day, the technique of using volunteer women (dedicated and intelligent as they were) to interact with the so-called hard-core problem girls was still a daring experiment.

I could sense the volunteer interviewer's shock as she read the number of days Loretta had been absent from school, but she merely smiled pleasantly at the girl and asked what sort of things interested her.

At an informal meeting of Teen-Aid later that day, we decided that Mrs. Ware, one of our Negro volunteers, should be Loretta's sponsor or immediate counselor. Mrs. Ware, a quiet, thoughtful housewife, had joined the organization out of her deep conviction that these "delinquent" girls had talent, energy, and strength, but that these qualities frequently withered because adults did not take the time to nurture them. Loretta gave Mrs. Ware her first opportunity to test this belief.

Three weeks later, when the older woman stood beside the girl at the second hearing of the delinquency charge, I could feel the friendly warmth that already existed between them.

Reading through a stack of pink sheets, Judge Hoffman shook his head in amazement and beckoned. "Come up here, Mrs. Richette —you, too, Mrs. Ware. I want you both to read these."

He was referring to Loretta's test results. She had scored over 130—proof that she was markedly superior in intellect and ability. The psychologist recommended a full college-preparatory course for her. He explained that Loretta knew she was bright, but had not been able to weave her interests and ambitions into the tattered strands of her family life. She had never known her father, a boyfriend of her mother's who had never really been a part of the household. Her two older sisters, seventeen and nineteen, had dropped out of school when they became pregnant and had never returned. They and her mother had encouraged her to be absent from school, saying that, after all, it was only a matter of time until she, too, had a baby. Loretta, the psychologist reported, wanted to be more than just a breeding machine, but the struggle to overcome her environment was too much to face alone.

Mrs. Ware's jaw tightened. Her usual reticence gave way to a quick flurry of emotion.

"I've been to the house, your Honor," she whispered. "Actually, just a three-room apartment on a very bad street. I think there are prostitutes on the first floor. The place is so cluttered and filled with baby things there is barely room to breathe. Even if Loretta were to go to school, I don't know where she would find a quiet corner to study. The whole family receives assistance; nobody works. They sleep late, get up, and do a few chores. Their days are unplanned and disorganized. And her mother laughs when I tell her that Loretta should study and maybe even go to college. 'Who's going to pay?' she keeps asking. When I tell her about scholarships, she looks at me and says that these things don't happen to colored children. It's going to be tough for Loretta in that house. If only there were a foster home or a halfway house—some decent place—where she could live."

"There isn't, Mrs. Ware," I said. "I've been through this many, many times, as you well know. The only other possibilities for a girl like Loretta are a jail or a training school. It's just a question of which is the least objectionable alternative, and that's her own home, such as it is."

Someday, I thought, we'll have a group of halfway houses in every area of Philadelphia, but Loretta will be middle-aged by then. However, with our help, this bright young girl might make it . . .

Under Teen-Aid's procedure, Mrs. Ware made regular reports on developments. First, she went to the all-girl high school that Loretta had failed to attend and talked at length with the principal. An exceptional woman and a Negro herself, she became immediately sympathetic when she realized Mrs. Ware's interest. There were hundreds of Lorettas scattered throughout her school, she said; but by the time they started junior high school, it was already impossible to reach them through conventional classroom channels. What the many girls like Loretta needed was exactly the one-to-one personal relationship that Mrs. Ware was successfully establishing. The principal promised that the school would help in every possible way.

Next, Mrs. Ware went to a Free Library branch several blocks away from Loretta's home and arranged to have a special study area made available to the girl; special library and borrowing privileges were also granted so that she could work at an accelerated pace to make up for years of lost time.

Every day until the end of the school year Mrs. Ware talked to Loretta. The girl's school marks soared to A's and B's; her final report qualified her for the honor roll. During the summer, she took a typing course at a center-city business institute; Mrs. Ware arranged for Teen-Aid to pay the bill so that Loretta would be able to type when she went to college.

This assistance plan was instituted shortly after we started Teen-Aid. We had realized what special needs *should* have been noted on the disciplinary forms: books, clothing, special courses, an occasional ticket to a play or movie, long-term dental corrective work. Since we were not recognized as an "agency" by the health and welfare establishment, we had no access to any Red Feather–Community Chest funds. Undaunted, we went to business and professional people for direct contributions; in special cases we told the potential benefactor the girl's whole story, omitting only her real name. Teen-Aid, Inc., is still one of the few child-service agencies in the nation that relies wholly on private support.

Never once in the next two years did Mrs. Ware falter in her belief that Loretta would continue her education after graduation from high school. And her faith was so compelling that the girl, too, began to believe that this dream could come true. Teen-Aid paid all the fees for Loretta's College Board Examinations, because there are no public assistance monies available for such "nonessential" items, and the principal wrote a number of letters of recommendation to help the girl obtain a scholarship. On graduation day Loretta—the first in her family to receive a diploma—learned that she had won a full four-year tuition scholarship at a college forty miles away. Her only problem now was to find the money to pay for her room and board, clothing, books, and other expenses.

However, Teen-Aid received annual amounts of money for higher education purposes from the Emergency Aid of Pennsylvania, an active private organization of socially prominent and socially minded women. From this fund, Teen-Aid loaned Loretta enough money each fall so that she could concentrate full time on her studies, dress suitably, and take care of her personal needs. Each summer, Loretta worked as a waitress, a camp counselor, or a secretary in order to pay back the year's loan.

In her sophomore year, because of her excellence in French, she was offered a six-week exchange fellowship at the Sorbonne. It was a tempting idea, but after a long discussion with Mrs. Ware, she decided that she was not ready to go abroad. Also, she needed to earn money during the summer. "I'll see Europe later, when I'm in a position to really enjoy it. After all, I don't want to do everything at once," Loretta said with a grin. "I want to have something to look forward to!"

During her last year at college she wrote the Teen-Aid president a long letter expressing her gratitude for the group's interest and help. Although the last three and a half years had flown by, she said they contained a whole lifetime's experience, and the fulfillment of a childhood dream as well. She recalled that the day she came to court had been like reaching the bottom of an abyss. Yet it had in fact been the turning point in her life. She ended by saying that after graduation she hoped to join Teen-Aid so that she could help girls as she herself had been helped.

Loretta is now a high school teacher in a predominantly black school, working to help children who come from her background tune in to the excitement and fun of learning.

Some children make it even when the bare glimmers of light and hope are missing. Early in 1968, as I was leaving juvenile court with a client, one of the psychiatrists told me about a sixteen-year-old boy who had been locked up for two months in the House of Correction's wing for teen-age boys on a truancy charge. The prison social worker had referred him to the doctor when he observed that the boy was becoming seriously depressed.

"No wonder he's low," the psychiatrist said. "Who wouldn't be? We put him in jail because he doesn't go to school. Nobody bothered to find out that this boy has been learning to be a butcher since he was thirteen years old. He actually saved his pennies—money he earned delivering food orders—so that he could go to an evening trade school when he was fourteen. He lied about his age and got himself a full-time job at a neighborhood meat market. He has been completely self-supporting: he lives alone and pays his own expenses. His mother threw him out last year because he wouldn't give her his whole pay—she's apparently quite an alcoholic. And how do we reward all this independence and initiative? We call him a delinquent and put him in a jail cell. Will you take this case and try to get him released?"

When I spoke to the recently appointed judge who had ordered him confined at Pennypack House on the recommendation of the school authorities, he was astounded. None of these facts had been presented to him; the boy had stood mute as the charges against him were read by the Board of Education representative. Unfortunately, he had not had a lawyer to speak for him because the prison, viewing the truancy charge as "non-serious," had not apprised the poverty program's handful of lawyers who try in vain to represent all poor children. After I intervened, the boy was released within a few hours. Since he was only sixteen and under the legal age for full employment, the Board of Education had to issue him a working certificate. As we filled out the forms I thought, How paper-obsessed we have become! Even when children escape the labyrinth, they continue to be pursued by paper demons!

In the past five or six years, many Americans have come to realize that poor children, especially the blacks, are pitifully short-changed and robbed of many birthrights we assume belong to all children. The complicity of unsympathetic and hostile teachers and school administrators in this spiritual larceny has become evident. In our work with children we have seen thousands of such instances. One ten-year-old was so convinced by his teachers that he was a dummy that he actually asked the staff supervisor at the Youth Detention Center for a book on dummies so that he would know how to behave correctly.

Dozens of strapping fifteen-year-old boys, although they were "technically" high school students, could not name the President of the United States, or even spell the most elementary words.

An alert sixteen-year-old girl told her probation officer that she had never heard of the United States Constitution or the Fourteenth Amendment. She had become interested in the legal battle to integrate Girard College, then a racially segregated boarding school for male orphans, and had read that the law on which the whole attack relied was something called the Fourteenth Amendment. Her probation officer, dismayed, began to poll other youngsters assigned to her. Not one of them knew what the Fourteenth Amendment says or means—or even what an amendment is.

No doubt many schools are beset by so many difficulties that it is easier to label troublesome students as *discipline* problems than to admit that some of them may have *learning* problems. But in that way the schools relieve themselves of the responsibility they have to *all* children, and to the community as well.

Another devastating anti-educational practice of school officials is to convey to a child their belief that he is worthless and hopeless, thus reinforcing the negative self-image the child has already developed outside school.

A friend who teaches in one of the best-rated junior high schools in Philadelphia told me that the school disciplinarian, who is just a tough teacher, *not* a counselor, has developed the following formula for dealing with problem boys. When the boy enters his office, the man does not invite him to sit down. He remains standing while the disciplinarian pores silently over a file—presumably the boy's dossier. Finally he looks up at the boy and says, "*I* know what you are. *You* know what you are. *You are a bum. A bum. Repeat after me, 'I am a bum.'*"

The surprised youngster chimes in and is instructed to keep repeating the words. After a dozen or so times the man says, "O.K. Now we're clear about what you are. If you give us any more trouble, off you go to Boone School!" (Most students know that this is a remedial-disciplinary school.)

Within the school system there are thoughtful, sensitive educators who shudder at the treatment meted out to disruptive, problem youngsters, who admit the system is but a step away from the whipping post. In their view, educators should help children to master their antisocial impulses, not treat them as pariahs. They believe that the present emphasis on lock-step conformity is destructive and self-defeating and that therapeutic techniques should replace the current policing and punitive measures.

Uniformed security officers are now assigned to patrol the movements of students in junior and senior high schools. Despite the fact that these students became accustomed to endless lining-up in their earlier grammar school years, they run wild and are unruly in and out of the classroom. If more thought had been devoted to proper "handling" of these children when behavior problems became visible at an earlier age, police officers would not have to patrol secondary schools. For years it has been apparent that ordinary classroom techniques alone could not do the job of helping these children develop inner controls, which they have failed to learn at home. While the Man is watching, there may be docile behavior and quiet corridors, but the police are not part of the learning team and their presence in schools is an open admission of the system's failure to provide a stable environment for all its youth.

Ironically, there are even situations when in order to learn a child must resort to criminal acts. Tall, somewhat gangling, neatly though shabbily dressed, Conrad Stanton seemed more embarrassed than any other fourteen-year-old thief we had ever seen. The charge on his court summary was larceny; the prosecutor, the Board of Education.

"What is this boy supposed to have stolen?" asked the judge.

The Juvenile Aid police officer shrugged his shoulders. "We have nothing on this case. The Board of Education filed the complaint with the Youth Study Center."

"I have the case, your Honor," said Mrs. Holmes, one of three Board of Education representatives who appeared frequently in court. Their deep compassion and interest in the children who came before the bar of juvenile justice was evident. Very often these trained guidance workers, through direct contact with the Board's Division of Pupil Personnel and Counseling, served as invaluable intermediaries between the court and the schools.

"Conrad is charged with stealing five art books from the Dobbins Vocational School. He took them over a period of time."

"Art books!" exclaimed the judge. "What kind of art books?"

"I don't really know," she replied. "I don't have a list. Perhaps Conrad can tell you, your Honor."

She signaled me with her eyes. I leaned over and she whispered, "He's a very good boy, and I think he must have had a valid reason for taking the books. The school counselor was very upset when I checked with her, but she said the vice-principal insisted on prosecuting."

"Conrad," the judge said, "you're charged with stealing art books. Do you want to tell me whether or not this accusation is true? And is there anything else you want to tell me about this? Speak up. This is your chance."

"Yes," the boy said quietly. "I'm ashamed that I'm here, but I did not really intend to steal them, Judge. I was just borrowing them for my own use. They are collections of reproductions of the Old Masters, and I wanted to copy them. There are good color plates that I needed especially."

"If you are interested in art, why didn't you ask your teacher?" queried the judge.

"That's just it. I don't have any art courses. They wouldn't let me major in art."

The Board representative nodded vigorously. "Conrad is absolutely right. There's a notation here that the boy is taking mechanical drawing and lettering, and that he had requested a transfer to Fine Arts but the head of the department did not approve it."

"Why not?"

"I'll tell you, your Honor," the boy said softly. "They don't think there's any future in it for a colored boy. The department head told me I should study something more practical. I don't like mechanical drawing and lettering and all that, although I'm doing well. I want to paint."

Close as he was to tears, Conrad threw his shoulders back with dignity and turned to look at the row of seats reserved for parents. A gray-haired, blue-denim-clad man sat by himself, clutching a large parcel.

"Daddy," said Conrad, "please come up here and show the judge."

The package was covered with crumpled brown wrapping paper and carefully tied with heavy, worn twine.

"What is in that package, Mr. Stanton?" I asked. "Has it something to do with Conrad's case?"

He nodded. "Yes, ma'am. These are his paintings and drawings. We brought them here to show you how hard this boy has been working, and how interested he is in art."

"Go ahead, untie it, sir," said the judge. "Conrad, it looks as if you have prepared a good defense." He smiled kindly.

"I hope so," said the boy, smiling back. He had an engaging, nice quality. The sheriffs, bailiffs, and other court workers moved closer as Mr. Stanton removed the wrappings.

On the bar of the court rested perhaps twenty-four paintings done in water color on the most unlikely surfaces: cardboard panels from soap cartons, corrugated paper wrappings, newspapers, even large pieces of heavily worn sheets. The boy had made use of anything he could find. These makeshift canvases were not an attempt to be original—necessity drove Conrad to seize whatever materials were available.

The paintings themselves were powerful and remarkably sophisticated. One still-life theme, a bunch of red flowers in a milk
bottle, recurred in several styles ranging from the strictly realistic
to a highly impressionistic treatment. There were many portraits, all
of them of famous white men and women. He had done a particularly
good head of John Glenn, the astronaut. As I bent over to look at it
more closely, Conrad said, "That's Colonel Glenn. I think he's great;
he has real courage. It's my favorite."

Even the most unknowledgeable among the court attendants
were nodding in amazement by the time we reached the last picture,
a painting of a sparsely furnished but cheerful living room. Tom
Gelson, the judge's official stenographer, was openly enthusiastic. A
connoisseur of the arts and a Negro, he was frequently appalled by
the social treatment of many of the poor children, black and white,
whose pathetic stories he recorded on his stenotype machine. His
generosity, like Judge Hoffman's, caused him to reach down into
his own pocket to pay for a needed "extra" which might help a child
over a hurdle. Although he never spoke of it, I knew he had offered
help to many children and parents.

"Your Honor," he said, "this boy has talent and drive. Since the
school won't teach him to paint, perhaps we can see that he gets instruction somewhere, somehow."

He got up and approached the judge, wallet in hand.

"I'd like to start a fund for this boy's art education," he said,
pulling out a twenty-dollar bill. "Maybe Mrs. Richette can suggest
a good place he can go after school or on Saturdays."

Several of the sheriffs and matrons reached into their pockets.
This boy had touched us all; we were determined to give him his
chance. Perhaps we were delighted to have found one youngster
whose need was simply an art course that money could buy. The
other children who moved us had deeper, more complex wants,
which, to their frustration and ours, were more difficult to fulfill. His
father lovingly collected the rags and cartons, rewrapped them, and
tied them.

"Your Honor, I wish I myself could afford to pay for lessons,"
he said, "but I'm receiving a disability pension. I try to do odd jobs
now and then. There are four other children at home, and my wife;
I just can't do it. I don't even have carfare to send Conrad to a
special course. I've gone to the school and begged them to let Conrad

change his major. They wouldn't budge. I didn't know he had taken those books. I don't approve at all, Judge. I've always trained Conrad to do right and obey the law. We'll return the books. I'm sure they are in good condition."

"Mr. Stanton," said the judge, "I don't have the power to tell the Board of Education what to do in this case. I can see from Mrs. Holmes' expression that it's hopeless to try. I think that Mr. Gelson's idea about arranging for art classes somewhere is a good one. I'm going to ask Mrs. Richette to look into this possibility. I take your word that the books will be returned immediately to the school. Conrad, I'm going to discharge you and order that all court records be destroyed. You won't be officially connected with juvenile court in the future, do you understand? We want to help you—but as friends and admirers! Good luck to you!"

Soon afterward I called Frank Graham, director of the excellent educational division of the Philadelphia Museum of Art. Before I could finish my résumé of Conrad's situation, he interrupted me to say that he was well aware of the bias against allowing disadvantaged children to study the fine arts. He himself had determined to admit as many of these children as possible into the various programs available at the Museum.

"Send him along this Saturday. There's only one problem: he'll need supplies, and we haven't any funds at the moment for that sort of thing."

As a past Sunday painter I knew how expensive a pursuit it was. I had a dear friend, a gifted lawyer, who was now devoting herself to painting. She was a woman of both means and compassion, and when I explained the problem, she agreed to establish a charge account for Conrad at a center-city art store on two conditions: that she remain anonymous and that the boy's purchases be restricted to twenty dollars a month.

"He should learn to buy what is essential. I don't want him to develop the bad habit of undisciplined spree-spending," she explained before she made the arrangements.

This subsidy continued for the remainder of Conrad's high school years.

One day, about six months after he had appeared in court, Conrad came into the judge's chambers with a package under his arm. He shyly presented it to the judge.

"I hope you like them, Judge Hoffman. I would be very proud if you would hang them here," he said. The package contained the striking portrait of John Glenn, but executed in oils this time, and a new painting of a woman in Elizabethan dress.

"Who's that?" asked the judge with a smile. "Conrad, I think she looks a little like Mrs. Richette. Was that intentional?"

"No," he said, "I don't think so. It's just a fantasy figure of a great lady. Like the lady who's paying for my supplies. I hope she comes in someday to see this painting."

After he graduated, Conrad served for two years in Vietnam. As soon as he returned, he came to see me. He had been wounded, but not seriously, and he had done many sketches of the war. He was uncertain about continuing with art school, although he said he would always paint. Finally he explained that he had to get a job to help his family. His father's health was worse than ever.

"What kind of job do you want, Conrad?" I asked.

"Oh, anything. Actually, I would like to learn about jewelry. I'd like to design, make, and sell it. Maybe open up a shop someday, with a gallery attached to it."

"That's a marvelous idea," I said. "Put me down as a reference if you need one."

Shortly afterward, I received a phone call from a bookkeeper for a large establishment on Philadelphia's Jewelers' Row. She wanted to know what kind of boy Conrad Stanton was. I gave her my most glowing recommendation.

"He hasn't been in trouble, has he? Not arrested for stealing or anything? You never know with *them*——"

I interrupted her, trying to contain my anger, "No, he hasn't. The boy is an artist, and he wants to learn to be a jeweler."

"Well, I hope you're right," she said dubiously.

After risking his life and his young manhood for his country, Conrad still had to convince people of his right to find the means to express his love of beautiful things.

With so many youngsters lost every year in the paper labyrinth of the public education system, it was exciting to learn in the early sixties of a new program launched at West Philadelphia High School by an English teacher, Mrs. Rebecca Segal.

Mrs. Segal, a dynamic, energetic woman, was distressed that the high school, once distinguished for academic achievement, in the past few years had failed to produce one student who was on the honor roll, much less one with the distinction of achieving a straight A average. She became convinced that many of the children could qualify for such honors, but they had simply given up trying.

In addition to her teaching duties, Mrs. Segal volunteered her services in setting up a program to search out and encourage talent in children during their early high school years. Such youngsters, selected on the basis of special tests and interviews she devised, would participate in an intensive program whose single goal was to motivate them to high achievement and spur them on to college and post-graduate work.

How to convince apathetic, discouraged pupils to take extra classes after school to strengthen their reading and mathematical skills? How to persuade them to spend some of their free time in the evenings or on week ends exploring new worlds—music, theater, art? Although Mrs. Segal did not start with any theoretical precon-ceptions, she was sure of one thing: the only way to make the pro-gram work was to love these youngsters, to care deeply what happened to them, and above all, to believe in their ability to grow and to learn.

The West Philadelphia Motivation Program, as it became known, was a smashing success. Knowing that these students also needed the support and encouragement of their parents, relatives, or foster parents, Mrs. Segal organized a parents' group which met monthly to share views and give each other assurance and support. Because many of the children lacked suitable adult models and did not know any college students, graduates, or professional people intimately, she also recruited prominent Philadelphians who agreed to open their homes to the youthful participants in the Motivation Program. Judge Hoffman volunteered his help and he and his gracious wife enter-tained informally many of these boys and girls.

As their horizons widened, these students became interested in politics, law, and government. Judge Hoffman conceived the idea of involving them in a television series entitled *Verdict by Another Jury*, sponsored by the local affiliate of CBS. Local attorneys and judges participated in the series, which consisted of miniature trials, complete with summations. The issues posed were the liveliest and thorniest currently in litigation. And the kids returned with their verdict.

I participated in several of these programs, and came away deeply moved by their responsiveness and their insight, and impressed by the factual knowledge they revealed. As we waited to tape the shows, they crowded around me and fired off civil liberties questions at me; then, even before I could answer, they would begin to debate the issues. They had poise, confidence; they were really attuned to everything going on about them. They were the first truly enthusiastic high school students from lower-class backgrounds I had met in years.

From an initial involvement with 475 students, the Motivation Program has expanded to include 4,700 teen-agers. Starting in one senior high school, it has now branched out to fourteen of Philadelphia's twenty-two high schools; even one technical school is now included. The whole structure is headed by its originator, Mrs. Segal, and each unit includes a coordinator, a cultural events liaison person, a secretary, a counselor, and special mathematics and English teachers.

Although the project has caught on, it is still struggling to overcome many limitations. For one thing, the selection process excludes children who may have the necessary qualifications but who have been repressed so long that they go undetected, despite the careful testing methods that have been devised. Also, there are not enough scholarships from private and public sources available for worthy but poor graduates. And, finally, many of the environmental struggles are so overwhelming that some youngsters who join the Program simply cannot surmount them. Very strong life lines are necessary to pull a boy or a girl back to safety, but they are not easy to find in this complacent throwaway society.

Mark Quincy, one of the children Mrs. Segal selected for the pilot program, almost slipped out of everyone's grasp. Unusual even in the circumstances of his birth, Mark was of Negro and Japanese ancestry, the natural son of an American Negro soldier serving in the Korean war and a Japanese mother. She abandoned Mark and his infant sister when he was two years old. Both children were rescued by another American Negro GI who arranged to adopt and bring them home to his wife in New York City.

He loved both children dearly, and they had a happy childhood.

Then, when Mark was eleven years old, the man died in an automobile accident, and his wife decided she could not keep both children. She sent Mark to Philadelphia to live with a girl friend and that friend's elderly aunt. When Mark entered high school, things were going smoothly. He had a week-end job at a neighborhood grocery store, and earned enough money to buy his own clothes. His foster mother and her aunt were happy with the situation and looked forward to the boy's leaving school and taking a full-time job as soon as he turned sixteen.

At West Philadelphia High School, Mrs. Segal immediately recognized Mark's potential and persuaded him to join the Motivation Program. He was articulate and very artistic. Without any lessons to speak of, he painted and sculpted creditably; soon he began to play several musical instruments. He particularly loved the theater and eagerly accepted a ticket every time they were offered to the students.

His foster mother, however, was annoyed with this change in activities and his loss of interest in his job and friends. She objected strenuously to his theater-going and to his new obsession with books. When he continued to pursue his new interests, the woman and her aged relative no longer wanted him around, and they sent him to live with a girl friend.

In that household, Mark's whole world began to cave in. His new foster mother, a nice enough person, lived with a wild, alcoholic, and violent boy friend who resented the boy's striking looks and intense, quiet manner. He began to berate the boy, accusing him first of being a faggot, then of seducing the woman. One wintry night a bloody battle raged; Mark, trying to protect the woman from the savage attacks of her wine-crazed lover, received a ferocious beating. Around midnight the man kicked him down the front doorsteps and locked the door firmly behind him.

Alone and desperate in the darkness of the ghetto streets, Mark walked to a nearby drugstore that was still open. With the few dollars in his pocket, he bought a large bottle of patent-medicine sleeping pills and a package of razor blades. Then he began to walk.

He walked for miles through the city streets until he reached Fairmount Park. He knew his way clearly now; he headed toward the area he loved best, the refuge he had found when he first came to Philadelphia: the beautiful Japanese Tea House donated by the citizens of Tokyo to the City of Philadelphia.

The house, nestling in a shady glen beside a shimmering pond, was locked, but the veranda was open. Its polished wooden planks gleamed in the moonlight. Mark sat down, opened the bottle, took eighteen of the tablets, and then slowly cut his wrists. He had finally come home, he thought, as he sank into a dazed sleep, hugging his bleeding, throbbing forearms against his body.

Toward early morning, a park guard found him half dead. His one wish, Mark moaned, was to be left alone to die. After a few weeks' convalescence in General Hospital, he was well enough to appear in juvenile court on a charge of attempted suicide.

Mrs. Segal, who visited Mark constantly in the hospital, realized that one glaring omission in her program—housing and foster homes —had very nearly been the boy's undoing. But there are no houses— nice or otherwise—for children who are rejected by everyone and literally thrown away into the streets like litter. Not in Philadelphia, not in any American city. Jails, detention centers, welfare and correctional institutions, yes. But a quiet, loving home where a boy or girl can live, study, and be understood is quite another thing.

Happily, one of Mark's teachers offered him a home. She and her husband appeared in court and advised the judge that Mark could live with them as long as he wished. With Mrs. Segal's support, and the opportunity to live in a household where learning was revered, the boy's whole outlook brightened. He received psychiatric counseling for a short period and then went on to graduate at the top of his class, winning a four-year scholarship to an outstanding college. He attends classes, lives at a Y, works in a professional theater group, and is very active in various cultural and political movements.

Mark the boy could find no other way to solve his problems than to use the ancient death ritual of the first culture that rejected him. Mark at nineteen is fully oriented to life and eager to explore the potential it holds.

It is absurd for adults—and tragic for children—to be deluded into believing that the present paper labyrinth is a feasible method for socializing and educating young people. Many alternatives are being put forward: decentralized schools, vestibule classes, community control of education, the Harlem street academies, and others. Despite the tumult and controversy raging about the American school system today, two major efforts must be mounted now to transform the labyrinth into a spacious air corridor for children and parents alike.

First: In addition to focusing on new facilities and the latest "hardware," educators must concentrate on teaching and helping all children to develop as worth-while human beings. They must give particular emphasis to those whose oppressed and difficult backgrounds have prevented them from developing a healthy image of themselves. Additional supportive services must be made part of the everyday school experience. Instead of writing off these children as uneducable or disciplinary problems, they must be recognized as special challenges that, unheeded, will jeopardize the future of the American educational system as a whole.

During the preparation of this book, senior high schools in several major cities were plagued by serious problems seemingly rooted in racial problems. Actually, turmoil has been seething in the labyrinth for at least a decade. Such thorny issues as desegregation and racial balancing of student bodies and faculties are important, to be sure; but they should *not* divert the community and the school planners from guaranteeing each child both the right and a genuine opportunity to learn, no matter what his social, physical, or psychological handicap—and no matter what militants on the right and the left proclaim.

Ten years ago, emotionally disturbed children who could not get into the one residential school that the Philadelphia Board of Education had to offer (built in 1928 and actually designed for truants) were locked out of all other schools under "medical exclusion" rules. A high Board official says that the total number of such evicted children cannot be calculated, but his best estimate is that between eight hundred and a thousand children were thrown out each year. In 1968, the Philadelphia system for the first time opened in various schools thirty-nine special classes, each consisting of eight emotionally disturbed children and one teacher. So three hundred and twelve— slightly less than one-third of the total—have at least a chance. What of the other two-thirds?

On an equally small scale, two other pilot ventures have been started: an experimental school for typical underachievers and an extended Day Treatment Center for adolescent boys on probation, run in cooperation with the juvenile court of Philadelphia.

These innovations are modestly calibrated, and it is too early to evaluate them. Nor should we expect dramatic overnight transformations. But these are good beginnings, and we must encourage them and other imaginative programs that will offer children a new chance to learn.

Get-Set and Head Start, the highly publicized preschool programs, have wide emotional appeal and community support. They are not a total answer, but two parts of it. Other enriching, individually geared projects are needed to build on this excellent base. Such programs must be locked into the system at every level, from elementary to junior and senior high school. It is not easy to persuade policy-makers and ordinary citizens that the millions of dollars they cost are monies wisely spent. Even success—the best evidence—sometimes fails to persuade.

For example, the Motivation Program established by Mrs. Segal received in 1967 a two-year Federal grant to sustain it. The initial budget in the first year was slashed from $685,000 to $440,000; during 1968, a further cutback reduced it to $284,000. The funds were expected to run out as of June 30, 1969, unless other sources—nowhere in sight—were found. Yet last year, over 700 students who graduated from the Program went on to college—students who, in Mrs. Segal's view, "never would have gone, wouldn't have wanted to go, and wouldn't have gotten the College Board scores they got unless it were for the Program."

Second: Like other components of the youth services establishment, schools must stop dispensing to children, and especially to adolescents, what Edgar Z. Friedenberg and others have characterized as the "full nineteenth-century colonial treatment." This means that schools must give up the old premise that children have no rights, that they are "nonpersons" lacking the credentials of full citizenship. This assumption has given rise to exclusionary and punitive school procedures that violate the democratic and humanitarian values summed up in the Bill of Rights' phrase "due process."

The Supreme Court has opened up a new issue in the schoolroom by imposing due-process requirements in the juvenile courtroom. Why shouldn't constitutional rights be observed by superintendents, principals, and counselors whose "conferences" often produce decisions that radically affect whether or not the child shall go to school at all—and where? Logic tells us that of course legal protection of the right to a free childhood must include the right to a full educational experience. So, increasingly, educators will find that their kangaroo court systems will be scrapped, along with the disciplinary schools, orthogenic classes, and other relics of a bygone era. In a 1967 New York case (*Madera v. Board of Education*) the Court of Appeals for the Second Circuit heralded this significant development by ruling that lawyers should be present at *crucial* confrontations between the child and school authorities when the child's right to continue his education in his present school setting is at stake.

In another vital area—students' constitutional right to freedom of political expression—the U.S. Supreme Court on February 24, 1969, ruled in *Tinker v. Des Moines Independent Community School District* (*No. 21, October Term, 1968*) that students do not leave their status as United States citizens at the schoolhouse doorstep. Said Mr. Justice Abe Fortas for the majority of the Court:

> In our system, students may not be regarded as closed-circuit recipients of only that which the state chooses to communicate. In the absence of specific showing of constitutionally valid reasons to regulate their speech, students are entitled to freedom of expression of their views.

This case, which involved the right of students to wear black armbands in protest of the Vietnam war, presages a new spirit toward youth and, hopefully, the end of the nineteenth-century colonial treatment to which so many American children have been subjected. The Court emphasized, however, that their free speech rights are limited to conduct that does not disrupt school discipline and functioning.

This introduction of orderly, fair procedures into the school system is part of a broader legal and social movement to secure the long-overlooked rights of vulnerable members of our society. And who are more vulnerable than children? By making due process part of our school system we educate ourselves as well as the children involved. Computers and other gadgetry socialize neither children nor adults. On the contrary, they dehumanize. As Mr. Justice Brandeis so perceptively observed, "the true measure of this civilization must be found, not in lifeless artifacts, but in the vibrant solicitude it exercises toward the weakest and most defenseless in its midst."

The throwaway answer to the question Who Can Be Educated? cannot work. The schoolhouse threatens to become a barricade unless we guarantee that children may extract from their school years a deep and lasting meaning. To accomplish this goal, we must begin by redefining our concept of a school. Be it a store front, a reconverted old house, or a multimillion-dollar complex, a school is not a labyrinth for aimless wandering, but an open meeting-ground where the child and the adult, the student and the teacher, find each other.

14 ‗‗

MINI-FLOWER
CHILDREN:
THE NEWEST THROWAWAYS

Whan they first surfaced sometime in the spring of 1965 on both American coasts, they looked like victims of a vast shipwreck: disheveled, unbarbered, their clothing an improvised, bizarre rag collection plucked at random from stray cargo. In those great American ports of call, New York and San Francisco, they appeared in great numbers.

Philadelphia, a declining and less important terminal, witnessed the arrival of a much smaller contingent, but they bore the same shipwreck stamp. First they sauntered onto center-city streets in pairs. More and more appeared and, all at once, fifty of these pairs had flocked like sparrows to the center of Rittenhouse Square, an elegant, historic pocket park nestling against towered luxury apartment houses, stately churches, and a fashionable hotel. And there they have remained, their numbers burgeoning as more and more young people join this unique rebellion against the mainstream shibboleths of the American middle class.

At first the passers-by dismissed them as latter-day Bohemians or beatniks, a residue of rebels left over from the mid- and late fifties. But as the months passed, many perceived that these unwashed, unkempt boys and girls (it was often difficult to distinguish between them) perched on the stone walls or huddled at the base of the flower pond were something else again. But what? And where had they come from? Why were they not safely tucked away behind school and college doors, or working for the Peace Corps, or at home with their families?

The mass media noticed them too. *Time, Look,* and *Newsweek* emblazoned their identity in cover stories that were read across the nation: Here come the Flower Children! Variously characterized elsewhere as "the Freudian proletariat," "the cultural expatriates," and "the internal *émigrés,*" hippies were given an in-depth treatment in *Time* (July 7, 1967); the movement was aptly described as ". . . a transplanted *Lost Horizon,* a Shangri-La à go-go, blending Asian resignation and American optimism in a world where no one grows old."

Unlike other American migrants, the Flower Children came to fulfill not the traditional dreams but their own highly private and controversial vision of a new Jerusalem: Psychedelia, U. S. A. Their gospel was threefold—love, poverty, and drugs. Joining them seemed the only chance to "do your own thing," to uniquely express your unique uniqueness. Love—be it the sensation of skin against skin or a wordless empathy with everything around you—was the guiding principle. Poverty meant to want and therefore to need none of the material symbols of the hollow, lonely rat race. This was liberation beyond belief. And drugs, in this loving, free atmosphere, offered a mind-expanding experience that led to that final self-fulfillment: a soaring to Himalayan peaks of brilliant clarity and delight from which you could survey both universe and self, and find meaning and peace.

This was the rhapsodic manifesto I heard the hippies proclaim when I stopped to chat with them in Rittenhouse Square. It was more than curiosity that impelled me to listen: I had begun to notice younger and younger faces in the throng. One day in early 1967 I asked a boy his age. When an older girl assured him I was "safe," he confessed that he was thirteen. I was shocked. And according to the March, 1968, issue of *Esquire* Magazine, such "teeny-boppers" were being superseded by the micro-boppers, eight-to-twelve-year-olds. However, these children sound more precocious than hippie-like. There is still another group to emerge, but it is impossible to predict the childhood and adolescence patterns of the hippie babies, weaned on psychedelic drugs and molded by the hippie environment.

In the next few months I could see that the Flower Generation was not a static band of hippies in their late teens and early twenties, but a dynamic group enveloping hundreds of troubled adolescent boys and girls who thought they had at last found a formula for rebellion. Eagerly they accepted its outer trappings and learned, too late, its inevitable aftermath.

A teacher from an elegant private school . . . a gifted sculptor whose warmth and compassion shone through stone and metal . . . a surgeon of international renown. A politician from the upper policy-making echelons in a nearby state . . . an intimate friend whose poise and sophistication were her trade-marks . . . a well-groomed stranger who had learned of my interest in the mini-flower children. These were the parents who came to talk to me about their suddenly unmanageable youngsters: "Find them. Talk to them. Tell us what to do." This was why they had come.

Then the middle-of-the-night telephone calls. Tense, cultivated voices using unfamiliar terms: police district, Narcotics Squad, marijuana, speed. ("What on earth is speed?") I had no time to explain that it was the hippie name for the stimulant drug generically known as methamphetamine, which is prescribed for obesity, narcolepsy, Parkinson's disease, and some cases of minor mental depression. (Other trade names are Methedrine and the less familiar Desoxyn.)

After the calls, all-night vigils in police headquarters, where expensive tweeds and soft silks or furs were in odd contrast to the harsh lighting and the hard wooden benches. And the dialogue: "Oh, here he comes at last! Handcuffed? Why, he hasn't had his hair cut in at least a year!" . . . "When did she eat last? And *where* did she get those horrible clothes?" . . . "Look at that hideous freak he's with!" . . . "Where did she meet a character like that?" . . . "Will he go to jail?" . . . "What can we do with a girl who beds down with——*them?*"

Today, a lawyer who represents young people must more than ever be shockproof and resilient. And ever more aware of the huge gaps in community sensitivity as well as services needed to rescue these latest throwaways—the mini-flower children.

It was early when I set out across the park, but the usual crop of week-end runaways—the Monday morning newcomers, I called them—had already settled in for the day. No welcome wagon was needed here: acceptance was easy in the Square. The older hippies were outgoing and curious; like islanders, they were happy to share their small domain with the transients. Perhaps the visitors would become permanent residents if they found the life attractive enough.

I saw Cynthia, a hunchbacked, cerebral-palsy victim who had been jostled in and out of correctional institutions by her ashamed parents. They had tried to keep her locked up at home, but at the age of ten she began running away whenever she got the chance. A few months earlier, I had walked out of Older Girls' Court with her; she had wept bitterly when her parents refused to take her back and instead sent her to live at a YWCA. Now she was "hippified"; laughing, high on at least marijuana, she waved cheerily as I passed by.

Halfway across the Square, and all about me was the sound of young voices chattering in a new language. Hippie talk—a patois of hipster terms, prison slang, homosexual argot, and ghetto jargon. With the exception of certain policemen, only a criminal lawyer or a former Assistant District Attorney could master this "underground" vocabulary, for we had penetrated the hidden world of rejects and outcasts. These once-protected children identify, not with the blacks, as Norman Mailer's term "White Negro" implies, but with an even more oppressed American minority; thus their self-image as "White Indians."

I wove a path through tunics, boots, capes, Navajo shawls, and beads. The clothing was as much a badge of identity as it was a thrifty solution to the problem of what to wear when money and laundry services are scarce. The dirt was the final layer that obscured their middle-class origins in the Land of Duz.

As usual, I was looking for a runaway child, this time the bright sixteen-year-old son of a policeman. The father had frantically recounted his difficulties with Larry, who had been suspended from school because of his long hair. He had been missing for almost a week; his mother, terminally ill with cancer, had thought of me as a last resort.

With two hundred thousand estimated runaways in 1967, finding a youngster is more difficult than it used to be. And, for the first time in America's history, runaway girls outnumber boys. Several years ago, Senator Abraham Ribicoff proposed a bill to establish a Federal bureau to help parents and communities locate their young strays. No longer alone and resourceless, the flower children have an effective underground system by which they move each other quickly out of a parent's range of vision. Once hidden in warrenlike "pads," they are safe from Mommy and Daddy.

I caught sight of DMZ, a wizened twenty-two-year-old Vietnam veteran who had started out on "grass" while in the service and had ended up following Timothy Leary's exhortation to "drop out." DMZ came to my rescue: it was no longer "Larry" I was looking for, he told me; it was "Lancelot," a new hippie name adopted to symbolize rebirth. (This new identity is so important that one San Francisco hippie staged a funeral for his former self.)

DMZ pointed to a barefooted youth sitting on the asphalt walk with several flower-kids, all of them listening to guitar music. At the center of this impromptu love-in was the musician herself, a pre-Raphaelite-looking girl whose wide capelike sleeves fell over the gleaming wood as she strummed. I recognized Cristine, young heiress to an old fortune and rebel supreme. For the past two years she had deigned to talk to her parents only through her lawyers and theirs.

Had his father not told me, I would have wondered if Lancelot's blond, shoulder-length hair was *really* his. He could easily have been wearing a hairpiece, a not uncommon practice that allows boys to conform to the short hair style required to stay in school or keep parents quiet. But they buy or borrow hair in order to make the hippie scene.

"Hi," I said to the boy. "I'm Lisa Richette, a lawyer, and I want to talk to you, Lancelot. Can we go sit down on that bench? The rest of you are welcome to come and listen. No secrets."

Hippie etiquette requires that discussion be public and free from hang-ups about privacy. DMZ nodded approval as the kids and I sat down on a park bench. A small, red-faced girl who seemed not much more than thirteen years old held Lancelot's hand and stroked his knuckle joints with her dirty fingers.

As though he read my mind, he said abruptly, "This is Rudolph . . . Rudi," indicating the girl beside him. "She always has a red nose, Christmas Eve and every eve!" He grinned.

I joined in the general laughter. "Are you local, Rudi?"
She shook her head. I saw she was one of the silent ones. Was
she too frightened or too angry to speak?

"She comes from faraway," volunteered Cristine. "Upstate New
York, near the Canadian border," she added admiringly. Cristine's
flight involved only a few miles of travel from her Main Line mansion to the Square. "She's been loose for more than a year."

I merely nodded, having learned to master my amazement at these
twelve- and thirteen-year-old wanderers. I knew the difficulties such
kids faced—where to sleep, keep warm, hide from threatening figures
from the adult world; how to get food and the other necessaries of
life. But I also knew how much the hippie world looked like the
answer to a runaway's prayer.

However, my business was with Lancelot and I turned to him
again. I was here, I said, to arrange a meeting, and perhaps an accord, between him and his father.

It was with great reluctance that Lancelot agreed to a meeting at
my home that evening. "It's useless. You'll see. He has a Nazi mentality—like the rest of the fuzz." The group tittered. "You promise
I can leave alone, I'll see him. No threats, no beatings, or I'll——"

He did not complete his ultimatum. Like so many children, he
had learned to manipulate, but he was scared.

That night Lancelot arrived thirty minutes late—a bad sign. I
had a feeling the meeting would be a difficult one for both father
and son. I was right. Lancelot's glare at the older man was his only
greeting. As I started to explain that his parent's concern was genuine, his jaw tightened and he cut me off with the gutter vernacular
that is the prize weapon of protesting youth:

"I won't listen to this shit. He doesn't give a fuck about me. He
just can't stand the thought of having a hippie son. And he can't
have me arrested. What would his superior officers say?"

He had flung down the gauntlet. To my surprise, his father, unlike most parents who encounter defiance, remained calm. He quietly
reminded the boy that he was a minor and had to live with his family
or be sent to an institution.

"Look!" Lancelot told him angrily. "I'm not coming home. I'm
staying with Aunt Peggy. And I don't have to cut my hair! I can
go back to school too. My marks are okay and I told the principal

he should worry more about what goes on *under* my hair. As long as I push it back, away from my face, the school district isn't going to make a test case out of *me!*"

The boy was right. In every hair case in Philadelphia, whenever a lawyer for the American Civil Liberties Union challenged a principal about a suspension, the child was readmitted; therefore the propriety of the school code regulations concerning dress and hair length had never been put to a court test.

"What's Aunt Peg like?" I asked.

"She's all right." The boy nodded to emphasize his words. "She tries to groove with me. She even took me to the shrink she works for. He's all right too. He gave me a letter—want to see it?"

As I unfolded the letter, his father explained that Peggy was a divorcée and childless. She was, I gathered, in his judgment also a stray.

The letter was authentic, signed by a well-known psychiatrist for whom Aunt Peg worked. The doctor said he had interviewed the boy and concluded that the home tensions were so great it would be best for him to live with his aunt. How clever of Lancelot to be armed with this safe-conduct pass. As long as he produced it, he was neither a runaway nor a vagrant. Aunt Peg undoubtedly would cover for him.

"And do you stay with her on week ends?" I asked.

He readily admitted that he frequently went to New York.

"It's unbelievable," said his father, shaking his head. "I went to New York for the first time when I was thirty, on my honeymoon. But then I had to work when I was a boy; I've worked all my life to——"

"Here it comes," said Lancelot disgustedly. "The Eroica Symphony. My father, the big, all-sacrificing martyr. Big shot. What about the time you left Mom for a month to go with that whore? And all your boozing! He's a head, too," he said to me, "a booze head."

And what kind of head are you? I wondered. (Head is jargon for an addict of any kind.) The best heads on the Square at that time were the "acid heads," the regular users of LSD-25 (d-lysergic acid diethylamide), the best known and most widely used of the hallucinogens, or mind-expanding drugs. (Others include Mescaline, a chemical derived from the peyote cactus, and Psilocybin, extracted from Mexican mushrooms.)

"Look, Lancelot," I said, "your father is trying to talk decently about this situation. Do you think it's fair to talk the way you have just now? Why don't you try to show some love for him? Isn't that a big part of your thing—loving everybody? Why not include your father?"

"I can't. I hate him. I know I shouldn't, but he won't let me alone. He wants me to go to college, to be a lawyer or an accountant or something. I want to write. He thinks that's just an excuse to be a bum."

"No, I don't," his father interjected. "If you want to be a writer, go ahead. But you need a college degree, maybe an M.A. too. Just sitting around in some filthy apartment doesn't make you a writer."

Lancelot got up and started to walk out of the room. His father clutched at his arm.

"Don't touch me," the boy said coldly. "Or do you want to beat me up again? Go ahead. I won't hit you back. You can beat me up, but you can't make me come back."

"What about your mother? You know she's got cancer. The doctor doesn't give her too much time."

"Damn you," whispered the boy. "I don't want to hear about her." He began to cry. "I nursed her for two years. I know she's going to die. There's nothing I can do. She just lies there and hassles me. She calls me a queer. Yes, she's dying, but so are babies in Vietnam. Don't pull that one, Dad!"

It was the first time he had acknowledged his father's relationship to him. And with that single "Dad," he ran out of the house.

Before Lancelot's father left, he shook his head in discouragement. "I don't know what to do. His mother doesn't want him to be put in a correctional institution, but I just can't sit by and let Larry do this to himself. What it boils down to, I guess, is that I'm really helpless. I can't win no matter what I do . . ."

Several weeks later Aunt Peggy called me: Lancelot had failed to return from his week-end trip to New York. It was Wednesday and she was worried. "He's never done this before," she added.

Was he with anyone? Yes, she thought he had gone with Jeff— did I know him? I had not spoken to him, but I had seen him in the park and knew he was an on-again, off-again flower child who shifted from the Square to his parents' country estate and back again. I told her there wasn't much we could do at the moment, but I'd ask around the Square.

The hippies confirmed that the two boys were missing. Their opinion of Jeff? He was a nice "plastic" hippie—an amiable fake who was not really committed to hippiedom but dressed and talked as if he was.

"He's never blown his mind," said Frog, an eighteen-year-old Negro whose chick, Daisy Mae, was a ringer for the Al Capp heroine, curves, tattered skirt, blonde hair, and all. "He's faked a couple of blasts, but he doesn't fool us! He's a good cat. He comes through with bread."

Obviously, Jeff was just a nice upper-middle-class boy who was generous to needy hippies. In order to be accepted in the group, he pretended to use psychedelic drugs.

I was relieved. Lancelot was in responsible company; he would bob up again in the park. So many kids do, unless . . . Unless someone knifes them or blasts them in some hideous tenement basement and they end up dead, like Linda Fitzpatrick and the famous New York hippie "Groovy," alias James Hutchinson. They had been murdered in New York's East Village, the large hippie gathering-place to which Lancelot and Jeff presumably repaired on week ends.

Late that same night, I was startled out of sleep by the pounding of my door knocker. Alone with my small son in the house, I went to the door somewhat apprehensively.

"It's Jeff," a voice called back in reply to my query. "I've got Lancelot. Please let us in."

I opened the door, and there stood Jeff in his usual violet tunic and black satin levis. He was holding Lancelot, but when the boy pulled away and staggered in, he fell down with a hard thud on the marble steps of our foyer.

"What's the matter with him?" I asked.

"Bad LSD trip," said Jeff. "He's been on it for three days. He seems really out of it. I didn't know where to take him. He wouldn't go to his aunt's. I thought you could help us."

"At two o'clock in the morning? The only place we could get him emergency medical care is a hospital."

I had read Fact Sheet Number 5 from the Bureau of Drug Abuse Control (August 25, 1966), and I knew what trouble we might be in for with Lancelot:

> Eating, inhaling, or injecting even as small a quantity of LSD as 1/280,000 of an ounce causes symptoms ranging from hallucination, distortion, and intensification of sensory perception to panic, impulses toward violence, suicidal acts, and psychosis. These effects, totally unpredictable and varying widely from person to person, may last from eight to ten hours, and recur without taking the drug again.

When I suggested to Jeff that we take his young friend to a near-by hospital, Lancelot pulled himself up. "I'll kill myself! I want to die anyway. Don't take me to the hospital! They'll call my father! I'll be busted [arrested]; he'll be disgraced—lose his job. NO! NO!" he screamed.

"He's been this way for days. He almost jumped off the eleventh floor at a friend's pad. Just now, while I was parking my car, he opened the door and jumped right out into the street. Good thing there's no traffic at this hour! He has a real big death-wish, this cat."

"Look, Jeff," I said. "My husband is away. I'm alone here with my little boy. Lance can stay here, but *with you here too*. It's too late to call a doctor—we'll wait until morning to work something out. Take him into the library while I make some coffee."

I returned to find Lancelot propped up on a couch. Looking at his ravaged face, I saw that underneath the dirt there were hard little pimples and a few running sores where he had undoubtedly scratched at them. His eyes alternately burned with exaltation and drooped with exhaustion.

"I'm brilliant," he suddenly cried, tossing his head deliriously. "Wait until you hear me. I sound like James Joyce. Example: in lawyer's lady-lair lies Lancelot all lots unlanced and lances unlotted, and God, the one-eyed Gorgon gasser, gasses off in gaseous great fart! . . . Oh," he wailed, "I'm melting into this sofa! God, I'm going to melt into one big gray and red glob! I feel my brain melting out of my head! Stop it! STOP!"

In the silence that followed his outburst, he wrapped both arms around his head and filled the room with a blood-curdling shriek, "*Aieee!*"

Then he looked up and went rigid, his hand pointing at the television set. "That monster! Look! He's going to devour me. Save me!" In terror he flung himself on the floor and lay there trembling.

"How long did you say he's been like this?" I asked, deeply concerned for the boy.

"Two or three days." Jeff paced the room worriedly. "He started this trip in New York—I don't know how I ever got him back here. I thought we'd both die in a wreck. On the turnpike I had to hold him down with one arm. Imagine driving all the way like that! Say, Mrs. Richette, don't you have *anything* to give him?"

I said I had nothing that would do the trick, but assured him that Lance would be safe until we got him to a psychiatrist, who would administer an antidote to the LSD.

It was a long, ghastly, and frightening night for all of us save my small son who never once woke up. Lancelot would not lie down or go near a bed. When he tried feebly to drink a small amount of milk, he began to retch violently. He had no control over urination or defecation. Once he rubbed against the refrigerator and said he was welding himself to it. "The ultimate cool!" he exclaimed. Then he opened the door and tried to sit inside.

As the Joycean stream of language continued to flow, I put on a tape recorder and filled one tape in less than an hour. I knew I could never remember that terrifying onrush of words. Finally, sometime near dawn, Lancelot stood wearily against the library wall, squinted one eye, and said he was going to try an owl-nap, a wise-sleep. Then he sank into a near-by chair and dozed fitfully for about an hour.

While he slept, Jeff and I, fortified by uncounted cups of coffee and each other's presence, talked quietly.

"What are you both doing in this scene?" I asked. "Listen to that boy; such a beautiful mind gone awry. And you, Jeff, you're not really in it—not yet. You're just flirting, but you're getting awfully close to the edge. I know your father slightly [he was general counsel for a large manufacturing firm] and I'm sure he isn't aware of what you're doing. What about your mother?"

"Look," he answered, "she's all right, I guess. But she's square. You know: horses, cocktail parties, dances, all that bit. God, the whole thing turns me off! I'm bored, I guess. I told Mom about Lancelot, how his mother is dying and all. She told me to invite him to live with us. Poor Lance! You know, I would never admit it, but I was afraid to blow my mind. Now I'm glad I didn't!"

A couple of hours later I called Lance's father, and he came for the boy and took him to the psychiatrist I recommended. Jeff's mother invited Lance to recover at their house. The visit extended into a long-term stay. Lance transferred to the high school Jeff attended, and graduated with decent marks at the end of the year.

The following year, both boys enrolled at a city college, Lancelot because he still thought he wanted to be a writer and Jeff for no particular reason other than that he was accepted. By the end of the first semester, Lancelot had decided to be a painter. After he transferred to an art college, Jeff stayed on and became part of an activist antidraft movement.

Although Lancelot no longer lived at Jeff's house, they saw each other frequently and came, singly or together, to visit me. The Damon-Pythias relationship was less strong, but it had helped each boy weather his adolescent crises. They went back to the Square nostalgically from time to time, but left quickly.

"It's changed," Jeff told me. "It's not a fun place any more. The kids freak out in frightening ways. Remember Rudi, the red-nosed reindeer? She's a total freak-out, a super speed-head. She was arrested with an older woman who was on scag [heroin]. Rudi jumped bail and blew."

The irony, said Jeff, was that he had given her a button that reads *Speed Kills.*

It is undeniably difficult for parents to maintain an understanding and flexible attitude toward children who, seemingly overnight, are transmogrified into rebellious, hairy strangers. More frequently, they panic and press all the wrong buttons, causing an already volatile situation to blow up in everyone's face. One button that triggers a backfiring mechanism is commitment of the child to either a detention center or a psychiatric hospital. Both types of "lock-up" take children on a parent's say-so. All they need to obtain are two affidavits by physicians requesting a ten-day emergency commitment. Private hospitals, although expensive, have a constant supply of available beds. The hope is that the youngster will come to his senses and "stop all this nonsense." Now the backfiring begins. The child usually cons everybody by accepting the bribes offered by the now-guilt-ridden parents and assuring the psychiatrist of a change of heart and high resolves. Once released, he goes right back to his old ways—but this time makes sure that his family doesn't find him so easily.

These youthful offenders do not find sympathetic response outside the home either. One talented young musician who had driven his parents to distraction with both his hair and his rock-and-roll combo found himself in Pennypack House as an "incorrigible." When the juvenile court judge, repelled by his behavior and appearance, ordered the boy back to jail "for further studies," the youth whipped out a straight razor he had wheedled out of an adult inmate and slashed his wrists at the bar of the court. At the city hospital he explained to the psychiatrists that he preferred *their* jail. They returned him to the court with the recommendation that his parents allow him to perform with his group. They did so, reluctantly. Today, he is an up-and-coming figure in the rock-music scene.

Lambchop, a shy, auburn-haired fourteen-year-old, had no problem eluding her parent. In the year that the girl was away from home, her mother made *one* inquiry at the Square. When the kids said her daughter was doing well, she turned on her heel and returned to her home community two hundred miles away, never to be heard from again. Even Lambchop's hand-drawn Mother's Day card, which bore a return address, did not evoke a response. But Lambchop had other big problems.

"I'm in trouble," she told me softly. "Maybe you can send me somewhere. I'm pregnant, and I think I have syphilis."

When Lambchop was eleven, her father, a factory supervisor, died. Within a year her mother remarried a widower with three children of his own. Lambchop did not get along with any of them, and she was blamed for the unhappy home life. Her mother, desperate to make the marriage work, told her she was sending her to a correctional school. Lambchop short-circuited that event by running away to Philadelphia.

At the bus terminal she met two kids who took her to the Square. Before nightfall she was the chick of a groovy spade cat who took her to a crash pad. (I knew this particular pad, having visited it in search of another runaway child. Ironically, it was in a slum area almost in the shadow of the courthouse. And with rows of mattresses lined up only a few inches apart, it looked like the gymnasium floor of the Youth Study Center where the overflow of throwaway children slept. The four-room apartment could accommodate up to thirty.) For about six months Lambchop lived there. She had sex with anyone who wanted to; it was nice to feel close. Then, one night she took too much speed and "zonked" (became deranged). She does not remember what happened, but she thinks that she turned on many men and boys for a couple of days. When she came to, the spade cat said she had to leave. Lambchop walked to the Square and met Stanley, a twenty-six-year-old white hippie who took her to East Village.

A hopelessly addicted ex-convict who needed several "fixes" a day, Stanley put Lambchop to work on the street. One day he just left without a word. Seemingly unmoved, Lambchop got a ride back to Philadelphia, where a kindly hippie couple took her in. She found a cat and called it "Happiness."

Now she stood before me stroking it, asking my help. She accepted my word that going to a clinic I recommended would not result in her being busted. Several days later she showed me a lab report indicating (a) she was pregnant and (b) she had a minor venereal disease. I could see that she was terrified, but she promised to return the next day to make future plans. She hurried off with her cat and never came back. The kids say she is not in New York either. Who can tell the end of her throwaway history?

Then there was Jonathan, a fifteen-year-old "speedster" and a self-proclaimed warlock. He read demonology and was convinced that he had actually made a four-year pact with the devil. Thus he had supernatural control and power over himself and others. Yet he carried a cane, a tacit admission that, the pact notwithstanding, he was crippled. After his last arrest, I was able to arrange for his evaluation at a psychiatric center. Although immediate therapy was recommended, the Mental Health Division advised me not to count heavily on its availability. Acutely schizophrenic children by the dozens were in line ahead of him. Nevertheless, by twisting an arm here and there, I finally got him a bed in an adolescent unit. In a few months, Jonathan improved noticeably and forsook witchcraft in favor of chess.

Lucretia is less lucky. A thin black girl with an elongated neck and a handsome natural cut, she became hooked at thirteen by her twenty-year-old white lover who pushed pills and hard drugs in a three-state area. She is the darkest member of his harem, and her position is shaky due to her youth. She has tried every "high," yet is constantly low-spirited. At her request, I asked her mother to take her back. A God-fearing fundamentalist, the woman said the girl was too full of sin to come home. When I suggested a Catholic training school, she smiled. Even though they used incense, she said, she was sure they, too, would find her "sinful." So Lucretia clings to the pusher, and to the needle, and each time hopes the hurt will be lessened and the "high" higher.

As toward other throwaway groups in this country, the community stance toward the flower children is negative, disapproving, and punitive. Apart from a handful of interested private professionals, who are the official intermediaries from the Establishment to this new group?

The emissaries dispatched to convey not greetings but displeasure are the gentlemen in blue—the police. Ordered to "clean up" the kids' meeting places, they plow in and try to make them leave. Encountering passive resistance, open hostility, or, occasionally, unexpected bursts of affection, the police have no choice but to place the youngsters under arrest and remove them from the scene forcibly for brief intervals.

The futility of such police–flower children confrontations is almost self-evident. Arrest, punishment, jails, mean little to youngsters who have already allied themselves psychologically with the untouchables of America. All that police interference does is reinforce their alienation and the accompanying negative self-image.

In the summer of 1967 the Philadelphia police authorities carried out mass arrests and mopping-up operations in Rittenhouse Square. Two raids, one on June 17, the other on July 15, brought in about thirty-five persons. Several nonhippie observers who protested the arrests were also taken in. After several hours of questioning, all were released.

After the second raid, David Pittinsky, a young Yale Law graduate associated with a large firm, volunteered his services to the local chapter of the American Civil Liberties Union, an organization that defends the constitutional freedoms of citizens. Together with Julian

Goldberg, general counsel for the chapter, he drafted a unique complaint filed by three hippies as representatives of the whole class of hippies against the Police Commissioner of Philadelphia and the Director and Superintendent of the Fairmount Park Commission in whose bailiwick the affairs of Rittenhouse Square fall.

The sixteen-page complaint charged the defendants with violating "under color of state law" Fourteenth, First, and Fourth Amendment rights guaranteed to all citizens. Under provisions of the Federal Civil Rights Act the hippie petitioners asked for a court order to restrain the defendants or their agents from further interfering, either temporarily or permanently, with these rights.

After the complaint was filed, the lawyers began to wonder: Would the hippies responsibly re-enter the inner sanctum of straight society—the courtroom? Above all, would they testify coherently in straight language comprehensible to a Federal judge?

At a preliminary conference on July 26, the Honorable John P. Fullam, Judge of the United States District Court for the Eastern District of Pennsylvania, refused to issue a temporary restraining order, but set the case down for hearing two days later.

David Pittinsky, who lives near the Square and visits it frequently, quickly notified the hippies that they would be expected at the United States Courthouse at Ninth and Chestnut Streets early on the morning of July 28. He could sense immediately a new excitement on their part, completely different from their usual "cool" state.

Pittinsky had warned Judge Fullam that he represented clients who did not dress conventionally.

"I don't think it will be a problem," the judge said calmly. "If it is, I will let you know."

But no one, including Pittinsky, was quite prepared for the action on the day of the trial. About one hundred and twenty-five hippies arrived promptly—indeed, some had been waiting for hours— and entered the courtroom barefooted, bearded, hair flowing. Two hippie girls scattered rose petals along the corridor, singing soft love songs as they pattered along the marble floors.

Judge Fullam's composure during the day-long hearing was exemplary; he seemed not to notice the bare feet and the dirty visages. That he was acutely "grooving" to every aspect of the hippies is evident in the gentle statement in his opinion that some hippies "have so completely rejected the middle-class value of cleanliness that their very presence in the courtroom was an olfactory affront."

But, clean or dirty, all the plaintiffs' witnesses recited essentially the same narrative. Repeatedly and almost on a daily basis, police and park guards took groups of hippies into the small guardhouse at one end of the Square. There they were questioned about their possible homosexuality, their views on the Vietnam war, whether or not they were Communists, and their general nonconformity. There were several isolated episodes of face-slapping, kicking, and other abuse. To all these indignities the hippies submitted rather passively.

Patrick Hughes, one of the plaintiffs, testified that on one occasion earlier in the spring the policeman interrogating him in the guardhouse smacked him in the face. When Hughes did nothing, the policeman asked, "You won't even throw up your hands, will you?"

Hughes' testimony continued. "And I said, 'No, I won't. It would be ridiculous.' He said, 'Why, you are a punk,' and I got smacked again. And I said, 'Now, you have four friends outside the door with sticks. I am not throwing up my hands to you or anyone else in this guardhouse.'"

Other nonhippie witnesses stated that on the evenings of the two mass arrests, no overt illegal acts had occurred: the Square had been peaceful and the plaintiffs had been suddenly set upon for no apparent reason.

On cross-examination of the police witnesses produced by the defense, it appeared that the arrests were carried out not because the police were looking for runaways (none of them had a list of runaways with them at the time) or drug pushers and addicts, but simply because several "known" homosexuals were talking to people who seemed to be juveniles. Some time before the trial, David Pittinsky had chatted with a park guard who said he was very upset because the lawyer seemed to be on some kind of "crusade" on behalf of the hippies. When Pittinsky said he was concerned that the hippies were being subjected to illegal harassment, the guard had replied that he was paid to harass them; those were his orders.

At day's end, the hippies left the courtroom in a happy frame of mind. They embraced Pittinsky and Goldberg and called them "groovy, beautiful people." And they promptly went back to the Square.

Although Judge Fullam did not hand down an opinion until April 11, 1968, and no restraining order had been issued, a marked easing occurred in the police–hippie confrontation. There were no more mass arrests and no more interviews in the guardhouse for the rest of the summer and fall. One or two isolated episodes of harassment were promptly reported to Judge Fullam, who called in the Assistant City Solicitor to see what could be done to work things out.

One problem worried both hippies and lawyers. Upon being taken into custody, the entire group had been photographed, fingerprinted, and questioned extensively about their sexual orientation, political affiliations, religion, and general habits. Photographs and interview sheets were locked in police files, available for any future use.

When Judge Fullam's opinion appeared, it completely vindicated the hippies' right to enjoy the Square, its walks, pool, and benches, without any police interference. Although Judge Fullam surveyed all the available literature on the hippie movement, he did not rule on whether or not the plaintiffs could bring action on behalf of the whole class of hippies. Since they clearly could sue in their own behalf, he would decide the issues posed by the case.

The police could not arrest individuals merely because they had adopted a life style that ran counter to prevailing mores. "It is not a crime to be a 'hippie,' " the opinion states firmly, "and the police could not lawfully arrest on the basis of suspicion, or even probable cause to believe that the arrestee occupied the status of being a homosexual or narcotics addict." On the principle that "our criminal laws are directed toward actions, not status," Judge Fullam effectively ruled illegal any future arrests of hippies carried out solely because they are the unwashed plague of the parks and squares.

"It is quite clear from the record in this case that the primary motive for the various arrests and interrogations referred to above was a desire to rid Rittenhouse Square of 'hippies' or at least those 'hippies' thought to be homosexuals, narcotics-users, or otherwise especially undesirable." Continuing, Judge Fullam notes that "there have been throughout our history, many analogous attempts to apply the police-power of government to protect the conventional majority from too-close association with the unpleasant or undesirable minority."

Reviewing many cases and authorities, the opinion concludes that this is an unlawful exercise of police power. Judge Fullam did not issue a permanent injunction, preferring rather to keep the matter open under his jurisdiction as "a precautionary measure." He stated that the police and Park Commission officials, as reasonable men, would take the proper steps to rectify the situation. And, finally, he ordered that all record of the mass arrests of June 17 and July 15 be expunged and that all photographs be returned or destroyed.

The police withdrew; the hippies jubilantly staged a love-in at A.C.L.U. headquarters; the matrons, bankers, and pensioners were more outraged than ever. No one stepped in to fill the vacuum left by the police withdrawal from the scene. During the late spring and summer of 1968, the kids lounged on the grass—some even smoked "grass"—and the hippie colony, confident that no further disruptions would occur, did its thing.

Once the police activities halted, the sullen community ran out of ideas. Yet, positive, nonauthoritarian programs were being tried elsewhere. These small-scale projects were designed to get at the underlying causes of alienation while attempting to reverse the polarizing life patterns that separate the hippies and their mini-friends from the adult world.

In San Francisco a medical clinic offered help to ailing love children suffering from hepatitis, respiratory infections, and venereal and other diseases to which this group is particularly susceptible.

In New York and California new techniques of therapy for young drug addicts were tried at Daytop and Synanon with strikingly successful results.

In Philadelphia in the late winter of 1968 a small pilot venture, Gaudenzia House, adopting the Daytop technique of "encounter group therapy," offered help to a score of self-referred addicts from the area.

In Washington, D.C., the "Mustard Seed" opened in the basement of a Georgetown Presbyterian Church to serve hot meals and offer counseling to hippies.

In Philadelphia one well-organized effort came from the hippies themselves in the form of a short-lived, self-help "Digger" operation that offered indigent hippie youth food and clothing.

The mini-flower children need what other throwaways need,

and much more. Father David Gracie, Philadelphia's Episcopalian Urban Missioner, sees their needs as fourfold: (a) legal representation and assistance in their confrontations with the law (in Philadelphia largely provided by the local A.C.L.U. chapter and a few individual professionals on a mainly volunteer basis); (b) medical treatment; (c) emergency and longer-term housing; and (d) an educational program based on noncoercive principles to teach them useful skills.

He sees the community's failure to fulfill any of these needs as part of a larger failure to implement its avowed ethical and moral beliefs. What is the hippie philosophy but a reaffirmation, in part, of the core of Judeo-Christian philosophy? That young people reject present-day society is more our failure than theirs to translate its precepts and directives into action.

Rittenhouse Square, a microcosm of the American scene, documents this nonfulfillment and tells us "where we are at." Within its perimeter, complacent, successful people sit, watching the well-cared-for toddlers—the "nice" children—at play. All around the park live and work some of the most talented, educated, and resourceful citizens of the community: doctors, scholars, lawyers, artists, executives, musicians.

In the center are the throwaway mini-flower children and their older companions, the hippies. The uncommitted all around the park scarcely look at or think about this bizarre, unwashed group: they feel no connection with them, no responsibility. Their only concern is that there be no unpleasantness, no disturbance of the peace.

And what about the four established and thriving religious institutions standing as cornerstones to the west, south, and east: an Episcopalian and a Roman Catholic church, a conservative synagogue, and a humanistic Ethical Society group? They seem as indifferent to human need and suffering as the private citizens. Their doors remain closed to the flower-tots. Late at night the kids sit on their steps, waiting . . .

Everybody hopes they will go away—but they won't. Until we invite them in, become involved, they will remain.

It is a scene whose dimensions were laid bare by T. S. Eliot in his masterpiece "Ash Wednesday," another expression of where we are as a compassionate, life-oriented society:

> Will the veiled sister pray for
> Those who walk in darkness . . .,

Those who are torn on the horn between season and season,
time and time, between
Hour and hour, word and word, power and power, those who
wait
In darkness? Will the veiled sister pray
For children at the gate
Who will not go away and cannot pray:
Pray for those who chose and oppose.

[Italics added.]

PART FOUR

THE LAW AND THE THROWAWAY PROCESS

PART
FOUR

PROLOGUE

O n June 4, 1959, a fifteen-year-old "model boy"—polite, attractive, an honor student at a private preparatory school—walked up to a detective and said, "I killed her. I stuffed her body in a basement closet in my house."

With those words, the ten-hour frantic search for a missing three-year-old girl ended. She was the child of the boy's neighbors: his older sister had been their baby-sitter.

As law enforcement officials, police investigators, and juvenile court personnel faced the task of preparing legal procedures against the boy, they and the shocked community searched for both an explanation of the terrible deed and a directive from somewhere as to what should be done with a model boy who suddenly, senselessly, kills a little girl.

From the most unexpected quarter of all, the victim's father, came their answer. In an open letter to Philadelphia—and America— published by the *Evening Bulletin* on the front page of all its editions that day, he pleaded for a change in the throwaway process that characterizes much of the law's stance toward deviants:

Dear People of Philadelphia:

I write to you this morning, at the rise of dawn, still in the midst of a tormented wake, of the most terrible grief which has ever seared my soul.

Yesterday afternoon, on June 4th (as you most certainly read in the papers), I lost the most precious thing that life ever gave me—a 3½-year-old girl child of surpassing purity and joy; a being profoundly close to the secret well springs of life itself—a closeness from which she derived great unconscious strength which made her irresistibly attractive to human beings with whom she came in contact.

She was murdered in the afternoon, in the basement of a house only a few doors away from ours, by a 15-year-old boy.

I beg your indulgence in speaking with what must surely seem like fatherly bias about my child that was killed.

I have mentioned her special qualities because I believe that they are essential to understanding what happened to her. My letter to you is motivated by an irrepressible wish to contribute my share of understanding to what has taken place in the hope of thus slightly increasing our understanding for one another.

The first most important facts to which to draw attention are the facts about the boy who did the deed, and his family.

So far as one could tell, the family was exemplary. In public appearance they have always been considerate and kind; their house has always seemed very well managed. People and property, both, always gave the appearance of great tidiness.

The daughter of the house—who is now studying nursing in Washington, D.C.—used to baby-sit for us last year, and always conformed to the highest standards of courtesy and efficiency.

The boy himself, as you read in the papers, has also always given an excellent formal account of himself—honor student, gentle in manner, handsome, and all the rest.

How then, you will exclaim in horror, can all this good come to such an ill result?

I would plead that it comes from a profound lack of comprehension and admission of the full range of feeling and emotion, which is our common human heritage, and which, for convenience's sake, we are so fond of denying.

For the sake of a most immature passion for self-esteem—perhaps immature in the development of our race rather than in the development of an individual human—we are wont to label everything which we prefer to stuff into a closet (even as was done to my child) as *"inhuman."*

So, for example, did we speak of the Nazis with their indescribably horrible concentration camps.

It is in this way that we permit ourselves to divide the fullness in each of our breasts into two dissociated parts—one part ascribed to the hero, the model boy, the ideal father, and the other part to the criminal, the deranged, the villain.

I am not—as you might wrongly conclude—suggesting that we are all fundamentally "bad" and should therefore spend our lives feeling guilty for what we are.

I say instead that it should be openly recognized that every human being *must*, by his nature, express hostility, rage, fear, destructiveness, as well as love, creativeness in action, pure joy of life, and other generally recognized desirable responses.

And in regard to the need for expressing these "positive" as well as "negative" responses, there is an iron-clad law according to which all that goes unexpressed will not thereby be eliminated, but will assert itself in often uncontrolled and uncontrollable ways.

Of course, one cannot reasonably argue for the uninhibited expression of *everything* in society. It is, perhaps, mainly a matter of degree—and most especially during the formative childhood years when basic response patterns are first being established and when the practical effects of "bad" behavior are generally not at all serious from the standpoint of society.

There is something truly terrifying about the model child—almost always well behaved, never or seldom a bother to his parents, very clean, and basically, very unexpressive.

Remember that when you punish a child for being "bad" you are using a double-edged sword.

On the one hand you are helping him to learn the rules of society by which he will have to live; but on the other you are pushing underground feelings of destruction and hostility which, if not skillfully and understandingly guided into the open, will become deep-seated festers—eventually wreaking a terrible vengeance on the individual and society.

It cannot be an accident that Germany, which has perpetrated some of the most brutal horrors humanity has had to bear, has also been most given to authoritarian and disciplinary up- bringing.

Remember, too, that the boy who throws a baseball bat through the window, or gives his baby sister a mighty wallop, usually does so for reasons he himself is not skillful enough to discern.

To simply punish him for his misdeed without attempting to account for his hostility to yourself and to him, to make him angry at you or to make him guilty about being what he is—none of these responses lead to healthy human beings.

Often, of course, the punishment will actually be necessary; but it should never be "simply punishment" with the implication of "I'm the *Good* father" and "you are the *Bad* child."

Let's face it. We must all be punished and yet loved and cherished. There is (or should be) no contradiction between these two.

The point I am arguing goes, of course, well beyond ques- tions of children's education.

Our habit of thinking in terms of villains and heroes extends well beyond our family management, but expresses itself in politi- cal attitudes and in the conduct of foreign affairs.

It is very hard to admit, but there are simply no villains on whom to blame it all. There are simply lots of human beings, all with a similar set of fundamental drives, all needing control *and* love in order to function in society.

And some of these human beings have had their basic drives so profoundly inhibited—often by being overwhelming goodies for much longer than health and sanity will permit—that the problem of their control poses a most serious problem for society, thus making police departments and armies an unhappy, weighty necessity until we can, as a race, grow up some more, and make them less weighty accordingly.

And now to return to the murderer of my daughter.

I am sure that his parents have been God-fearing, upright citizens, too uneducated in matters of the human soul to have recognized the plight of their child during the years of his growth.

They undoubtedly took naive pride in his *constant* good be- havior, neat appearance and good performance at church and school, never suspecting that this very goodness was a serious cause for worry in the light of what must have been left unaccounted for.

It is, of course, worrisome, from the social point of view that there are parents with such lack of understanding.

It is, I submit, much more profoundly worrisome that it should be possible for this boy to go through his whole 15 years without *anyone* who was responsible for his upbringing—such as his school and his church—having taken note (out of uncaring or lack of understanding) of the danger signals before the tragedy.

Beware, citizens. The human animal cannot be cheated forever. *It will have love, or kill.*

You will understand that I am not lecturing to you for the pure joy of sounding wise. I am hurt to the depths of my being, and I cry out to you to take better care of your children.

My final word has to do with the operation of the machinery of justice. Had I caught the boy in the act, I would have wished to kill him. Now that there is no undoing of what is done, I only wish to help him.

Let no feelings of caveman vengeance influence us. Let us rather *help him* who did so *human* a thing.

A Sick Father

15

FROM JANE ADDAMS
TO CHARLES ADDAMS:
A SUMMING-UP

U ntil the twentieth century, the Western world, despite its highly vaunted claims to civilization, made no fundamental legal distinctions between children and adults accused and convicted of criminal acts. Boys and girls as young as ten or twelve years huddled in overcrowded, fetid jails awaiting their trials. Afterward, if they were lucky, they returned to these human pigpens to rot away the rest of their childhood. The less fortunate child convicts were hanged, lashed, burned at the stake as witches, physically branded, mutilated, or sold as indentured servants. In the early nineteenth century, a boy under ten years of age was hanged in England for stealing a letter from a mailbox—a crime which then invoked the death penalty.

The community accepted this system of justice. Law and order, and the protection of private property (including letters), were then, as now, society's top priorities. Courts existed to uphold them by meting out swift and sure punishments that would both deter the criminal from future misbehavior (even if he had to be killed in the process) and give would-be offenders serious pause.

Poor children, working side by side with adults in workhouses and factories, and as illiterate as their parents, were blurred into the mass of humanity that had to be kept in line to serve the social order. In the Northern cities of America, white children had no special legal rights. In the slave society of the South, by the time they reached the age of six, black children were working in the cotton fields under the same relentless supervision their elders endured. When they reached adolescence many of them were sold, often at good prices. Only with the Emancipation Proclamation did they lose their status as work animals.

Spurred by the example of the English penal reforms which had begun with the great Bill of 1832, responsible citizens in the North cried out against the conditions in the jails and criminal courts. They sought first to move the children out of the prisons and jails and later to hammer out rules and regulations that courts would follow. These nineteenth-century counterparts of today's so-called bleeding-heart do-gooders were amazingly effective. Among their accomplishments: the abolition of slavery, the creation of a mental hospital system, the cleaning-up of prisons, the crusade against child labor, and the adoption of compulsory education systems for all children. Simply to get the children away from hardened criminals and to reduce the length of their confinements was considerable progress.

One of these crusading citizen-reformers had a more ambitious vision of justice for children. Jane Addams (1860–1935), called America's first social worker, founded the nation's first official neighborhood center, Hull House, in the very heart of the Chicago ghetto. To the troubled children who came to this settlement house she offered help and understanding. It became clearer and clearer that environmental and social factors contributed markedly to the behavior of these children. Asking herself why society's legal system could not underwrite a more compassionate and constructive- treatment for *all* children in difficulty, she hit upon the idea of a Juvenile Court. With the indefatigable zeal typical of her breed, she mustered a group of prominent citizens under her banner, and in 1899 succeeded in pushing through a law that set up the first such court in America in Cook County, Illinois, a political subdivision then encompassing Chicago. Straddling the very crossroads of the nation, Chicago, the scene of riots and turbulence by alienated youth during the 1968 Democratic National Convention, was then in Carl Sandburg's phrase, "hog-butcher to the world." Ironically, then, the Juvenile Court was midwived in a prototypical American big-city setting very like those that now witness the effects of a throwaway philosophy.

Between 1899 and 1920, juvenile courts sprang up in every state. Jane Addams's ideas filtered down to the most remote hamlets, and indeed penetrated into every corner of the globe governed by Anglo-Saxon and even Continental systems of law. The founders and supporters of these courts had high hopes. By finally liberating the judge from the straitjacket of the old criminal system that had permitted him to move only in the single direction of punishment, reformers were sure that he would forge individual rehabilitation programs for the children who came before him. He would become a beacon light to his black-robed brothers, and soon *they*, too, would forgo the prison cell for the treatment center. They, too, would view the adult men and women before them as complex human beings needing help, not hate. They, too, would focus their attention on the offender instead of the offense. Rehabilitation would become the avowed goal.

The juvenile court judge himself was the cinch-pin of the system. Lawyers drafting juvenile court laws searched out possible precedents for the almost limitless new powers the judges would need to carry out the mission of transforming delinquent children into good citizens. They found them in the special powers bestowed by English kings on their courts of Chancery, the hated rivals of the English Common Law system. These Chancery judges were authorized to protect the property of children, and even the children themselves. This power to play "Big Daddy" sprang from an ancient doctrine whose Latin name was *parens patriae*. And by dusting off this phrase the juvenile court judges in America received unparalleled powers. In 1967, Justice Abe Fortas, in his opinion handed down in the *Gault* case, summed up the doctrine with these words: ". . . its meaning is murky and its historic credentials are of dubious relevance."

Armed as they were now with this less-than-impeccable power, what other credentials should these new juvenile court judges possess? In a 1909 *Harvard Law Review* article entitled "The Juvenile Court," Judge Julian Mack, one of the first judges of Chicago's new court, declared:

. . . because of the extent of his jurisdiction and the tremendous responsibility it entails, it is . . . absolutely essential that [the juvenile court judge] be a trained lawyer thoroughly imbued with the doctrine that ours is a "government of laws and not of men . . ." He must be a student of and deeply interested in the problems of philanthropy and child life, *as well as a lover of children*. [Italics added.] He must be able to understand the boys' point of view and ideas of justice; he must be willing and patient enough to search out the underlying cause of the trouble and to formulate the plan by which, through the cooperation, ofttimes, of many agencies, the cure may be effected.

Many juvenile court judges *have* been lovers of children. Many have not, concealing hostility and even sadism behind a mask of benevolence. But the failure of the court in late twentieth-century America goes deeper than the mistakes of individual judges, no matter how well-intentioned their protests. It has occurred as a result of two vicious community practices, interrelated and rampant on a national level.

First: communities have used the juvenile courts as dumping grounds for *all* unruly children—a practice made possible because the originators, in their missionary zeal to rescue *all* children from troubles big and small, insisted upon broad definitions of delinquency. This fervor rested on the untested assumption of Jane Addams and others that the court would, with new tools at its disposal, produce genuinely workable solutions to the variety of problems that beset youth.

With a naïveté that today seems quite incredible, many of these kindly Victorian reformers saw juvenile delinquency as the result of a child's conscious decision to go bad. And they perceived dimly— if at all—the possibility that future generations would produce millions of delinquent children whose lives and behavior patterns would be the consequence, not of willful perversity, but of what the President's Commission on Law Enforcement and the Administration of Justice has characterized as "a multitude of pervasive societal influences well beyond the reach of the actions of any judge, probation officer, correctional counselor or psychiatrist."

Second: social workers, who had unwittingly supplied the gigantic litter basket, soon found that they, along with the rest of society, could use the court to rid themselves of troublesome cases they could not handle or did not want.

"Why is this child in juvenile court?" Judge Hoffman would ask many times each day. Honest agency and Welfare Department social workers would answer directly, "Because we have no other plan for this child."

For example, consider the children who from birth have been pushed in and out of foster homes and dreary institutions. Some of them run away, running for their very lives, in search of unknown parents or a better existence. Inevitably caught, they are brought to court as "delinquents" because they are runaways from placement. Instead of facing up to the reasons for the youngsters' actions and making determined efforts to improve the system, social workers leave them at the steps of the juvenile court and walk away.

In March of 1968, *Look* Magazine published an article about Teen-Aid entitled "Philadelphia's Friendly Arm of the Law." Shortly afterward, I received telephone calls from distraught court workers in such states as Florida, Kansas, and Nevada who wanted more detailed information about this private volunteer agency. The callers reported that the jails in their communities were filled with homeless runaway teen-age girls from other states. All of them had been made wards of the juvenile court.

Parents, teachers, and psychologists—all have played the dumping game with increasing enthusiasm. In fairness to juvenile court administrative staffs, I must point out that many have been long aware of this practice and have tried to resist it. But the dumpers have the law behind them, and the court officials and judges feel a sufficient sense of responsibility to at least try to help these children.

Perhaps this has been a mistake on their part, an act of complicity which in the long run has done more harm than good. Maybe they should have herded these children into public view, screamed more loudly, even marched them into the halls of the legislatures and the city councils, into the offices of governors and mayors throughout the land. Activist protest, however, is not the life style of either lawyers or social workers. Nobody else has cared enough, or known enough about it, to give the matter a second thought.

And so for years children who needed homes, education, and people to help them create a new, positive self-image to replace the battered negative one they carried about like an albatross have found themselves instead shipped off to correctional institutions, often located hundreds of miles away from familiar faces and landmarks. Parents who could afford to make monthly visits to them often had great difficulty finding the places. Families with no money for fare (and many, on meager public assistance allowances, did not) never saw their children during the entire period of institutionalization. For these youngsters, together with the orphans, visiting days were waiting days—for adults who never showed up.

Thus have human castoffs been left to this fate for months and years while the probation officers and the psychiatrists have tried to resolve what happens next. In Philadelphia, many have remained in the Youth Study Center. One thirteen-year-old runaway girl from Rhode Island sat for *two years* in the Center while the Pennsylvania and Rhode Island state welfare authorities sent each other reports and polite letters. But in most communities, they have been kept in jail, rubbing shoulders with bona-fide delinquents who have committed one or a series of antisocial acts.

Despite the upward-spiraling numbers of delinquent children thrust upon the juvenile courts, no equivalent or even relative increase in probation officers, supervisors, or judges has been forthcoming. Legislatures and city councils alike continually turn deaf ears to requests for additional personnel and facilities. When they do listen, their skepticism about the legitimacy of the need leads them to adopt defensively negative attitudes. I recall the prominent upstate legislator who asked me seriously after I had presented my case to him, "Why are you so interested in creating new jobs for social workers?"

Both the children and the community have been the real victims of this neglect. Institutions bursting at the seams have had to resort to highly regimented management to handle the overload. Prematurely released children, sent back to unsatisfactory home conditions with no aftercare plan, have kept getting into further trouble. Children on probation have turned up in court on new charges even before their first scheduled probation visit. Sometimes these repeaters do not know their probation officer's name.

Recidivist rates have continued to soar. The FBI's 1967 *Uniform Crime Reports* show that of *all* young offenders under twenty released from institutions in 1963, 70 per cent have committed new crimes for which they have been arrested, many as adults.

Jane Addams's dream of individualized personal justice has become a nightmare. To relieve the overcrowding and to release from detention the innocent children and the minor offenders, Philadelphia judges have sat long hours, hearing from *forty* to as many as *eighty* cases each day. Under the unbearable weight of these heavy lists, the informality characterizing juvenile court procedure has occasionally sagged into formlessness, devoid of resemblance to any known legal procedure. One Roman Catholic judge confessed to me that before going into court each morning he recited a rosary, in the hope that divine intervention would prevent him from making a serious error that might hurt a child. Soon afterward he requested and secured a transfer to an adult court.

On the wall opposite my office desk during the period I served in juvenile court hung a brightly colored poster. From an eloquent sketch of a child in the center radiated eight wheel spokes, each ending in a single word. Under the bold-faced title, WHAT EVERY CHILD NEEDS FOR GOOD MENTAL HEALTH, these eight words seemed to sum up, both when I first read them some fourteen years ago and now as I write them, what the juvenile court should have been trying to secure as part of every child's birthright:

Love	*Security*	*Acceptance*	*Faith*	*Control*
	Guidance	*Independence*	*Protection*	

For years this poster lacerated my conscience.

It is easy to achieve one of the eight goals—control. Despite the reluctance of most judges to institutionalize children, and despite the dedicated efforts of court administrators, like John A. Rosica and Dr. Leonard Rosengarten in Philadelphia, to find other solutions, invariably none materializes. Many youngsters have been and continue to be scarred and mutilated for life by this hasty surgery, which tears them away from their homes and their families. Older youngsters with television-based concepts of fair legal procedures compare their one-sided "quickie" hearings with Perry Mason's courtroom scenes and bitterly decide that justice is a fraud, that no adults connected with the system can be trusted. Emerging embittered from confinement, they adopt either defiant or hypocritical stances toward well-meaning probation officers and community workers assigned to help them.

Rhetoric and high-sounding phrases aside, the best that juvenile courts are doing is exactly—and only—what the adult criminal courts have done with children since time immemorial: locking them up in jails. While mouthing the language of the reformers, the juvenile court has become, in many cases, the legal strong arm of the community. And the kids know the score.

How do trained and sensitive child workers, probation officers, judges, and lawyers keep their sanity under grotesquely sinister conditions reminiscent of a Charles Addams cartoon?

Some quit in disgust.

Others do the very best job they can during working hours, and use their scant leisure time hammering away at civic groups, seeking to enlist their help in setting up new projects that might rescue throwaway children.

Some highly trained social workers, surveying the wreckage from insulated agency offices and research-geared niches, retreat safely behind their academic exercises. In talking to *Look*'s Senior Editor Daniel Chapman, I called them present-day "mandarins—the empire is collapsing, and they worry about calligraphy."

Unfortunately, almost everyone connected with the system must finally develop varying degrees of autoanesthesia. They simply numb themselves in order not to be torn apart by the painful spectacle in the juvenile arena. Some, steeling themselves against overreaction, become immured.

Early in the spring of 1968, I stumbled upon a most shocking example of a throwaway child. I had been visiting a client at an adult state mental hospital. As I was preparing to leave, a nine-year-old Negro boy alighted from a school bus that pulled up to the main administration office. He walked jauntily into the building with an air of belonging. Incredulous, I asked the supervisor who he was and why he was entering the hospital with school books under his arm.

"He lives here," she told me. "Believe it or not!"

"Who sent him here?" I demanded.

"The State Department of Welfare, if you please," she replied.

A throwaway by birth, at age seven he had been handed over by his mother to an alcoholic friend who, in a moment of sobriety, realized that she could not keep him either, and put him out on the street. The police soon picked him up and brought him to the Youth Study Center. Through the Social Service Exchange the probation officer learned that a prestigious children's aid society indeed knew the family and had, at one point, "worked" with the boy's mother. The agency now said it would not accept him for foster-home placement until the court psychiatrist had made a thorough study, since it was not in business to handle disturbed children.

The court medical report described the boy as a tense, anxious child who wet his bed, chewed his nails, and could not concentrate for very long. Despite the psychiatrist's conclusion that the youngster was not psychotic, the agency decided he was "too disturbed" to be eligible for placement, and flatly refused to take him. The only place left for the court to look was in the state's bare cupboard of foster homes or schools.

After a year and a half of fruitless search by the probation officer, the boy was still at the detention center. One day a State Welfare Department supervisor visited the place on other business and learned of the boy's plight. He promised to move him out before the week was over.

He telephoned the state hospital supervisor, a warmhearted mother herself, and begged her, as a personal favor to him, to accept the boy as a patient, despite the fact that he was not mentally ill and that the hospital she ran had no section for children.

When the frightened boy arrived, she took him under her wing, arranging that he be kept away from disturbed patients and that he be enrolled in grammar school in a town some miles away. She became his substitute mother, signing his report card, helping him with his lessons.

"I don't think that anyone really looked at that child too closely," she said as we walked to my car. "Last summer I took him on a vacation trip with my husband and children. After all, I couldn't leave him here all alone. The first day we went swimming, I saw his little body. His chest and belly were severely scarred by what must have been repeated belt-buckle beatings. Yet there isn't a single mention of this brutality in any of the agency reports! His mother has four young children living with her, I'm told. I wonder what's happening to them?"

The next day I attended a conference at which the top state welfare administrator assigned to Philadelphia was present. I spilled out my story. He looked at me calmly as I described the boy. Finally I asked angrily why he was put in such a place.

"Your story proves," he said, shaking out the ashes from his pipe, "that we really are resourceful people."

If that is the best we can do for that boy and thousands like him, then it is no wonder there are so many forgotten throwaways. But then, how can a system built on unfulfilled goals and broken promises rescue and rehabilitate children?

Despite the impassioned outcries of a few top professionals like Dr. Harold Lewis, Professor of Social Research at the University of Pennsylvania's School of Social Work, social workers generally, as part of the Establishment, were not likely to rock the leaky boat.

No; challenge and change originated elsewhere. This time the attack upon the *status quo* was mounted by lawyers, so long unwelcome in juvenile court because of their purported failure to understand the real purposes of the court. In the end, the lawyers were to prove that they understood only too well.

16 ══

HALT—
IN THE NAME
OF GAULT!

Gerald Francis Gault, a fifteen-year-old boy on probation to an Arizona Juvenile Court because he had been with a boy who snatched a purse, had a Damoclean sword hanging over his head.

For him, as for countless other under-eighteen probationers, one misstep could cause the sword to fall, slashing away family and school ties. Although neither he nor his parents realized it, his probationary status had placed him in the constant shadow of the reformatory.

Undoubtedly Paul and Marjorie Gault, like most other middle-class American parents, believed that the courts were the best shelters available to citizens whose personal freedom was in jeopardy. They did not conceive the possibility that the juvenile court had become, not a haven, but a casualty zone.

Early in the summer of 1964, one of the Gaults' neighbors received several obscene telephone calls. One day, listening hard, she thought she recognized Gerald's voice. Aware that he had been in juvenile court, she did not bother to call the police. Instead, she spoke to the boy's probation officer.

Shortly after her report, while both of his parents were at work, Gerald was picked up by that officer and taken to the juvenile detention home. This peremptory action, taken without notifying parents, was not an uncommon practice, but it was hardly in accord with our notions of justice and respect for the individual's rights and freedoms in the United States. It was hours before his distraught mother found out what had happened. She was also told that Gerald was to appear before the juvenile court judge the next morning; the probation officer implied that the boy was in serious trouble. All would be explained in court, he replied in answer to her worried questions.

The next day, when Mrs. Gault walked into the judge's chambers, she saw only three people present in the room: the judge, the probation officer, and Gerald. The officer repeated the neighbor's complaint. The boy's accuser was nowhere in sight. No one was taking notes of what was being said; thus we will never know for sure whether at that "hearing" Gerald admitted holding the telephone while a friend of his dialed the neighbor's number, as his mother maintains, or whether in fact he admitted using lewd language.

The judge finally ended the meeting by saying that he would make up his mind in a few days what to do with the boy. Until then, Gerald was to remain in detention. Mrs. Gault went home, reassuring herself that the judge was merely trying to shake Gerald up, to put a good scare into him. After all, the court was there to help teen-agers like her son sustain the rougher bumps of growing up.

A few days later she was called back to court. Again only the judge and the probation officer were present. Again she arrived without a lawyer because no one had told her she needed one. The judge had reviewed Gerald's whole record, he said, and had decided that the best thing to do for the boy was to send him to the state training school for an indefinite term that could extend until Gerald reached his twenty-first birthday, *six years hence.*

Stunned momentarily by the severity of the sentence, Mrs. Gault recovered enough aplomb to say that she would hire a lawyer to appeal the ruling. The court responded with the curtly delivered information that it would be to no avail because under Arizona law there was no provision for appeals from juvenile court rulings.

Mrs. Gault's attorney, Amelie D. Lewis of Sun City, Arizona, believed that it was worth a good try. On the Gaults' behalf she filed a writ of habeas corpus declaring that Gerald's commitment to the training school had been illegal because the boy had never had a real hearing with a lawyer present to cross-examine his accuser and present his case properly.

Opposing her, state attorneys argued that juvenile court proceedings by law were informal, that the boy was not standing trial as a criminal, that he was not being sent to jail for punishment, but to a school where he would better himself. The court turned thumbs down on her plea.

Undaunted, Mrs. Lewis went "upstairs" to the next level of justice: the Arizona Supreme Court.

The American Civil Liberties Union had long been opposed to the kind of juvenile court practices that Mrs. Lewis and the Gaults were protesting. After they lost again in the state's highest court, two of the Union's most able lawyers—Professor Norman Dorsen of the New York University School of Law and Melvin L. Wulf, its Legal Director—joined forces with Mrs. Lewis as she prepared to knock on the doors of the United States Supreme Court.

These doors had been closed to lawyers seeking to correct injustices meted out by juvenile authorities. Such pleas had been so consistently turned down that some lawyers believed that a sign reading *Children under 18 not admitted* should have been hung above the Supreme Court's massive doors.

Most consistently excluded were cases involving direct challenges of juvenile court rulings. The few scattered appeals that were granted to young people sprang from errors or abuses inflicted upon them by adult criminal courts to which they had been transferred by the juvenile court when charged with felonies or murder.

Against such a background, Gerald Gault's chances of being heard receded into wafer-thin slimness.

But a careful reading of *Kent v. United States* (383 U.S. 541) gave the Gaults' lawyers encouragement as they prepared to file their papers. This Supreme Court ruling of 1966 established that children must receive a full and fair hearing in juvenile court before being transferred for adult trial. More especially did the words of Justice Abe Fortas, speaking for the majority of the Supreme Court in 1966, give them hope:

There is evidence . . . that there may be grounds for concern that the child receives the worst of both worlds: that he gets neither the protections accorded to adults nor the solicitous care and regenerative treatment postulated for children.

Their hunch proved correct. The Supreme Court agreed to hear Gerald Gault's appeal.

On May 15, 1967, with Justice Fortas again serving as spokesman for the eight-man majority, the United States Supreme Court struck down the boy's commitment.

The Court said that the boy had not had the fair trial guaranteed him under the Sixth Amendment of the Bill of Rights; and certain of his rights under the Fifth and the Fourteenth Amendments had also been violated.

Following are the four essential rights that Gerald Francis Gault was denied:

1. Notice in writing, at the earliest possible moment, of the specific charges against him and the factual allegations on which these charges were based—and sufficient time to allow for the preparation of a defense. Said the court:

> Due process of law requires notice of the sort we have described—that is, notice which would be deemed constitutionally adequate in a civil or criminal proceeding. It does not allow a hearing to be held in which a youth's freedom and his parents' right to his custody are at stake without giving them timely notice, in advance of the hearing, of the specific issues that they must meet.

2. The right to be represented by a lawyer, either of one's own choosing or appointed by the court if the circumstances warrant.

> We conclude that the Due Process Clause of the Fourteenth Amendment requires that in respect of proceedings to determine delinquency which may result in commitment to an institution in which the juvenile's freedom is curtailed, the child and his parent must be notified of the child's right to be represented by counsel retained by them, or if they are unable to afford counsel, that counsel will be appointed to represent the child.

3. Guarantee of the rights of confrontation and cross-examination of hostile witnesses.

4. Guarantee of the privilege against self-incrimination. Again the Court spoke clearly:

> It would indeed be surprising if the privilege against self-incrimination were available to hardened criminals but not to children. The language of the Fifth Amendment, applicable to the States by operation of the Fourteenth Amendment, is unequivocal and without exception.

The inclusion of children within the meaning of "persons" under the Fourteenth Amendment is perhaps the most important thing in the Gault opinion. Although the Gaults' lawyers raised the issue of the need for appeal procedures to make the state law provisions comply with our notions of "due process," the Court did not decide this issue, relying on an earlier 1956 opinion (*Griffin v. Illinois*, 351 U.S. 12), which stated that the due-process clause did not require states to provide defendants the right to appellate review. After all, the trusty old tool of habeas corpus is always readily at hand under the Bill of Rights. But the Court did point out how difficult it is to make even this tool effective when notes of testimony are not transcribed or opinions written setting forth the reasons why a judge reached a particular decision.

> As the present case illustrates, the consequences of failure to provide an appeal, to record the proceedings, or to make findings or state the grounds for the juvenile court's conclusion may be to throw a burden upon the machinery for habeas corpus, to saddle the reviewing process with the burden of attempting to reconstruct a record, and to impose upon the juvenile judge the unseemly duty of testifying under cross-examination as to the events that transpired in the hearings before him.

Fortas's opinion attacked firmly the prevailing view that because juvenile courts were virtually therapy clinics, children who came before them did not need the protection of the Bill of Rights of the American constitution. The reality, he declared, was that these courts frequently imposed more drastic and severe punishments than their adult counterparts. Witness Gerald Gault's sentence of *six years* for a crime which, for adults, carried a five- to fifty-dollar fine and a maximum sentence of two months! It is interesting to note that Gerald is now a student at a junior college in California, and is "making it." According to Mrs. Lewis, his old "record" still haunts the present: the Army is hesitant about accepting his enlistment.

Fortas concluded that children charged with juvenile delinquency needed constitutional protections as desperately as, if not more than, adults standing trial. Children can no longer be dismissed as non-persons or legal mutations not included in the Fourteenth Amendment guarantees that prevent the various states from depriving American citizens of life, liberty, or property *without due process of law.*

Partly because the Court was unwilling to disrupt law enforcement efforts struggling to cope with rising juvenile crime rates, partly in observance of a self-imposed rule to say no more than necessary under the facts of a given case, the Supreme Court did *not* pass judgment on the broader system of juvenile justice of which juvenile court proceedings were an important, but not exclusive part. It remained silent on such controversial questions as:

1. When should a child be informed of his rights? When taken into police custody, as is the case with adults?

2. Why hasn't the child's lawyer the right to examine the official court record in order to prepare and conduct a proper defense?

3. How long can a child be confined before his punishment becomes "cruel and unusual" under the Eighth Amendment?

4. Is it *legal* for states to dispatch children to correctional institutions where they mingle with older criminals?

5. May children be tried in a juvenile court without a jury and their guilt decided by a preponderance of evidence rather than by the "reasonable doubt" standard applied in adult criminal trials?

This last question, representing perhaps the most frontal assault on juvenile court philosophy and procedure, was granted an audience by the U.S. Supreme Court on February 24, 1969, when the justices agreed to consider the case of *Debaker v. Brainard* (*No. 662, October Term, 1968*).

The Supreme Court's focus in the *Gault* case was confined to a single question: *What kind of hearing should a child receive in juvenile court?*

Informal chats between a fatherly judge and the defendant resulting in the child's imprisonment are now definitely out. Juvenile courts are law courts and should behave accordingly, giving children careful and fair hearings. However, the Supreme Court did not include in its opinion a How-to-Do-It set of instructions to juvenile courts. Presumably, they will get the message without such a kit.

Six months after the *Gault* decision, I represented a boy charged with a series of burglaries in an outlying suburb of Philadelphia. On the day of his hearing, several local lawyers came up to me in the courthouse corridor and, knowing that I was a stranger, warned me that the judge had his own way of doing things, the *Gault* decision notwithstanding.

"Above all," they advised, "don't be too legalistic. He doesn't like lawyers to argue too hard."

Armed with this good advice, I walked into the hearing room. The detectives who had arrested the boy prepared themselves to testify. We all waited for ten minutes while the boy's probation officer, seated next to the judge, spoke to him in a low voice. I could not make out his words, but observing the judge's head-nodding, his thumbing of a mass of reports, and his occasional glances in our direction, I knew they were discussing the boy.

Knowing that to protest at this point would start me off on *two* wrong feet, I nevertheless stood up to object.

The judge told me to sit down. I held my ground and explained that the court was receiving possibly prejudicial information which I could neither challenge by cross-examination nor answer in rebuttal.

"Don't worry," said the judge, "I always keep an open mind. Just remember, young lady, that you're going to have a hard time convincing me that I shouldn't send him away for at least a year." (After several other "hearings" in which the judge remained adamant, he ordered the boy off to a training school.) As I left the courtroom, I marveled at the neat irony of the situation: the very courts which had in the past expected immature children from devastating backgrounds to change overnight into good little boys and girls were now discovering how difficult, even distasteful, is self-reform.

In the years 1956 through 1966, Philadelphia's juvenile court judges had adopted a hearing format which, as it turned out, paralleled the *Gault* hearing format in all but one respect: the right of children to remain silent. In omitting the privilege against self-incrimination, the court was following the 1954 directive of the Pennsylvania Supreme Court, which ruled in the *Holmes* case that children were *obliged* to testify and that their failure to do so would *in itself* be an act of delinquency.

Lawyers privately retained by parents with means appeared frequently on behalf of children. In the late 1950's, prodded by Judge Adrian Bonnelly, Presiding Judge of the County Court, the Philadelphia Bar Association set up, in addition to its existing Lawyers' Reference Service, a special panel drawn from the Junior Bar to represent children whose parents could pay a nominal fee of twenty-five dollars or more. From time to time the Voluntary Defender Association (V.D.A.), which gave free legal representation to indigent adults charged with crime, lent a hand in juvenile cases of special hardship. But it had neither the manpower nor the funds to assume this responsibility for children on even a part-time basis. In the fall of 1968, the always acute problem of money became overwhelming and the acting director of the V.D.A. announced that no new adult cases could be accepted. Thus, when the *Gault* decision was handed down in 1967, Philadelphia juvenile judges asked themselves where they would find lawyers to represent the thousands of indigent children who faced commitment to institutions.

Less than a year earlier, the Philadelphia Anti-Poverty Action Committee, funded mainly by an Office of Economic Opportunity (O.E.O.) grant, and the Philadelphia Bar Association (which supplied 10 per cent of the community contribution required by Federal law) had jointly launched Community Legal Services, Inc., a new program of legal assistance for the poor. One section of this new group, consisting of four lawyers, had been assigned to represent juveniles. To these few lawyers, and to others who came forward to volunteer their services, the judges began to assign cases.

It was an impossible mission, doomed from the outset. Neither four nor even forty lawyers could represent even a significant percentage of the children needing counsel. While they waited for lawyers to interview them, or their cases to be listed for hearing, children remained in detention. In December, 1967, the Community Legal Services lawyers closed their doors to any more court-appointed juvenile clients. Shortly afterward, the head of that group resigned.

The situation was described in the Philadelphia *Evening Bulletin* as one of "turmoil at the County Court." Between February 4 and March 24 of 1968, four able judges tendered their resignations from duty in the Juvenile Division because they could no longer endure the daily frustrations in court. Judge Charles Wright, the last one to resign, called for a "grand jury investigation of our whole Juvenile Court proceedings."

Early in 1968, the Philadelphia Bar Association Chancellor, Lewis H. Van Dusen, taking stock of the chaotic condition in the juvenile courts, appointed a blue-ribbon committee to devise a comprehensive plan for legal services to indigent children facing delinquency charges. As chairman of this new group he appointed Robert M. Landis, long active in social agency affairs and a partner in a large Philadelphia law firm. While Landis's committee deliberated which group should be given charge of the proposed program, the O.E.O. announced that it would no longer supply monies for lawyers because the *Gault* decision had made each state responsible for such funding. In April, 1968, Judge Frank Montemuro, now presiding judge of the Family Court Division of the Court of Common Pleas of Philadelphia County, appointed a lawyer for a poor child and sent the bill for the service to the Commonwealth of Pennsylvania. Although the legislature had set aside funds to compensate lawyers appointed by courts when no other resource could be found, the state balked.

The final recommendations of the Landis Committee that the City of Philadelphia appropriate $350,000 annually for public defenders for children may also fall through, because, at this writing, the city is grappling with a school-budget crisis and other fiscal difficulties.

These roadblocks faced by Philadelphia have sprung up all over the nation. In large American cities with great numbers of poor families—and in rural areas as well—"due process of law" for children still remains a faraway goal.

Despite the grumblings of some lawyers who think that as long as the Supreme Court was deciding the *Gault* case, it should have gone ahead and given children automatic rights to appeal juvenile court rulings, and despite the dismay of others with the Supreme Court's ruling that individual states should decide whether or not to make the decision apply retroactively to children committed before May 15, 1967, on the whole the lawyers legitimately congratulated themselves on a signal victory which could launch a new effort to secure justice for children.

By enhancing a child's innate dignity, due process of law—one of society's most profoundly civilized values—may mean more in the life of all children than all the rhetoric of the therapists. The

Gault decision may also help to prevent adults from future lapses into authoritarian techniques—even in the name of "human progress."

However, the *Gault* case does not authorize us to transform the juvenile court into a miniaturized version of adult criminal court. On the contrary, it serves as a spur to all who care deeply about the future of children to work hard to make juvenile courts a place where a child can receive both just *and* compassionate treatment.

Yet lawyers alone cannot change the whole *system* of juvenile justice; they will do what they must in the courtroom. But who will come forward to do the rest?

In the April 22, 1967, issue of the *New Republic* (shortly before the *Gault* opinion was handed down), Judge David Bazelon terms this system one of "blindness and insensitivity" in which "everyone . . . had become society's janitors, fixing a pipe here and there, sweeping the floor, making sure the heat was on, but never once suggesting the structure was faulty."

Surely we Americans, living in the most affluent nation in the world, can do better than repair hit-or-miss plumbing. Instead of tinkering, we should all be thinking creatively about the entire juvenile justice system and how to make it really work.

For too long we have been content to delude ourselves that the experts had the situation well in hand. They didn't. Now that we perceive the chaos, we must not stop to ascribe blame; with each passing day the toll of wasted youth mounts. Yet very close at hand are new techniques for reclaiming our young people. The name of the game is *children;* the object—to reverse the throwaway process.

PART FIVE

REVERSING THE THROWAWAY PROCESS

PART
FIVE═══

PROLOGUE

Many American middle-class reformers, having a penchant for self-hypnosis, tend to become mesmerized by their own rhetoric. Once they have issued a report on a social problem, they persuade themselves that they have solved it. The thicker and more jargon-laden the document, the more apt the solution, they tell themselves. During the years I have served on state and local planning commit-tees and city-wide health and welfare boards, I have often felt in imminent peril of drowning in a Sargasso sea of mimeographed studies.

Every now and then out of the welter of surveys and "white papers" comes an incisive, brilliantly conceived and articulated pro-gram for action such as the report prepared by President Johnson's Commission on Law Enforcement and the Administration of Justice. Like some of its excellent predecessors, that report, *The Challenge of Crime in a Free Society*, may suffer mummification rites.

In Philadelphia, one classic example of a buried report involved shocking conditions in foster homes and institutions for neglected and dependent children. A distinguished lawyer, E. Calvert Cheston, headed a 1962 Philadelphia Citizens' Committee that conducted a thorough probe into these services. Their recommendations to the mayor and the city fathers included an immediate plan to replace the bungling operation. Six years later, all knowledgeable Philadelphians agreed that the Cheston Report tells it like it really was—and still is. Not one of the basic reforms it urged has been carried out.

There is an equal threat of oblivion hovering over the juvenile justice reforms lucidly expounded in the President's Commission Report, discussed in the next chapter. Even if the machinery is quickly revised by flurried activity in state legislatures and local councils, the juvenile courts themselves will still be handicapped by the tremendous shortage of judges, probation officers, therapists, and lawyers to handle the daily case loads created by burgeoning crime rates.

Even if organized community groups quickly set up Youth Service Bureaus to fill the vacuum created by a new delimiting of the juvenile court's scope of jurisdiction, they will find the community cupboard of youth services quite bare when they actually try to fill their young clients' needs.

What then?

Shall we all shrug our shoulders and go home, leaving the bureaucrats to continue muddling through and the new Bureaus to become the litter baskets of tomorrow?

If we do, we make a tragic decision that will condemn millions of future Americans to a country increasingly beset with violence on the one hand and police repression on the other. How long, we must ask ourselves, can a free society survive these polarizing tensions?

We must face up to two very hard facts now. *One:* The entire country is at least thirty years behind in its social planning. *Two:* Without massive volunteer citizen effort we will be unable to implement the programs that emerge as we try to close the gap. The entire delinquency field has been so scantily supported by both the public and the private sectors that it will take us a full generation to train the professionals we need. For example, at the present time, 77.56 per cent of all the juvenile probationers are supervised by probation officers with case loads of from 51 to 100 children, even though the most feasible total should not exceed 35 children. According to the Commission Report, the present total national number of 7,706 probation officers should be almost doubled immediately to provide 13,800 workers. By 1975, more than 23,000 probation officers will be needed in American juvenile courts. As matters now stand, they will not be forthcoming.

How then shall we proceed?

Even the longest journey begins with a single step. It was John F. Kennedy's favorite Chinese proverb.

We must all decide to take that first step on America's journey to a better future for all children.

17 ====

AMERICA'S
UNFINISHED HOMEWORK:
A REPORT WE OVERLOOKED

W hy didn't Americans rush forward in 1967 to purchase (at nominal cost from the United States Printing Office) *The Challenge of Crime in a Free Society*, a publication of vital national importance? The reason could not have been a general aversion to Presidential Commission Reports, because one year later another such tome, the Koerner Commission's survey of the causes of rioting and racial disorder, became a runaway best seller—thereby adding to the various astonishments of the year 1968 in American life.

If, as the political slogans of the 1968 election campaigns indicated, law and order was the main preoccupation of the American people, virtually outranking the Vietnam war, why does the report of President Johnson's Commission on Law Enforcement and the Administration of Justice gather dust while the Koerner report is still selling in corner drugstores?

Both reports were frankly intended to jolt Americans into awareness of the need for change. We seemed willing enough to listen when the race issue was the topic. Why, then, are we so reluctant to face the realities of crime?

Were Americans antagonized by newspaper summaries of the crime report's conclusions that rising crime rates were the result of decades of failure both to provide full opportunities for millions of Americans and to update and reform the traditional systems of criminal justice dealing with juvenile and adult offenders? Certainly, many Americans would have preferred to hear that crime rates were mounting because recent Supreme Court opinions permitted the "coddling" of criminals or because the "moral" fiber of the nation was unraveling. Yet the Koerner report with equal bluntness told Americans that race riots were their own fault and not the work of outside agitators and infiltrators, who had served as convenient scapegoats in the past.

It is true that dramatic events witnessed on television sets in every part of the nation moved relations between blacks and whites to center-stage in America's consciousness. For all of us the memories are searing: summer nights spent viewing wordlessly the devastation in Detroit, staring in disbelief at the silhouettes of helmeted soldiers standing guard in the nation's capital as night fires cast their eerie glow on familiar landmarks and monuments. Perhaps it was only natural that, shuddering, we sought answers to all our questions in the report submitted by the top-level experts President Johnson had summoned in the aftermath of the 1967 summer riots.

There have been few such vivid confrontations with crime, and especially with youth crime, to intensify our curiosity and concern. Ignorant about the inner workings of criminal justice, many of us are content with the worn-out plots and the catsup shoot-outs on our television screens. What's the big fuss about? If we need more prisons, penitentiaries—warehouses—let's build them. What else does a nation do with its thugs, hoods, and long-haired juvenile punks?

Yet in 1964 Americans responded to the vision of a "Great Society" by giving Lyndon B. Johnson a mandate to make it come true. It seemed then that everyone wanted the country to move forward and remedy what the President termed in a message to Congress "ancient evils."

Interpreting this national mood toward renewal and change as a green light, the President, on July 23, 1965, issued Executive Order No. 11236, establishing an eighteen-man commission to make specific recommendations to him—and the nation—on ways to curb crime and also improve the administration of justice for both juveniles and adult offenders. He wanted fast action; the deadline gave the Commission less than eighteen months to complete its work.

The Commissioners, headed by Nicholas de B. Katzenbach, then Attorney-General of the United States, later to serve as Under-Secretary of State, completed their assignment in record time, and their pace did not in the least impair the quality of their work. These Commissioners (among them Pennsylvania's former Secretary of Internal Affairs, lawyer Genevieve Blatt), assembled over forty full-time staff members from various professions and workposts. Cadres of lawyers, police officers, prosecutors, sociologists, psychologists, and authors were formed to serve as advisers and consultants. The Commission's final roster of staff members and part-time experts read like a *Who's Who of American Criminal Justice*.

Its magnum opus, *The Challenge of Crime in a Free Society*, belongs on the bookshelf of every American home that has one. One chapter, "Juvenile Delinquency and Youth Crime," should be condensed to hand-bill and pamphlet proportions and made available everywhere: supermarket counters, theaters, churches—any place where Americans gather in large numbers to satisfy their material and spiritual needs.

This well-documented and perceptive survey of juvenile justice in the United States describes in detail how our throwaway children hunger not only for justice but for the same opportunities for human fulfillment that others in our society enjoy.

But the Commission, aware that even the most authoritative presentation of facts does not automatically lead to changes in firmly entrenched policies, prejudices, and practices, did more than catalogue the problems that beset the nation. It examined the causes and effects of juvenile misbehavior and made specific recommendations and proposals to relieve the immediate stresses within society and outlined a long-range national strategy for achieving the desired goals to which a truly free society must be dedicated. The seven-point plan set forth in the report recommended:

1. That full opportunities open up in social and economic areas for millions of Americans now shut out of society's existing channels for self-advancement.

2. That new ways be sought to cope with juvenile and adult offenders.

3. That unfairness and discrimination be eliminated in the legal treatment of offenders by police and by courts.

4. That job conditions within the correctional system and other phases of criminal justice administration be improved so that high-level, creative persons will be attracted to these careers.

5. That basic and other research be done into the reasons for crime and the techniques for controlling it.

6. That huge sums of money be poured into the entire system to strengthen, improve, and when necessary, revamp it.

7. That all Americans become wholeheartedly involved in a national awakening of interest to the problem, and that they commit themselves to sustain this involvement until the changes and reforms are accomplished.

The report advances over 200 specific proposals logically and realistically related to the present situation.

The proposals that affect youth lend themselves readily to action now. It is unreasonable to demand or expect communities to change long-standing attitudes and policies overnight. But it is important that Americans begin to respond compassionately to the plight of the young; too few of us realize how many of the scarred derelicts who pass through the halls of adult justice today were yesterday's throw-away children.

Whatever we do to revamp the present system of handling youthful offenders will reverberate elsewhere. If millions of American children can be helped, the criminal court workloads may be so drastically reduced that even with their present limitations, these courts will do a more effective job.

Throwaway children are the spin-offs of a society that is failing to do its best for young people. These deficiencies are apparent on legal, social, and cultural levels. All we have to do is take a look at the actual conditions under which we ask these children to live, to learn, to develop into whole human beings, to prepare themselves for the future. Time after time, the report cites examples of everyday circumstances of life that confront many American children—circumstances so adverse that delinquent behavior is virtually inevitable. It will require a sustained, multipronged effort to provide these young members of society with adequate homes, decent communities, wholesome, affectionate family lives, and good schools where they can breathe freely—grow, play, study, and aspire to an adult life that will be remunerative and rewarding. Government, private industry, social, professional, and other groups can play a vital role in creating and maintaining this kind of environment for all children.

The Commission then asks the key question: What kind of system should a compassionate democracy dedicated to humanitarian ideals devise to deal constructively with those children who fail to conform, even under improved childhood conditions?

Whatever techniques we apply should rescue them and at the same time protect the community from their destructive acts. The present juvenile system has failed to do so, and the overhauling and redesigning it needs is long overdue. For almost three-quarters of a century it has pivoted on one axis: the Juvenile Court. Serving in most American communities as the sole control center for delinquent and troublesome children, it was inevitable, considering its lack of resources and a coherent philosophy, that this court would yield to community pressure and become a dumping ground. Now that the *Gault* decision has thrown the Juvenile Court into a state of crisis, the Commission's critique (written while the case was still pending before the U.S. Supreme Court) is even more sharply to the point.

The juvenile court, the report suggests, should stop trying to be all things to all children. Realistically, it should supervise a *legal* control system, as the adult courts do, reserving its services and skills for the children it can most effectively handle: those who repeatedly and seriously endanger the rights and safety of other citizens and the security and stability of the community.

The diagram opposite, reproduced from the Commission's report, shows how the proposed new system shifts many therapeutic services sought by parents, school officials, and even police away from the Juvenile Court—thereby eliminating the necessity of filing formal delinquency petitions and declaring children to be offenders as a prelude to obtaining help for them. This new plan is based on a broad spectrum of community rehabilitative, *not punitive*, services. At the same time it preserves a direct route from the police to the juvenile court, for serious offenders.

Proposed Juvenile Justice System

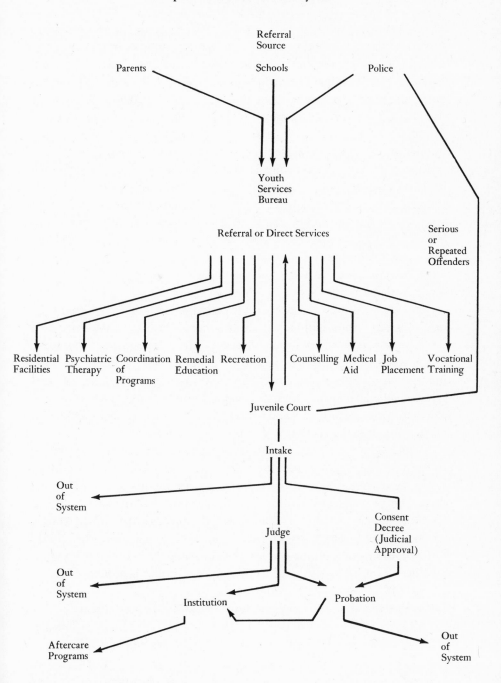

The number one task is to up-date and revise our juvenile laws so that they reflect the philosophy and guiding principles of a democratic society. The Commission counsels lawmakers to redefine "delinquent conduct"—at present a term loosely applied to all kinds and degrees of undesirable or bothersome youthful misbehavior. Experience should have taught us by now that the more we brand children as delinquent, the less likely they are to respond positively to our ministrations. Many children become permanently antagonistic to authoritarian techniques; they form rigidly negative self-images that lead to future antisocial behavior. Court intervention should be restricted to acts punishable as crimes when committed by adults. If legislators insist on giving courts jurisdiction over children who misbehave in noncriminal ways, then the Commission recommends that this power extend only to repeated serious misconduct and not include trivial escapades or parent-child conflicts that belong more properly in other hands.

Whatever sanctions are employed against children should be different from those applied to adults; moreover, they should be used only as a last resort— not indiscriminately under the guise of "therapy." The Commission urges us to see the "commitment" process for what it really is: deprivation of liberty for varying lengths of time not subject to outside review. Present-day institutions being what they are, they do little more than keep a child under lock and key. Thus it is the community that benefits temporarily, not the child.

Children should receive the same legal protection that adults do when they face judge and jury. Due-process guarantees should be written into these new juvenile laws, together with clear-cut procedures the courts are to follow in hearing and deciding all cases. The Commission believes that a child's formal court hearing should consist of two separate and distinct parts: the first to establish the child's guilt or innocence under the specific charge; the second, after guilt has been legally determined, to arrive at a proper sentence. Only in the second phase of the hearing should community and school reports be considered along with the findings of the probation officer.

Children who are "dependent" in the sense of having no proper guardians should be the concern of social agencies, not juvenile courts. The court itself should refuse to extend any special "courtesies" to such agencies and not permit them to file their own petitions to have the child declared delinquent. Social workers should be bound by the juvenile court law as readily as the police or parents are.

The court should step in when neglect is alleged against the parent because a legal decision is necessary: whether or not to remove the child from the parent's custody because he is failing to protect his child's all-important rights to health, proper education, or a wholesome childhood.

Juvenile court judges should arrange prehearing detention only for youngsters who absolutely need this kind of custodial care. In 1965, two-thirds of all children apprehended in the nation spent an average of twelve days in detention at a cost of fifty-three million dollars. Over half of them were detained in county jails. Even in affluent communities, no separate juvenile facilities were available to children; the citizens of Du Page County, a wealthy suburb west of Chicago, offered its children in trouble the doors of the county jail.

Another vital question is: Should these new juvenile laws treat children's court records more confidentially than is currently the practice? The Commission favors the principle of releasing the child's *legal* record only to other legal agencies; outside persons should receive such information only when the court is convinced that the individual youngster will not thereby be harmed. The social part of the record, covering intimate family background, psychiatric diagnoses, and school reports, should be given over only to reputable therapeutic agencies to which the parents themselves have gone for help or to which the court has referred the child.

The Commission believes that a juvenile court probation staff should devote more time to counseling sessions and informal arbitration meetings as an alternative to the filing of formal delinquency charges against the child. Using the technique of a preliminary conference (currently a part of New York practice), probation officers would bring together, on a voluntary basis, the child, his parents, the complaining witnesses, the police, and other interested parties, and proceed to work out a treatment plan acceptable to all. The juvenile court judge would have to approve the plan; his consent decree, embodying the agreement, would extend over a one-year period. If the child proved uncooperative or the treatment unsuitable for other reasons, the alternative of the formal delinquency process would then be available.

In Philadelphia, an informal Counselling and Referral Service similar to the Commission's recommendation has worked very well for several years. Funded by a private local foundation, the unit has been manned by specially chosen probation officers. In 1966–67, over four thousand Philadelphia children received help without being stigmatized as delinquents.

Once the catch-all delinquency category disappears, either by changing juvenile court laws or, more immediately, by juvenile court judges' own rulings, police officers, school authorities, and parents will need another supervisory agency to handle problems posed by troublesome and disturbed children. What new and different agency will replace the Juvenile Court?

The Commission wants every American community to create what it calls—somewhat unimaginatively perhaps—the Youth Services Bureau. Since the Commission conceives this agency as neighborhood-based, informal, and somewhat freewheeling in its work-style, a snappier name would be desirable, preferably one with initials forming a catchy acronym that young people could incorporate into their jargon.

Run by a board composed of community leaders from the area it serves, and using professional and volunteer consultants, each Bureau would offer a broad range of services to young people as well as perform certain "mandatory" functions. The Commission hopes that the agency would be so outreaching, many-sided, and enterprising in its bid for young clients that most of them would be self-referred. But a certain percentage of young people would come to its attention through either police or juvenile court intake channels.

Within a specified period of time (the Commission suggests thirty to sixty days) the Bureau would report to the court whether or not its services are proving adequate for court-referred children. If they are not, the Bureau would recommend other informal or more legalistic action by the court authorities.

To all young people living in the geographical area it serves, the Bureau would offer individually tailored, nonauthoritarian advice or help on such matters as housing, jobs, recreation activities, and educational or vocational programming.

Bureau-sponsored programs could be launched to assist needy youth. It could seek out empty, low-cost housing units that could be converted into youth centers with sleeping facilities for homeless or temporarily estranged young people. Other neighborhood store-fronts and apartments could become mental health clinics manned either by volunteers or by professional staffs hired and paid by the Bureau from its own funds or from monies obtained through foundation and other private sources.

The Bureau could set up "mini-schools"—small, informal classes held wherever space is available to give children extra help in reading, mathematics, English, and business training subjects. Courses could be conducted after regular school hours or on some other prearranged basis that enables both regular and volunteer teachers and students to meet conveniently. Whenever possible, National Teacher Corps personnel could be used, and the mini-schools would give these trainee-teachers invaluable classroom experience in a unique setting that offered them the freedom to experiment with new approaches.

The Bureau could place teen-agers in part-time jobs in neighborhood business enterprises and couple its job-finding efforts with those of professional employment agencies or Neighborhood Youth Corps programs if these already exist in the community.

Arrangements could be made with little theater groups, museums, music centers, and recreational facilities to set up leisure-time activities for youngsters. Poor children need the opportunity to putter freely, participate in creative writing, modern dance, and other self-expression classes, and attend good-grooming and charm courses. These and other stimulating projects could be developed by the Bureau either under its own aegis or through settlement houses and adult clubs equipped to supervise such programs.

Bureau members themselves could organize local committees to watch for signs of trouble in neighborhoods and to single out for help children who seem to be slipping or who live under blatantly impossible conditions. Here the Bureau could form its own unique "case work" approach by organizing neighbors to help faltering families—getting an alcoholic father to seek medical help, showing a mother how to shop and keep a neat house, for example. Older experienced women could be recruited to offer homemaking services.

Many ghetto parents, overwhelmed by their own inadequacies and frustrations and hampered by lack of funds, do not know how to share meaningful experiences with their children. They do not take advantage of their community facilities—parks, museums, zoos, and other fun places. The Bureau could set up weekly calendars to inform such parents of interesting events and even provide free transportation when possible. As these programs begin to catch fire, newly formed neighborhood social committees can take major responsibility for planning and carrying out some of these recreational or culturally enriching excursions.

Neither the concept of such a Bureau nor the many services it could perform are new. In many cities and smaller communities the nucleus of such enterprises exists. Many poverty-program groups have been engaged in similar activities for several years. The plethora of Federal programs like Get-Set and Upward Bound have shown strikingly good results with this type of dynamic programming.

During the administrations of Mayors Joseph S. Clark and Richardson Dilworth (1952–61), the City of Philadelphia had its own comprehensive Youth Services Board. Unfortunately, this effort did not continue after the advent of Federally subsidized youth programs oriented toward the poor. Newly established community agencies, funded modestly by foundations and church groups, are already doing some of the work of the proposed Youth Services Bureau.

In one of Philadelphia's most neglected slums, Herman Wrice, a young Negro father of six, himself a former gang member, has spearheaded a freewheeling community-service program called "The Young Great Society." Its store-front doors are open to everyone in the entire neighborhood—young and old alike. No human problem is outside its range of interest, whether it be a child's failure in school, building-code violations by a landlord, unfair police handling, arbitrary ruling by welfare officers, or any of the myriad troubles that plague the poor. Wrice's energy and dedication have enabled the project to survive several financial crises.

In Philadelphia and elsewhere, local poverty-program councils and more traditional citizen groups such as Health and Welfare Councils and residents' organizations have begun to draft plans for a broadly based Youth Services Bureau, but at present these efforts are uncoordinated and short-term in scope.

Without waiting for mandates from above or the official blessing of the power structure, existing community groups should explore the possibility of obtaining Federal funds to open full-fledged Youth Bureaus wherever needed. The Delinquency Control bill passed by Congress in 1968 appropriates limited monies for this purpose. If

Federal funds prove unavailable, these groups should persist in seeking other sources of assistance.

Side by side with juvenile court reforms and new community youth service groups, public programs should spring up to improve family, school, and work-placement opportunities for young people.

Although government agencies cannot order people to be good parents, they can, in the Commission's words,

> . . . develop and provide the environment and the resources and opportunities through which families can become competent to deal with their own problems. Better housing, better recreational opportunities, increased employment opportunities, assistance in family planning, increased opportunities to function as a family unit rather than as a divergent collection of autonomous beings—all these can create the independence and security that are prerequisite if relationships within the family are to be a source of strength.

One of the programs most urgently in need of reform is the current public assistance–welfare concept. Not only does this form of help weaken family life by keeping fathers away from homes and perpetuating apathy and dependence on the part of mothers, but it fails even to provide adequate food, clothing, and medical care for many children. Social workers are meshed into this system to function as bookkeepers and spies, when they should be devoting themselves to providing genuine counseling and using their skills to help solve their clients' problems. Current assistance laws and techniques, rooted in Elizabethan Poor Laws, reflect the ancient hostility and distrust of a less enlightened society toward its economically handicapped members. They have no place in a sophisticated twentieth-century civilization with claims to understanding complex social and economic causes of poverty.

When a family begins to fall apart, courts and public agencies should make their best efforts to recement it and to prevent further fragmenting of family relationships, especially between parents and children. Expanded marriage counseling and family service clinics should adjust their working hours to suit the needs of their clients. Too often a husband or wife is forced to miss work to talk to a social worker. Evening and week-end hours would bring in many more clients under relaxed conditions that might often make professional guidance more effective.

Present-day domestic relations courts should be expanded into family courts concerned not solely with how much support the father should be made to pay, but also with what *both* parents can do as human beings to give their children a good childhood. The outcome of divorce and separation procedures should hinge on whether —and how—the children will be affected. Courts should compel husbands and wives who have children to submit to short "cooling-off periods" after filing divorce petitions, or make other similar arrangements designed to prevent "instant" divorces.

The Commission believes that government and community agencies can and should do much, much more for young people. Because the public services that exist to help boys and girls make the transition from childhood to adulthood are so inadequate, millions of American children experience the intense frustration of forming vague life-goals without the means to clarify and achieve them. To relieve their anguish, they turn to their peers for guidance. Often the neighborhood reception committee is the gang. The ghetto offers little else. The gang setting provides ready-made, easily achievable roles. The chief recruiters have been described as drug peddlers, pimps, and petty criminal czars by James Baldwin and other articulate graduates of this environment.

Yet many gang members have displayed energy, intelligence, and an amazing desire for conventional recognition and success. These qualities can be channeled into constructive outlets: given even half a chance, many of these young people show fantastic ingenuity, responsibility, and leadership ability. The Commission's report underlines my own observation that we generally underestimate just how much young people can do for themselves, if adults will let them. Ghetto youth have shown mature responsibility in civil rights and activist movements—just as sheltered, middle-class college students astounded their parents, and the nation, by their efforts on behalf of Senator Eugene McCarthy in the 1968 Presidential campaign.

What most children need is positive direction, job training, and encouragement to get them through the dangerous adolescent years. Instead of condemning citizens who try to reclaim youngsters—as recently occurred when a Chicago clergyman was excoriated by a Congressional Committee for "fraternizing" with gang members— public agencies should lead in such efforts and expand work opportunities. The Neighborhood Youth Corps program in Philadelphia has successfully trained delinquent youngsters for jobs in social agencies. They should also be employed as aides to police and probation officers, not only because their own background gives them special insights, but also because such a program would help bridge the chasm that exists between these children and law enforcement agencies.

Recently, New York City announced a plan to use Federal, state, and local funds under a Model Cities program to train Brooklyn slum youths as police cadets and private guards to help protect merchants and residents in their areas. These young men, to be known as community service officers, will be trained for high school equivalency and civil service tests, so that they will be eligible later to enter Federal, state, or local police service. This plan is being patterned after a successful experiment, conducted in Harlem in the spring of 1968, in which a forty-two-member Community Patrol Corps toured the streets and proved their mettle in combatting crime.

One of the nation's most outstanding advocates of self-help programs for the poor is the Reverend Leon H. Sullivan, a Philadelphia minister and founder and chairman of Opportunities Industrialization Centers, Inc., a community-owned enterprise which trains adults and young people for skilled jobs. Heavily supported by Federal monies, the OIC has given many of these people the boost needed to lift themselves out of their trapped existences. Dr. Sullivan's activities are extending to a community-owned and -operated shopping center and a cooperative apartment development, both located deep in the Philadelphia ghetto. Similar programs tailored specifically for young people would achieve parallel success, given the kind of public support that Dr. Sullivan's charisma engenders.

To children still of mandatory school-attendance age, public boards of education must offer radically improved programs. The Commission notes that for slum youth, many American schools have become jumping-off points into delinquency, rather than stepping stones to a better way of life. Many students from the ghetto are already scarred by their early experiences and they have learning problems. Understanding, patience, and extra help, as well as excellent teaching skills, are essential if the school experience is to help reverse the throwaway process. The Commission concludes that by failing to teach these educationally handicapped children, public schools actually "can sap the child's confidence, dampen his initiative, and lead him to negative definitions of himself as a 'failure' or an 'unacceptable' person."

Most slum schools have nothing more to offer their pupils than inappropriate and out-of-date texts, battered and inadequate buildings, and poorly trained, often indifferent teachers. Many idealistic young novice teachers are horrified when they discover that school bureaucrats and administrators often *want* these children to fail, to prove they are subhuman, to turn them into resigned and apathetic adults.

Instead of teaching, public schools in the past concentrated on disciplining and policing. Failing to recognize outrageous or defiant behavior as one of the few defense mechanisms available to a rejected child, they take a hard line with "problem" students. Slum school officers should know that being "tough" is a necessary bit of role playing for adolescent boys growing up in the culture of poverty. It is not surprising that as soon as possible these children take off, leaving the classroom behind forever.

State and local governments should make slum schools chief targets for improvement. They should also seek ways to accelerate racial integration in the entire school so that all children may be enriched. In Chief Justice Warren's words:

> To separate them from others of similar age and qualifications solely because of their race generates a feeling of inferiority as to their status in the community that may affect their hearts and minds in a way unlikely ever to be undone. Social and economic separation compound the educational obstacles of racial segregation in many schools today.

The Commission urges American boards of education to put aside their present punitive approaches to children with behavior problems and to experiment instead with new techniques, such as assigning them to "lead" teachers who can work with them in small "vestibule" groups attached to larger classes. Rejecting the need to segregate mentally retarded and emotionally disturbed pupils, the Report also advances this suggestion as an effective way to handle these children.

Motivation programs and counseling services to encourage individual students to seek higher goals are educational rarities. Several years ago I participated in a panel discussion on this topic on a radio program where listeners called in their comments. For almost three hours the station was deluged by calls from black parents recounting instance after instance of how school personnel discouraged their children from seeking higher education or further job training. One parent, proudly announcing that all five of her children were college graduates, said she had to spend most of her life fighting the school board.

After they have left school, young people need the help of government employment programs. Unemployment rates soar highest for boys in the sixteen-to-twenty-one-year-old group. Of the 26 million young people who entered the labor force during the sixties, only 45 per cent were high school graduates. One-quarter of the group had not even completed high school.

For most of these youths, finding a job through conventional channels is harder than it sounds. For one thing, 50 to 90 per cent of all males who grow up in American slums have been arrested, and many employment agencies refuse to accept applications that indicate prior arrest records. State employment application forms should be changed to conform to the recently revised Federal employment Form 57, which requires an applicant to state whether or not he has been *convicted* of a crime, rather than the usual question about arrest. This revision would also help thousands of children adjudicated of delinquency and hence technically "arrested," though not "convicted."

Among the Commission's excellent recommendations for opening up new work opportunities for throwaway youth is the proposed Youth Service Corps, molded in the pattern of the Peace Corps and VISTA. Older boys and girls recruited to work in projects designed to alleviate social and economic misery would have the opportunity to seek careers in community service or government agencies.

Americans will find that all of the Commission's recommendations for legal reform and new government programs are worthy of serious study. Apart from being constructive and practical, they have the kind of panache that attracts young people and enlivens their sense of belonging and fulfillment. Even if only a handful of these paper programs become immediate flesh-and-blood realities, this country will have taken a first step toward safeguarding its most precious resource—its youth.

18 ═══

INVOLVEMENT—
NOW!

In virtually every American community, groups of intelligent, concerned men and women meet regularly in clubs and associations based on economic, social, or sentimental ties. They have good dinners or coffee hours, listen to "interesting speakers," become temporarily enthusiastic about a new idea—or angry about an old injustice—and then resume their patterned lives without considering how they can change the patterns. A terrible consequence of living in a complex, increasingly depersonalized society is that mass communications media dramatically project social problems, but the institutionalized machinery affords no room for effective citizen participation.

The long record of neglect that characterizes the social treatment of troubled children is thus part of a social pathology that requires, like the neurosis of an individual, an act of will as the first step to recovery. Just as the therapists require that an ill patient feel "motivated" to improve, so too the entire community must wholeheartedly want to discard its old throwaway habits, its neurotic refusal to face the real causes of crime and delinquency. And in so doing, it must ask itself what more profitable, more human solutions it can mobilize at once to end the paralysis of will.

Change, as Dostoevsky reminds us, is the most painful demand human beings can make of themselves and each other. The vast network of American citizens' associations, composed of well-meaning individuals, must assume a dual activist role of pressing for social change and joining community service programs.

"Community service." Even the term we use to describe a vital human function sounds dreary, do-goodish, and dull. Call it rather an adventure in living in a new dimension. Perhaps the solution to the malaise, the general sense of rootlessness, lies in our reaching out to its youngest victims to succor them. And in the process we will find new vitality, fulfillment, and joy.

Old established "roles" need to be humanized and updated so that the functions they serve are not limited to merely preserving status but are expanded to meet human needs. The traditional insistence of private social agencies on autonomy of operation has led to fragmenting and duplication of services. Citizens serving on these boards should urge that all agencies coordinate their programs.

Another Establishment practice that must be scrapped is the policy of maintaining Y's for "nice" boys and girls without arrest records and turning away homeless youths on probation or parole. Instead, these community hotels, supported largely by public contributions, should open their doors to all young people.

Men's and women's clubs should consider in their projected programs the selection of a correctional institution for delinquent children as a focus for special activity. They will find the warden or matron eager to cooperate in assigning one child to any club member willing to become a sponsor and visit that child at the institution. At the important moment of release, this sponsor, backed by the resources of the club, would help the youngster find a place in society.

Businessmen and corporate executives should earmark a specific number of jobs for young people with police and juvenile court records and follows through by hiring and training them.

Trustees of educational or charitable institutions that presently exclude Negro or other minority-group children should abandon their exclusionary policies, which do violence to democratic principles. For more than a century, Philadelphia Negro male orphans could not attend a top-level free boarding school, Girard College, because the trustees and alumni stubbornly clung to a phrase used by its founder in 1843—"for white male orphans." Long legal battles extending over fifteen years ended in victory when the U. S. Supreme Court refused to review a lower court ruling that the restrictive policy violated the Fourteenth Amendment.

New work opportunities for youths in the now-closed crafts and trades *can* be opened up by majority vote of members. Apprenticeship training programs should include young men from the ghettos and reformatories, regardless of racial or other background factors.

The Columbia student revolt triggered by the administration's indifference to its Harlem neighbors highlighted the isolation of universities from their communities. One way of ending this insulation is for these institutions to bring bright poor children of all ages— black and white alike—onto their ivy-covered campuses for special cultural and recreational programs—films, lectures, workshops, field trips, sports events, social activities of various kinds. Both administrators and faculty can spark in these children a feeling of belonging, an appreciation of the education process, and a desire for learning. They can also tutor them for College Aptitude examinations, a goal which their past school experience has not encouraged. There are myriad ways in which the great resources of learning centers can be used imaginatively to relieve the bleakness of many young lives.

In addition, university trustees and alumni groups should give priority to establishing special fully paid scholarships for institutionalized children showing special promise.

Many university students have already taken a good first step by working as tutors or counselors in juvenile detention centers and other institutions. Acknowledgment of their efforts should be made, and colleges and universities should encourage such involvement.

Why haven't scouting and campfire group leaders vigorously recruited both children and adults who live in poor communities? Their need to participate in wholesome group activities is as great as, if not greater than, that of other youth. If costly uniform and equipment requirements make membership impossible for the poor, then these outer trappings should be discarded in favor of a more simple approach. This new policy involves no change in structure—

merely a change in values. With a little effort, projects can be developed to fit the needs and capabilities of low-income families.

Existing settlement houses and community centers should launch aggressive, interesting programs that will attract large numbers of alienated children. Especially should they aim at communicating with them, not moralistically, but in very sophisticated terms about the whole problem of drug-taking and addiction. In this enterprise they could cooperate with school officials and counselors in setting up educational programs that present solid information to young people in a lively way.

Of late I have been aware that, at the end of lectures on socio-legal problems of the "now" generation, parent groups with greater frequency ask why so few efforts are being made to introduce drug education courses into the curriculum in junior and senior high schools. Alarmed by the skyrocketing trends in narcotics arrests, these concerned parents believe that drugs has replaced sex as the unmentionable topic between adults and adolescents. Just as parental pressure was a great impetus in getting sex education into the school's course of study, so, too, citizens' demands for high-level, intensive education programs on narcotics can bring about healthy, open discussions on the physiological effects of drug use and the underlying psychological causes and consequences. Such programs should not be conducted by police personnel, who view the problem legalistically. The ghastly film and the accompanying blood-curdling lecture that is representative of the Army type of approach to the subject should also be avoided, since young audiences tend to dismiss the presentation as adult propaganda.

Every American community has a public library. Unfortunately, it is often allowed to remain a dull, unappealing place that children shun except for visits made necessary by special homework assignments. Librarians should take a less conventional, more creative approach to their surroundings: inaugurate special activities; take down the SILENCE PLEASE signs and instead feature the kind of bright, eye-catching displays and decor that enhanced the Children's Room in the Nashville (Tennessee) Public Library:

> . . . colors dazzle the eye; fish and birds twirl overhead; hand-made flowers of paper, feathers, sequins and wood bloom in every

corner; trains trundle over little tracks . . . Gay yellow stacks
radiate from the main desk like wheel spokes . . . Even books are
color-coded with spots to indicate category . . . so that a child
must learn the color-code in order to find his favorite subject
. . . Highlight of the tour is a trip through the huge,
squeaking castle doors into the Story Room, panelled in dark
wood and complete with large open hearth . . .

Nashville children's introduction to the wonderful world of books is
thus described in the October, 1968, *Roadrunner's Report*, issued by
the Library Service Department of J. B. Lippincott Company.

Church activities for young people should be directed sensitively
at the intelligence, not feelings of evil and guilt. A very important
on-the-spot service that all churches irrespective of denomination
should establish is a counseling service manned by volunteers within
the congregation who have been briefed on such problems as job,
school, and personality development. These adults should be actively
recruited and if necessary trained for this work, which is often too
demanding and time-consuming for busy church administrators who
are immersed in pastoral programs.

All skilled professionals within a community should ask themselves how they can most effectively use their skills *outside their
regular commitments to their own work* to improve the lot of young
people. Especially is this self-confrontation necessary in the case of
therapists—psychiatrists, psychologists, and special case workers—
with lucrative middle- and upper-class practices. Such men and women
are desperately needed to train volunteer lay counselors for troubled
children and parents who have not the means to pay for professional
help. The professionals themselves need not engage directly in face-
to-face encounters with clients if time does not permit, but their
participation as consultants and guides is urgently needed.

Richard Cornuelle's valuable book *Reclaiming the American
Dream* is a mine of timely suggestions, telling how individual citizens can offer themselves to this vital task on which America's future
depends. A recent editorial in *Glamour*, a fashion magazine for young
women, listed, along with the usual beauty check-outs and shopping
suggestions, a series of immediately needed volunteer services in
which bright, "with it" young fashionables can participate. These
excellent ideas—ranging from tutoring ghetto children to organizing

groups to start day-care centers for working mothers; from running job-finding centers for teen-agers to investing in small Negro business ventures—should inspire women, and men, to a new usefulness in their communities, regardless of size or geographical location. Cornuelle's thesis is that neither the public sector (official government agencies) nor the private sector (industry, business, and existing agency structures) can satisfactorily meet the current needs. A third sector, encompassing the vast body of American citizens, is the force needed to make a breakthrough successful.

Not everyone can adopt a homeless orphan or become a foster parent to a troubled child, but all of us must give serious thought to launching out in such new directions. After children grow up and leave home, years of invaluable experience remain locked up inside their parents, never to be utilized again, except in later years and then on a different level as grandparents. How tragically wasteful to let their knowledge and insight remain untapped when there are broad socially useful ends to which this experience could be applied. Agencies that have foster-home programs should re-examine both their eligibility provisions (especially concerning age) *and* their recruiting programs.

The spring and summer of 1968 saw many Americans quietly and without fanfare reaching out for ways to help reverse the throwaway process. Suburbanites who had seen the New York ghetto only from commuter-train windows on their way to and from neat communities alighted now, and joined store-front recreational and tutoring projects for children imprisoned in the city slums.

In the elegant Washington suburb of Potomac, Maryland, an "In the Swim" project initiated by a wealthy couple the preceding summer spread to include fifty pools in Maryland, Virginia, and the District of Columbia. To these lovely private estates came 850 ghetto children once a week. Refreshments, games, and a sense of freedom made these outings a wonderful experience for deprived youngsters. Although the project began simply as a recreational program, the affluent men and women who contributed their money, their time, and their homes soon found a deeper meaning in the experience: how to involve themselves as suburban dwellers with inner-city people.

Such gaps in American life need to be bridged, not by words, but by deeds—by actively "living" the beliefs to which we have all too often given *lip* service, not *heart* service.

For every American there is at least one opportunity for involvement now—if only he or she will take the first step to find it.

Very well, one may say, suppose we all get busy and inundate our communities with good works that will actually *prevent* future adolescents and young adults from developing a sense of isolation and despair. What about those silent armies of delinquents in our midst who are already exhibiting antisocial attitudes and behavior, already branded, already institutionalized?

Here, too, citizens can step directly into the mainstream and work within the juvenile justice system, with all its deficiencies and contradictions. This direct contact, apart from the immediate benefits accruing to individual children, may lead to broadly based efforts to improve the administration of justice throughout the country. For once they enter the rooms behind the closed doors, citizens will experience at first hand both the gross and the subtle flaws and inadequacies described in this view of throwaway children; they will actively support essential reforms and vote for increased appropriations needed to improve operations at every level.

Let us consider, for example, the organized bar and the legal profession to which I belong. Both figure prominently in the throwaway indictment. Perhaps in a sense they are principal codefendants, for they have allowed the perversion and corruption of justice to creep into the system by being too selfishly preoccupied with their own aggrandizement and professional success to challenge unsatisfactory appointments to the bench in juvenile courts and to denounce abuses rampant in the system. Many lawyers have never set foot in the courtrooms of the poor because they mistakenly believe they have no business there. And for decades law schools have been training law students to deal with the problems of the "cake and caviar" set rather than with the life struggles of the "day-old bread and oleo" masses. Fortunately, movements are afoot to remedy the situation. The Ford Foundation has subsidized a grant-dispensing Council on Legal Education for Professional Responsibility for the express purpose of underwriting teaching programs of "clinical" law that will bring the students into shoulder-rubbing contact with the poor in much the same way that medical-school students obtain firsthand experience in hospitals. And through Bar Association efforts and the establishment of Community Legal Services offices, experienced lawyers are volunteering their services in juvenile courts.

Other programs need to be developed to involve senior and junior bar members in sustained year-round relationships with poor families. Judge Clifford Scott Green of Philadelphia, an able and sensitive Negro judge with long experience in juvenile matters, announced at a 1968 Bench-Bar Conference held in Atlantic City that a retainer plan for poor families which would provide them with skilled legal counsel would dramatically reduce the number of the so-called "hardcore" families that every juvenile court carries in its files not just from year to year but from generation to generation. This retainer plan, and others like it, needs to be activated by bar associations, private legal societies, and law schools.

Citizens need not be lawyers in order to apply their skills and interests in direct service. As subprofessional aides to probation departments, they can assist overloaded court workers and also introduce the personal human element that is so manifestly lacking in the juvenile justice structure. Not only can these volunteers relieve some of the burdens of regular probation workers, but many can be trained to help establish experimental community-based treatment programs.

Individual citizens can lend support to projects similar to New Jersey's Highfields program whereby twenty delinquent boys work and live in special institutions, largely governing themselves. Or under the direction of court probation departments in their own communities, they can set up organizations similar to the Draper Youth Center in Alabama, where inmates from several institutions receive instruction, aided by students from a nearby university.

In Philadelphia, William Freeland, owner of a small business, established the Lakeside Youth Service, a week-end program for boys aged sixteen to eighteen who had been sentenced to Pennypack House on delinquency charges. By special arrangement with the juvenile court and the prison, small groups of these boys spent their week ends in Freeland's modest camp in an outlying rural area, receiving counseling, job training, and remedial reading services in an informal setting. In three years, sixty-eight boys have passed through the program; fewer than ten have returned to court after being discharged in Freeland's care. Late in 1968 the Lakeside program was extended to include detentioners. In this new phase, a work-release program is evolved so that at the boy's hearing in court a full plan is presented as an alternative to institutionalizing him.

Ian H. Lennox, Assistant Director of the Crime Commission of Philadelphia, who has worked with Freeland, underlines the need of a halfway-house arrangement for many of these boys who lack adequate homes. Like other experts, he stresses that this does not require millions of dollars and years of paper planning. They can be launched immediately, with modest contributions. The most costly item, human service, is the gift that caring, responsible men and women can make.

In this technology-oriented, expertise-venerating era, we tend to overlook or minimize the historical importance of the amateur, the volunteer. We forget, for example, that the whole concept of probation in America was the brain child of a Boston cobbler, John Augustus, who over a century ago went to the criminal courts as a spectator and was aghast at what he saw. Like Freeland, he offered his services to jailhouse inmates, found jobs for them and drew up a constructive plan for their return to the community under his supervision. From his efforts came a viable alternative to long-term confinement, especially desirable for young, resilient offenders. Today, his spirit is still needed.

Teen-Aid, Inc., began with six women who had come together to start a new service for delinquent teen-age girls on probation. In less than ten years, under the guidance of court personnel and with the help of interested professionals, the organization has grown to encompass several hundred volunteer women. Its multi-faceted program includes individual counseling, job placement, and vocational guidance as well as visiting schedules and supplemental courses in girls' training schools and detention centers.

Women seem naturally adept at this work. After a six-week training program, Teen-Aid volunteers come forward eagerly to meet their young court-referred "friends"; often they find that the relationship continues beyond the girl's probation term. The warmth and sympathy of these volunteers evoke a response of loyalty and gratitude in the girls which helps them to find emotional freedom, so basic for healthy relationships based on mutual love and respect.

Teen-Aid volunteers find that their good influence often extends to other family members as well. Younger children as well as parents modify some of their behavior patterns as they see evidence of real change in the delinquent girl. One mother who had felt utterly defeated by her failures was so uplifted by the kindly interest of the Teen-Aid worker that she put aside pennies from her meager household budget and when she had accumulated five dollars' worth, sent the money to the Teen-Aid office as a token of gratitude.

A Teen-Aid type operation is simple to organize. Money for salaries for a professional director and a clerical assistant can be raised within the community by direct appeals by the volunteers themselves. Businessmen respond to the call of women who are giving their time, their hearts, and their minds to the vital work of reclaiming children. Fund-raising projects such as movie benefits, card sales, remembrance fund cards that can be sent out on occasions when flowers are ordinarily the rule, and other projects that involve the community, both swell the treasury and win recruits and supporters.

For years the Big Brothers' Association has done similar work with fatherless boys. Teen-Aid, a relative newcomer, has proved that women can work effectively with the so-called "bad girls," for whom in the past only institutionalization seemed to be a feasible answer.

Although money is a necessary ingredient of all these reaching-out programs, we must do more than write out checks. Only by direct and active participation can Americans humanize the institutions and enterprises set up to serve this country's citizenry. As we nurture throwaway children, we help them and ourselves to grow to new stature as responsible citizens. John W. Gardner, former Secretary of Welfare and now Chairman of the Urban Coalition, states in his new work, *No Easy Victories:*

> The release of human potential, the enhancement of individual dignity, the liberation of the human spirit—those are the deepest and truest goals to be conceived by the hearts and minds of the American people.

This vital offering of oneself as a private citizen committed to an ennobling, voluntary effort cannot come about by acting in the manner of a Lady or Lord Bountiful dispensing chocolates to needy urchins. For anyone afflicted with this reflex, the checkbook is a safer outlet.

Nothing alienates needy children—and adults—more than patronizing insensitivity. They ask only that they be treated with dignity and consideration and that they be given genuine reason to hope. Patience, perseverance, and self-discipline must be the volunteer's key words.

Melvin Floyd, a young Negro police officer who is also a Baptist minister, attests to the good results such an approach can effect. As resident supervisor of Teen Haven, a small settlement house located in a Philadelphia slum area, he has reached not only individual boys and girls but also hardened gang leaders who have waged relentless warfare in the neighborhood. In the summer of 1968 he brought together rival gangs in a truce that has lasted longer than anyone dared hope it would.

Founded in 1963 by a Negro evangelist, William Drury, Teen Haven has its counterpart in the Fourteenth Street area of Washington, D.C.—the scene of 1967's summer riots. Strongly religious in approach, the group works to help youngsters accept Christ as their Saviour; it also offers teen-agers cooking and sewing classes, Ping-pong, pool, chess, and trips to a camp it maintains in the Pocono Mountains. Maintained, as Teen-Aid and Lakeside are, by private contributions, Teen Haven has a community relations program through which it projects its story to interested groups. Slides of photographs taken by a thirteen-year-old boy depict the history and workings of the organization. In 1968 the Bell Telephone Company agreed to cooperate with Teen Haven by hiring and training the many hardcore high school dropouts who seek its help.

Youngsters are enthusiastic about Teen Haven. In a recent interview in the Philadelphia *Tribune,* one thirteen-year-old boy said: "I come from a large family and I am grateful that Mr. Drury and Miss Ruth Young of Teen Haven took an interest in me. I talk to my buddies and tell them to come to Teen Haven." And a fifteen-year-old girl observed, "It's a shame that there are not more Teen Haven houses around our city. I find that such programs have helped to keep poor children off the streets and out of trouble."

In recent years, encouraged by poverty program goals and inspired by the leadership of men like the late Dr. Martin Luther King, the parents and siblings of many throwaway children have organized themselves into action groups seeking to remedy injustices in welfare laws, housing code enforcement, and job discrimination. Such groups need the support and assistance of middle-class professionals and civic leaders. Here it is important for outside volunteers to play their limited roles as sensitively as possible. The poor do not want to be led by the hand; they are ready to walk alone, if necessary, although they welcome companions from other social levels who want to accompany them on their hard road of self-advancement.

For years, many white middle-class Americans have told themselves that poor Negro and other mothers receiving public welfare funds are riding a gravy train and leading idyllically happy existences. In the last two years, to their amazement, these so-called "pleasure-loving," "irresponsible" women have organized themselves into Welfare Rights groups. All over the nation, they are demanding improvements and changes in their status. In Philadelphia a group of these women conducted a dramatic experiment to prove how badly undernourished they were under present Public Assistance food allotments. When they tried to sell their blood to local hospitals, they could find no buyers because so many of them were anemic. Today the Welfare Rights group is in the vanguard of citizens working for reforms in the entire welfare system.

Another stunning example of what these women can accomplish, despite community hostility and with minimal help, is Philadelphia's unique New Horizons Center, a mini-school for unwed adolescent mothers, run in large measure by ghetto women who were themselves in many instances youthful parents of illegitimate children.

Beginning as a pilot program in 1959 under the joint auspices of the Philadelphia Board of Education and the City Department of Welfare, the New Horizons program recently reorganized itself into a community trust, whose officers include the president of City Council *and* the parent of one of the school's many successful alumnae. A local businessman donated a dilapidated, once-grand mansion. Borrowing money from a local bank, the group secured the volunteer services of an outstanding architect, Oskar Stonorov, and refurbished the house into a cheerful, airy place where the girls come daily with their babies. The Center's gifted Executive Director, Mrs. Cornelia T. Biddle, a social worker, consults constantly with the parent-group.

New Horizons offers basic academic courses as well as dressmaking, cosmetology, and secretarial courses. Since the entire focus of the educational program is on the development of a salable skill, the Center pays for its students to attend specialized courses in areas of their own choosing. One fifteen-year-old school-dropout mother of a bouncing two-year-old wanted to study television repair and electronics. She enrolled in an all-boys' program and with the encouragement of Mrs. Biddle graduated and found a good-paying job in her off-beat chosen field. Today she supports herself and her boy.

New Horizons students are encouraged to take care of themselves and their babies. For example, they shop for hot lunches, prepare them, and serve them under the guidance of a competent housekeeper. They are responsible for the upkeep of the cheerful new school and plan their own special programs, teas, and parties. The girls gain two important unique experiences: a sense of mastery and a sense of participation in a warm, positive community life.

Again hope has proved contagious. Their mothers, heartened by the prospect of "new horizons" for their daughters, have broadened their own life goals. Although most of them receive welfare funds, they have earned, by running a volunteer catering service, enough money to buy play equipment and books for the school. Several of them have gone back to school, and now have good jobs.

Dr. Samuel T. Bullock, an eminent Philadelphia psychiatrist who has served as New Horizons' consultant since its inception, describes the function of the Center as that of seizing upon the "moment of hope" that each of the girls feels when she gives birth to her child and sustaining it until it becomes the core of the girl's whole way of life. Since the Center, like the Vista Delmar project in California, encourages the fathers of these babies to participate in school dances and other social events, and invites them into counseling sessions, these young boys show love and responsibility for their children. Many of the young couples reach the mature decision to marry.

Human problems need human solutions. Human solutions need the involvement of ordinary people as well as experts and professionals. The problems of America's young people are deep-seated and tough-hided, encrusted by decades of neglect. Yet, America's young people—delinquent and law-abiding—are precious, exciting, brimming with human potential. A civilization that deserves to endure cherishes its young. A society that rigidly and shortsightedly relegates millions of children to jails and institutions may find that it has lost more than a small percentage of its citizens. It may be that it has also thrown away its claim to moral leadership in a troubled world.